D1737159

Nature and the Godly Empire

Nineteenth-century historians have described how science became secular and how scientific theories such as evolution justified colonialism. This book changes this narrative by offering the first sustained account of the relationship between nineteenth-century science and Christianity outside the Western world. It focuses on the intrepid missionaries of the London Missionary Society, who reverently surveyed the oceans and islands of the Pacific and instructed converts to observe nature in order to interpret God's designs. Sujit Sivasundaram argues that this knowledge functioned as a popular science that was inextricably linked with religious expansion. He shows how Britain's providential empire found support from popular views of nature as much as elite science, and how science and religion came together in communities far from the metropolis even as disputes raged in Europe. This will be essential reading for historians of empire, science and religion, cultural historians, environmental historians and anthropologists.

SUJIT SIVASUNDARAM is College Lecturer and Director of Studies in History at Gonville and Caius College, Cambridge.

Cambridge Social and Cultural Histories

Series editors:

Margot C. Finn, *University of Warwick*
Colin Jones, *University of Warwick*
Keith Wrightson, *Yale University*

New cultural histories have recently expanded the parameters (and enriched the methodologies) of social history. Cambridge Social and Cultural Histories recognizes the plurality of current approaches to social and cultural history as distinctive points of entry into a common explanatory project. Open to innovative and interdisciplinary work, regardless of its chronological or geographical location, the series encompasses a broad range of histories of social relationships and of the cultures that inform them and lend them meaning. Historical anthropology, historical sociology, comparative history, gender history and historicist literary studies – among other subjects – all fall within the remit of Cambridge Social and Cultural Histories.

Titles in the series:
1 Margot C. Finn *The Character of Credit: Personal Debt in English Culture, 1740–1914*
2 M. J. D. Roberts *Making English Morals: Volunteer Association and Moral Reform in England, 1787–1886*
3 Karen Harvey *Reading Sex in the Eighteenth Century: Bodies and Gender in English Erotic Culture*
4 Phil Withington *The Politics of Commonwealth: Citizens and Freemen in Early Modern England*
5 Mark S. Dawson *Gentility and the Comic Theatre of Late Stuart London*
6 Julie-Marie Strange *Death, Grief and Poverty in Britain, 1870–1914*
7 Sujit Sivasundaram *Nature and the Godly Empire: Science and Evangelical Mission in the Pacific, 1795–1850*

Nature and the Godly Empire

*Science and Evangelical Mission
in the Pacific, 1795–1850*

Sujit Sivasundaram

CAMBRIDGE UNIVERSITY PRESS
Cambridge, New York, Melbourne, Madrid, Cape Town, Singapore, São Paulo

CAMBRIDGE UNIVERSITY PRESS
The Edinburgh Building, Cambridge CB2 2RU, UK

PUBLISHED IN THE UNITED STATES OF AMERICA BY CAMBRIDGE
UNIVERSITY PRESS, NEW YORK

www.cambridge.org
Information on this title: www.cambridge.org/9780521848367

First published 2005

Printed in the United Kingdom at the University Press, Cambridge

A catalogue record for this publication is available from the British Library

ISBN-13 978-0-521-84836-7 hardback
ISBN-10 0-521-84836-9 hardback

Behold yon rustic temple, pillared round
With stems of stately tamanu and bound
With wattled boughs, and white and shining wall,
And wicker doors, thrown wide to welcome all
And graceful cocoa-plumes and plaintain leaves
Crowning its roof and drooping round its eaves!
The pulpit steps are propt on warriors' spears –
The peaceful badge of sanguinary years!
While poisoned shafts and hatchets hung on high,
And clubs like votive tablets, catch the eye –
And gods, whose demon-dynasty is o'er
Support the roof or fence the sacred door –
Like vassals conquered in the field of war,
And chained like trophies to the victor's car […]
Such is the temple of the rising state!
The pledge and promise of a happier fate! –
An infant Zion pointing to the skies,
To melt the heart and 'draw the wondering eyes!' […]
How sweet, how lovely, in this isle remote,
The first fair landmark raised to holy thought!
Fresh as a fountain in the wilderness,
Its living springs shall heal the land's distress! […]
All – all is changed! Where'er I turn mine eyes,
The monuments of peace and love arise! […]
Little he deemed, who led the first enterprise,
To watch the wheeling worlds that light yon skies –
How soon – where thirst of science paved the way –
The 'Men of Peace' should bring a brighter day!
How soon – attracted by a brighter star,
The light of Faith should follow from afar,
Divulge new worlds – the slumbering isles arouse,
Decked like a bride to meet her heavenly spouse!

Extracted from, Anon, *Polynesia, or Missionary Toils and Triumphs in the South Seas, A Poem* (London, 1839), 75–81. The author refers to the chapel of Raiatea, which was built by the missionaries who are at the focus of this book (lines 1–22) and to the voyages of Captain James Cook, which provided the inspiration for missionary work in the Pacific (lines 25–30).

Contents

Illustrations

Acknowledgements

On the shores of Colombo, alongside the rocks that stud the seashore and the railway line that transports hundreds into the city, there is a school called St Thomas's Prep. Every morning, at seven-thirty, the bell tolls and hundreds of boys dressed in white and blue make their way in perfect lines to the chapel. It was at this school that I learnt my first lessons, and it was here that I was first introduced to the rudiments of Christianity.

As I think about the long journey I have made since then, I have many people to thank. But the ever optimistic teachers of St Thomas's Prep, who kept to the task of educating their charges, regardless of the rude interruptions from bomb blasts, curfews and riots, must come very close to the top. My parents, Siva and Ramola Sivasundaram, have been unstinting in their support and encouragement, and have coped remarkably well with a son who never emerged from university. I am also indebted to my grandparents, Mano Muthu Krishna and George Candappa, from whom I learnt to write.

Cambridge – so different from Colombo – has now become my home. This book first took shape as a doctoral dissertation in the Department of History and Philosophy of Science, where the staff and students provided me with a setting to explore my ideas without the limitations of disciplinary boundaries. Jim Secord was the perfect doctoral supervisor. I have benefited enormously from his meticulous attention to detail, his unrivalled familiarity with scholarship, and his unfailing generosity. It can safely be said that this book would never have seen the light of day without his friendship.

More recently, the Master and Fellows of Gonville and Caius College appointed me to a Research Fellowship. I am grateful for the time this has given me away from full-time teaching to pursue a course of publication. I would not have been able to write a doctoral thesis without the financial support of the following sources: the Lord Mountbatten Memorial Fund; Christ's College, Cambridge; the Overseas Research Studentship Scheme; the Cambridge Commonwealth Trust; the Divinity School, Cambridge; the Edith and Raymond Williamson Fund; and the Holland Rose Fund.

x

My research has taken me to a number of libraries and archives, where I have valued the dedication of individuals who spend so many hours fetching, shelving and preserving the tools of history. I wish to acknowledge the assistance of: the Australian National Library; the Joseph Banks Archives, the Natural History Museum, London; the British Library; the British Museum, London; the Cambridge University Library; the Royal Commonwealth Collections; the Council for World Mission Archives at the School of Oriental and African Studies, London; the Sutro Library, California; the Whipple Library, Department of History and Philosophy of Science; and Dr Williams' Library, London.

Many people have provided invaluable comments and helpful suggestions. It would be impossible to name all of them. I would like to mention: Terry Barringer, Chris Bayly, Susan Bayly, Michael Bravo, Joe Cain, Geoffrey Cantor, Richard Drayton, Patricia Fara, Aileen Fyfe, Bernhard Fulda, Jill Hassell, Amiria Henare, Nick Jardine, Bernie Lightman, David N. Livingstone, Peter Mandler, John MacKenzie, Mark Noll, Andrew Porter, Sadiah Qureshi, Hazel Rendle, Jane Samson, Simon Schaffer, Anne Secord, Charlotte Sleigh, Brian Stanley, John Stenhouse, Nicholas Thomas, Jonathan Topham, Stephen Tuck, Glyndwr Williams, Andrew Zurcher and the two anonymous referees for Cambridge University Press. Margot Finn's enthusiasm for the idea of this book, and the encouragement and efficiency of Chris Harrison, Frances Nugent, Isabelle Dambricourt, Jackie Warren and Michael Watson, at Cambridge University Press, were vital in easing the manuscript's journey to press.

There are many friends here in Cambridge and beyond, who have ensured that I have retained my sense of perspective, without losing myself in the nineteenth century. But the friendship that I value most is that which I share with Caroline; this book is dedicated to her in appreciation of her love. Without her steadfast support it would not have been completed.

Introduction

Almost half a century had passed since the violent death of Captain James Cook, when Revd William Ellis of the London Missionary Society sat in a house on the island of Oahu in Hawaii with several local chiefs, a folio edition of Cook's *Voyages* spread before him. While poring over the image of the navigator's demise together with the chiefs, Ellis observed that they were 'greatly affected' by what they saw. 'More than once when conversing with us on the length of time the missionaries had been in the Society Islands, they have said, "Why did you not come sooner? Was it because we killed Captain Cook?"'[1] Ellis intended to convey how times had changed: the Hawaiians had converted and adopted the civilised manners of the British. Their absorbed interest in Cook's *Voyages* supplied evidence of how they could read and write. By describing the Hawaiians' remembrance of Cook, Ellis also testified to how their emotions had been tamed. He added that a missionary station had been built near the village where Cook had been killed. The cave where Cook's remains were deposited for a while was said to be of 'volcanic formation' and 'one of those subterranean tunnels so numerous on the island, by which the volcanoes in the interior sometimes discharge their contents upon the shore ... The roof and sides within are of obsidian or hard vitreous lava.'[2] Redeeming Cook's memory involved the rearrangement of the landmarks of the bay of the murder, the conversion of the islanders, and the entry of the site and its people into Western knowledge.

The evangelical missionaries who oversaw a dramatic change in the culture of the South Pacific drew the first idea for their campaign from reading Cook's journals. In London, the published narratives of travel were received in a climate of acclaim and controversy. After the journal of the first voyage was published, not a day passed without letters appearing in the press about its contents. Polite readers blushed as they read of the

[1] William Ellis, *A Narrative of a Tour through Hawaii or Owhyhee* (London, 1826), 102.
[2] William Ellis, *Polynesian Researches During a Residence of Nearly Six Years*, 4 vols. (London, 1829), vol. IV, 130–1.

sexual exploits of their countrymen; while a 'lax magazine culled from the *Voyages* all the warmest passages to make a new art of love'.[3] Cook's achievements were fairly summarised by an anonymous seaman who wrote to the *Public Advertiser* that it was a very 'edifying and entertaining Account of the most extraordinary Voyages ever attempted'. In its pages he had found 'new Features of human Nature'.[4] Cook's description of these far-removed human beings prompted the thought of mission. Among the unlikely readers of Cook's explorations was Revd Thomas Haweis, an Anglican minister with Methodist sympathies. So taken was the cleric by those he described as 'dusky islanders, so favoured by nature' that a mission to the region became the cherished purpose of his heart.[5] When the London Missionary Society was formed, Haweis singlehandedly persuaded its patrons to choose the South Pacific as the first location for missionary labour.[6] Cook's legacy passed therefore into the hands of evangelical missionaries, who subscribed to a form of moderate Calvinism, and who prayed fervently for the moral foundations of the South Pacific to be transformed.

At first the genres of exploration characterised by scientific explorers and evangelical missionaries seem quite distant from each other. Cook's voyages may be cast as romantic, while evangelical mission is now associated with a rational theology and an ideology of improvement.[7] Yet the observation, collection and signification of nature served as an important bridge between the two. Cook set the precedent for an empire of science, and the missionaries became active practitioners of this new knowledge.[8] Cook's ships were fitted with the best scientific instruments and on board his vessels were draughtsmen who invented a new genre of scientific vision and painting. One of Cook's crew on his first voyage wrote to Carl Linnaeus,

---

[3] The details of the reception of Cook's journals are taken from Helen Wallis, 'Publication of Cook's Journals: Some New Sources and Assessments', *Pacific Studies* 1, no. 2 (1978): 163–94. This quote from p. 166. For more on the reception of Cook's travels, see Bernard Smith, *Imagining the Pacific: In the Wake of the Cook Voyage* (New Haven, Conn., 1992).

[4] Wallis, 'Publication of Cook's Journals: Some New Sources and Assessments', 173.

[5] Richard Lovett, *The History of the London Missionary Society*, 2 vols. (London, 1899).

[6] Haweis' speech to the London Missionary Society will be discussed in detail in chapter 1. See *Sermons and Report of the Missionary Society for 1795* (London, 1795).

[7] For more on Cook's views of nature see the work of Bernard Smith, *European Vision and the South Pacific* (New Haven, Conn., 1985). For evangelical theologies of improvement, see David Bebbington, *Evangelicalism in Modern Britain: A History from the 1780s to the 1830s* (London, 1989), Boyd Hilton, *Age of Atonement: The Influence of Evangelicalism on Social and Economic Thought, 1785–1865* (Oxford, 1988). For more on evangelical science, see D. G. Hart, David Livingstone and Mark Noll, eds., *Evangelicals and Science in Historical Perspective* (Oxford, 1999).

[8] For Cook's science, see Margarette Lincoln, ed., *Science and Exploration in the Pacific: European Voyages to the Southern Oceans in the Eighteenth Century* (Woodbridge, Suffolk, 1998), David Mackay, *In the Wake of Cook: Exploration, Science and Empire* (London, 1985).

the celebrated natural historian: 'they have all sorts of machines for catching and preserving insects; all kinds of nets, trawls, drags and hooks for coral fishing, they have even a curious contrivance of a telescope, by which, put into the water, you can see the bottom at a great depth, where it is clear'.[9] All the instruments, the natural historians and artists came under the direction of Joseph Banks, who upon returning to London became the central figure in a network of field collectors and scientific correspondents. Banks became President of the Royal Society and a guiding force of the London Missionary Society.[10] He advised Haweis on how to conduct the South Pacific mission.[11]

The categories of science and religion occupy a central place in our world. The present work is a concerted attempt to examine the emergence of science and religion and their interdependence outside the West. In doing this it attempts to stretch the burgeoning historiography of science and religion outside its traditional focus on Europe and America.[12] It is my claim that the missionaries who followed in the wake of Cook saw themselves as practitioners of science, while their knowledge was avidly consumed by a religious populace. Today evangelical mission is still justified on the grounds of the introduction of science, the spread of literacy and the extension of Western medicine. By historicising the conduct of global evangelism, it is possible to show its peculiar relations to knowledge and empire, and its moments of strength and weakness. The missionaries who travelled to the South Pacific operated on the premise of a trans-oceanic network of exchange. Commodities such as arrowroot were grown in the islands and sent overseas, even as clothes, livestock and printing presses were imported into the Pacific. The missionaries believed that as the whole world was brought together, civilisation and Christianity would prosper and the millennial return of Christ would be hastened. Universal visions of

---

[9] Cited in Patricia Fara, 'Images of a Man of Science', *History Today* (October 1998): 42–9.

[10] For the biography of Banks, see John Gascoigne, *Joseph Banks and the English Enlightenment: Useful Knowledge and Polite Culture* (Cambridge, 1994), John Gascoigne, *Science in the Service of Empire: Joseph Banks, the British State and the Uses of Science in the Age of Revolution* (Cambridge, 1998).

[11] Banks's correspondence with Haweis will be discussed in chapter 3.

[12] The study of 'religion and science' is a thriving area of research. For the current state of the field, see the edited volume of essays, John Hedley Brooke, Margaret J Osler and Jitse M. van der Meer, 'Science in Theistic Contexts: Cognitive Dimensions', *Osiris* 16 (2001): 1–376. Good introductions to the issues are John Hedley Brooke, *Science and Religion: Some Historical Perspectives* (Cambridge, 1991), John Hedley Brooke and Geoffrey Cantor, *Reconstructing Nature: The Engagement of Science and Religion* (Edinburgh, 1998), Charles Gillispie, *Genesis and Geology: A Study in the Relations of Scientific Thought, Natural Theology and Social Opinion in Great Britain 1790–1850* (Cambridge, Mass., 1996), David C. Lindberg and Ronald L. Numbers, eds., *God and Nature: Historical Essays on the Encounter between Christianity and Science* (Berkeley, Calif., 1986).

science's powers to solve the world's problems might be traced back to science's theological foundations in the colonial period. The story revealed here shows that the quest for an improved world linked by knowledge and commerce has an evangelical ancestry.

Missionaries' enthusiasm for science and scientific methods should be placed in the context of the Enlightenment. The notion that evangelicalism was shaped by the Enlightenment runs contrary to the traditional historiography. Yet, following a recent volume of essays edited by Brian Stanley, a case may be made for how the missionary movement was remoulded in the light of new philosophies in the eighteenth century.[13] The theological study of nature, for instance, attracted unprecedented interest at this time. In addition to gentlemen of science, clergymen and even the working classes could summon the confidence to theorise on nature in a spiritual vein.[14] Recent work by Bernard Lightman has shown that evangelical meditations on nature continued to be popular until nearly the end of the nineteenth century.[15] Re-evaluations of the metanarrative of how Darwinism disentangled science from religion are therefore needed. Instead of proposing a clean account of how science became secular in the nineteenth century, historians are emphasising the diversity of contexts in which the relations of knowledge and belief were forged. Learned scientific societies were distinct from popular periodicals, schools and lending libraries or the pulpit, as the work of William Astore, Aileen Fyfe and Jonathan Topham has shown. In each of these contexts the history of science and religion could take a distinct trajectory.[16] The missionary settlements of the Pacific provide another venue for locating the tense cohabitation of these intellectual traditions.

---

[13] Brian Stanley, 'Christian Missions and the Enlightenment: A Reevaluation', in *Christian Missions and the Enlightenment*, ed. Brian Stanley (Richmond, Surrey, 2001). See also chapter 1 below.

[14] For the popularity of natural history in relation to religion, see Brooke, *Science and Religion*, Aileen Fyfe, 'The Reception of William Paley's *Natural Theology* in the University of Cambridge', *British Journal for the History of Science* 30 (1997): 321–35, Nicholas Jardine, James Secord and Emma Spary, eds., *The Cultures of Natural History* (Cambridge, 1995), Jonathan Topham, 'Science, Natural Theology, and Evangelicalism in Early Nineteenth-Century Scotland: Thomas Chalmers and the Evidence Controversy', in *Evangelicals and Science in Historical Perspective*.

[15] Bernard Lightman, 'The Visual Theology of Victorian Popularizers of Science: From Reverent Eye to Chemical Retina', *Isis* 91 (2000): 651–80.

[16] William J Astore, *Observing God: Thomas Dick, Evangelicalism and Popular Science in Victorian Britain and America* (Aldershot, 2001), Aileen Fyfe, *Science and Salvation: Evangelical Popular Science Publishing in Victorian Britain* (Chicago, 2004), Jonathan Topham, 'Science and Popular Education in the 1830s: The Role of the Bridgewater Treaties', *British Journal for the History of Science* 25 (1992): 397–430.

The missionaries' science and religion could come together at a number of different levels. Science provided a natural philosophy that complemented evangelical theology at an ideological level: missionaries believed that their account of God and the creation was more rational than that possessed by islanders. As practitioners of science they also presented themselves as more civilised than their charges in the manner in which they related to the material world. In addition to this, the study of nature provided a pool of similes and metaphors that pervaded missionary texts. More particularly, the cyclical processes of nature could provide an analogy for the progress of the spiritual life from conversion to death. There was thus a discursive unity between the representations of science and religion. Institutional links with figures such as Banks, and the transfer of accounts of nature back to the metropolis, allowed the later nineteenth century's professional science to be built upon the edifice of missionary knowledge. In all of these ways – ideological, discursive and empirical – missionaries' views of nature could operate quite distinctly from the emerging genre of professional and elite science. The intimacy of these links between science and religion make it anachronistic to clinically separate the two categories. The passing assumption, made by the prominent historians John Hedley Brooke and Geoffrey Cantor, that views of nature were shared between missionaries and local peoples needs modification.[17]

To understand missionary views of nature, it is necessary to leave behind us a modern understanding of scientific knowledge. It was only by the later nineteenth century that the categories of natural history and natural philosophy gave way to specialist disciplines.[18] By this time, the professionalisation of science led to the exclusion of amateurs from contributing to it. If modern science was forged to take this form at this historical juncture, it is reasonable to assume that there were many local contestants to this emergent knowledge in the earlier century.[19] Expert and amateur science, secular and religious science, elite and popular science, took on contesting

---

[17] Brooke and Cantor, *Reconstructing Nature*. On p. 27 they write: 'Design arguments might assist the religious apologist in attacking the atheist. They might even help to establish common ground in the context of missionary encounters with other cultures.'

[18] Andrew Cunningham and Perry Williams, 'Decentring the "Big Picture": *The Origins of Modern Science* and the Modern Origins of Science', *British Journal for the History of Science* 26 (1993) 418. For more on the definition of science, see Richard Yeo, *Defining Science: William Whewell, Natural Knowledge, and Public Debate in Early Victorian Britain* (Cambridge, 1993). See also Simon Schaffer, 'Scientific Discoveries and the End of Natural Philosophy', *Social Studies in Science* 16 (1986): 387–90.

[19] For popular science and its contestation of emergent elitism, see Roger Cooter and Stephen Pumfrey, 'Separate Spheres and Public Places: Reflections on the History of Science Popularization and Science in Popular Culture', *History of Science* 24 (1994) 242. For more on popular science, see Roger Cooter, *The Cultural Meaning of Popular Science: Phrenology and the Organization of Consent in Nineteenth-Century Britain*

existences amongst distinct practitioners. Each of these sciences utilised different forms of material production, while occupying separate spaces of activity. Missionary natural history was one such contestant; it sought to encompass the whole of life within its symbols and theories. Since scripture provided the ultimate word on how evangelicals should govern their lives, missionary science gave language and interpretation a central place. In adopting a distinctive style and starting from a firm belief in its reliability, missionaries hoped to provide a Christian alternative to the proliferation of accounts of exotic nature.

Amongst evangelicals, Pacific islanders were thought to be superstitious cannibals who worshipped nature, and who could not respect the body as the site of the soul. Nature had been benevolent to them; yet they had chosen to worship the created without recognising the Creator. Driven by this characterisation, missionaries hoped to point Pacific islanders to an alternative theology of nature, and away from what was said to be an irrational attitude to the environment. They instructed Pacific islanders to study nature, imitate the European missionaries, convert to rational religion, cultivate the spirit, and become missionaries to other islands. Evangelicals wanted nature to embody theology without drawing adoration. On one occasion, Revd John Williams, who became the foremost missionary to the South Pacific, taught Samoans to see their former god, the sea-eel, as the Serpent.[20] Williams was ecstatic to witness a local chief spear and eat an eel in the presence of all his people, with the statement, 'I have become a *lotu* or Christian.'[21] It was the Serpent that had tempted Adam and Eve, and by eating the eel the Samoan demonstrated his rejection of sin and the devil. Speaking of the eel as the Serpent rather than god and eating it could signify conversion, literally and metaphorically.

(Cambridge, 1984), Adrian Desmond, 'Artisan Resistance and Evolution in Britain, 1819–1848', *Osiris* 2nd series 3 (1987): 77–110, Iwan Morus, 'Currents from the Underworld: Electricity and the Technology of Display in Early Victorian England', *Isis* 84 (1993): 50–69, Anne Secord, 'Science in the Pub: Artisan Botanists in Early Nineteenth-Century Lancashire', *History of Science* 24 (1994): 270–315, Larry Stewart and Paul Wiendling, 'Philosophical Threads: Natural Philosophy and Public Experiment among the Weavers of Spitafields', *British Journal for the History of Science* 28 (1995): 37–62.

[20] Letter dated 8 June 1821, from Revd John Williams, cited in Niel Gunson, *Messengers of Grace: Evangelical Missionaries in the South Seas, 1797–1860* (Melbourne, 1978), 247. For more on Revd John Williams, see Gawan Daws, *A Dream of Islands: Voyages of Self-Discovery in the South Seas: John Williams, Herman Melville, Walter Murray Gibson, Robert Louis Stevenson, Paul Gauguin* (New York, 1980), Niel Gunson, 'John Williams and his Ship: The Bourgeois Aspirations of a Missionary Family', in *Questioning the Past: A Selection of Papers in History and Government*, ed. D. P. Crook (St Lucia, Queensland, 1972), Sujit Sivasundaram, 'John Williams', in *Dictionary of Evangelical Biography*, ed. David Bebbington, Timothy Larsen and Mark Noll (Leicester, 2003).

[21] Ebenezer Prout, *Memoirs of the Rev. John Williams* (London, 1843), 367.

Ideally, this work would benefit from a study of how islanders responded to these instructions. Despite the constraints imposed by the sources, it is possible to see how local factors always modulated the spread of missionary science, subverting the simple diffusion of knowledge from Britain to the Pacific. For instance, chapter 2 demonstrates how the practices of writing, reading and preaching about nature were resisted and reinvented by islanders. Chapter 6 suggests that when evangelicals sought to distinguish stealing from trade, and to put into force a defined view of exchange with respect to natural commodities, Pacific islanders set up a heretical sect that took a different view of material culture. Elsewhere in this work too, attention will be paid to the fragility of missionary practice. In the process of cultural contact, knowledge about how to relate to nature was changed and reinterpreted through dialogue. The tradition of contemplating nature that predated the arrival of Europeans in the Pacific had an impact on missionary science. Upon evangelisation, local peoples came to an altered view of their environment, which was a mixture of previous customs and evangelical belief. The manner in which colonisers and colonised exchanged scientific ideas is well documented in the historiography of other regions. Christopher Bayly and Fa-ti Fan's work provide excellent examples.[22] This argument has recently been stretched further: it is said to be unhelpful to distinguish indigenous traditions from Western knowledge. Rather, according to Eugene Irschick, coloniser and colonised exchanged views about nature in the same epistemic field.[23]

In studying the place of science in missionary practice, it is possible to intervene in the thriving historiography of science, nature and cultural contact. This body of scholarship has until recently been heavily influenced by the developmental models proposed over the past few decades.[24] According to Roy Macleod, for instance, a chronology might be drafted of

---

[22] C. A. Bayly, *Empire and Information: Intelligence Gathering and Social Communication in India, 1780–1870* (Cambridge, 1996), Fa-ti Fan, *British Naturalists in Qing China: Science, Empire and Cultural Encounter* (Cambridge, Mass., 2004). For the incorporation of indigenous knowledge into Western science, see also Richard Grove, 'Indigenous Knowledge and the Significance of South-West India for Portuguese and Dutch Constructions of Tropical Nature', in *Nature and the Orient: The Environmental History of South and South-East Asia*, ed. Richard Grove, Vinita Damodaran and S. Sangwan (1998), and Deepak Kumar, *Science and the Raj, 1857–1905* (Delhi, 1997).

[23] Eugene Irschick, *Dialogue and History: Constructing South India, 1795–1895* (Berkeley, Calif., 1994). For a theoretical account of how to speak of the relations between science and indigenous knowledge, see Richard Gillespie and David Wade Chambers, 'Locality in the History of Science: Colonial Science, Technoscience, and Indigenous Knowledge', *Osiris* 2nd series 15 (2000): 221–40.

[24] The model proposed by George Basalla continues to influence the field, despite being grossly outdated. George Basalla, 'The Spread of Western Science', *Science* 156 (1967): 611–22. See also Roy Macleod, 'On Visiting the "Moving Metropolis": Reflections on the

how science was transported from Europe on exploratory voyages, such as
Cook's travels, until it was successfully institutionalised in the colonies.
Non-European science was first controlled from the metropolis, until there
was leverage for greater local independence, which eventually gave way to
co-operation between the centre and the periphery. Many have followed
Macleod's lead by focusing on expeditions and the formation of disciplines, careers and formal institutions, in order to come to an idea of
science's relations with empire.[25] Instead of interpreting science as a dis-
crete body of ideas that could justify colonial expansion and strengthen
governance, I hope to pay serious attention to the symbolic and material
functions of natural knowledge. For my purposes, science and missionary
practice were so closely entangled that it is difficult to speak about the
relations between science and empire. Missionary science does not fit a
model of diffusion and institutionalisation: it existed in tension with more
elite knowledges and it drew on local traditions. It was a popular and
religious view of nature, a way of seeing as much as an exercise in theoretical speculation.[26]

Richard Drayton's suggestion, that Christian ideologies of man's place
in nature lay at the taproot of imperial expansion, provides a valuable
starting point for this work.[27] Drayton uses botany and Kew Gardens as
vehicles to explore how Britons attempted to find nature's divine laws and
to apply those principles in ordering human social arrangements. For
Drayton, Christian theology appears as a primal cause in scientific imperialism. In my work the focus is enlarged. Adamic responsibilities to subdue
the earth also had their place in the ideology of Christian missions.
Furthermore, in bringing agronomy, mapping and the display of nature
together with botany, it is possible to subscribe to a wider notion of

Architecture of Imperial Science', in *Scientific Colonialism: A Cross Cultural Comparison*
(Washington, 1987), Roy Macleod, 'Passages in Imperial Science: From Empire to
Commonwealth', *Journal of World History* 4 (1993): 117–50.

[25] See, for instance, the recent *Osiris* volume: Roy Macleod, 'Nature and Empire: Science and
the Colonial Enterprise', *Osiris* 2nd series 15 (2000): 1–317. For other valuable work on the
history of science, nature and empire, see Saul Dubow, ed., *Science and Society in Southern
Africa* (Manchester, 2000), M. H. Edney, *Mapping an Empire: The Geographical Construction
of British India, 1765–1843* (London, 1997), Richard Grove, *Green Imperialism: Colonial
Expansion, Tropical Island Edens, and the Origins of Environmentalism, 1600–1860*
(Cambridge, 1995), John M. MacKenzie, *Imperialism and the Natural World* (Manchester,
1990), D.P. Miller and P.H. Reill, eds., *Visions of Empire: Voyages, Botany and
Representations of Nature* (Cambridge, 1996), Alex Soojung-Kim Pang, *Empire and the
Sun: Victorian Solar Eclipse Expeditions* (Stanford, Calif., 2002), and Gyan Prakash,
Another Reason: Science and the Imagination of Modern India (Princeton, N. J., 1999).

[26] For the placement of vision in relation to colonial nature, see Mary Louise Pratt, *Imperial
Eyes: Travel Writing and Transculturation* (London, 1992).

[27] Richard Drayton, *Nature's Government: Science, Imperial Britain and the 'Improvement' of
the World* (New Haven, Conn., 2000).

nature's improvement. My suggestion is that the Christian rhetoric, to which Drayton pays heed, did not become a secular utopia as the century progressed. Christian ideologies of nature continued to have a crucial place in the public sphere even after they had ceased to hold credibility in the circles that Drayton discusses.

I am heavily indebted to the work of Niel Gunson, who has provided a detailed history of the South Pacific mission in its social context. Because the current work is primarily concerned with the status of natural knowledge, it is possible to rely on Gunson for a wider account of the character of the evangelists sent to the Pacific, and the challenges that awaited them there.[28] Gunson has also published an article on the scientific contributions of these missionaries, but has focused specifically on their role as guides and advisers to visiting naturalists, and their stance with respect to Darwinism.[29] I take a different route in discussing how missionaries saw their science as more credible than that of the secular visitors. In addition to Gunson, Rod Edmond, Vanessa Smith and Nicholas Thomas provide useful moorings for a study of the material culture of the South Pacific mission.[30] These scholars have pioneered the discussion of how the production, consumption and display of artefacts allowed meanings to be changed and exchanged in the context of the London Missionary Society's operations in the islands. Their methods are useful in making sense of missionary science as material culture.[31]

Through reading, writing, observing and collecting, the missionaries generated artefacts which made faith take form. The material culture of the missionary movement provides useful insights that help explicate how evangelicals ticked. A history that focuses on the production and reception of such objects can clarify the reasons for the popularity and pervasiveness of evangelicalism. There is much value in attending to the theological debates that framed this movement, yet it is the burden of this work to identify how missionaries regulated their time and lives in relation to the world around them.[32] Throughout this work a practical definition of evangelicalism will therefore be adopted, which takes the lived experience

---

[28] Gunson, *Messengers of Grace*.

[29] Niel Gunson, 'British Missionaries and their Contribution to Science in the Pacific Islands', in *Darwin's Laboratory*, ed. Roy Macleod and Philip Rehbock (Honolulu, 1994).

[30] Rod Edmond, *Representing the South Pacific: Colonial Discourse from Cook to Gauguin* (Cambridge, 1997), Vanessa Smith, *Literary Culture and the Pacific: Nineteenth-Century Textual Encounters* (Cambridge, 1998), Nicholas Thomas, *Entangled Objects: Material Culture and Colonialism in the Pacific* (Cambridge, 1991).

[31] For a starting point for science as material culture, see Robert Darnton, *The Kiss of Lamourette: Reflections in Cultural History* (London, 1990).

[32] For a start in the cultural history of evangelicalism, see Doreen Rosman, *Evangelicals and Culture* (Aldershot, 1992).

of believers more seriously. In this mode of analysis a missionary becomes an individual who meditated on nature, educated children, translated scripture and preached on the Sabbath. Such practices defined his sense of self and the community to which he belonged. The intellectual life of British expansion has often been restricted to studies of abstract theories and elite debate. But the knowledge that missionaries cultivated can also be understood if belief is seen as embodied activity.[33]

The way in which missionaries engaged with nature was central to the articulation of identity, and the first part of this book is concerned primarily with such private practices. Chapter 1 sets the context of the London Missionary Society's emergence, considers its attitude to learning, and the composition of its membership. The manner in which colonialism is used as a category in relation to missions will be explained here. Chapter 2 then considers how nature was implicated in the making of evangelicals, by considering how scientific methods were employed in education. Chapters 3 and 4 widen the discussion by suggesting how, upon conversion, meditations on flowers, oceans and the seed were vital in coming to terms with the passage of the spiritual life. As these chapters suggest, the practices of reading, writing, preaching and meditating on nature allowed missionaries far away from home to define their identity. This private and theological language of nature was also adopted by converts. But the process of replication was not simple; it involved creative appropriation and defined resistance. A close reading of objects exemplifies these claims. Chapter 2 analyses the depiction of a sloth and a beaver in order to show how natural historical creatures fitted into a typology of progress in education. A portrait of a Pacific islander called Temoteitei who was brought to London for conversion and treated like an animal is discussed in chapter 3. By studying an engraving of the demise of John Williams at the hands of alleged cannibals, chapter 4 suggests how a natural history of the environment was linked with notions of demise. The naturalisation of ideas of conversion, civilisation and death indicate how the religious self was linked with nature. Paying heed to the religious and the natural is vital in bringing to light forms of self-definition that operated side by side with race, gender and class.

---

[33] This theoretical move is inspired by the work of Barry Barnes, 'Practice as Collective Action', in *The Practice Turn in Contemporary Theory*, ed. Karin Knorr Cetina, Eike von Savigny and Theodre R. Schatzi (London, 2001) 19. The term 'practice' is borrowed primarily from the work of Pierre Bourdieu, *Outline of a Theory of Practice*, trans. Richard Nice (Cambridge, 1977), Pierre Bourdieu, *Distinction: A Social Critique of the Judgement of Taste*, trans. Richard Nice (London, 1986), and Pierre Bourdieu, *Rules of Art: Genesis and Structure of the Literary Field* (Cambridge, 1996).

The second part of the book uses nature in a different way: as a public arena that could be ordered and displayed to promote missionary rhetoric. Here also the 'thick description' of particular cases is of value. Chapter 5 considers the representation of one mission station named Huahine, while chapter 6 discusses a museological artefact now called A'a. The manner in which mission settlements were arranged denoted how the 'saved and the damned' were separated in physical space. Missionary stations epitomised British agrarian patriotism and provided proof of the efficacy of conversion in ordered paths and radiant chapels. The missionaries' documentation of an island's agricultural resources corresponded to the categorisation of islanders on a scale from barbarous to converted. When clothing their converts, missionaries did not use the raw produce of nature, but preferred to teach islanders to be industrious in growing cotton and weaving. Public practices of natural history could also encompass display: missionaries transported artefacts of war and livelihood back to Britain and placed them in a museum, alongside natural history specimens, demonstrating how unbelievers could not distinguish nature from culture. The environment of the islands, articles manufactured from nature, and commodities extracted from nature could all be used in the same rhetorical differentiation of converts and 'heathens'. The accessibility of nature, and the possibility of transporting artefacts between London and the Pacific, meant that the environment could serve as a common ground of knowledge between missionaries, their converts and their supporters. Nature became a means of engaging with Pacific thought, while appropriating and reinventing it. Relations with nature were invested with meaning in the public domain.

I will present these natural historical practices – both private and public – as a form of knowledge that eludes categorisation as science, religion or colonialism. The history of cultural contact is often plagued with questions of cause and effect.[34] What was the driving force of mission in the South Pacific? What was the relationship between the missionaries' theology and their politics and science? Such questions are too simple. Evangelical practice could encompass a range of different knowledges which were inherently and yet not fatally contradictory. Our modern classifications were still undefined, and so science was indistinguishable from religion or empire. The avalanche of diaries, letters,

---

[34] For example, see the premises of the exchange between Brian Stanley, 'Commerce and Christianity: Providence Theory, the Missionary Movement and the Imperialism of Free Trade, 1842–1860', *Historical Journal* 26 (1983): 71–94 and Andrew Porter, 'Commerce and Christianity: The Rise and Fall of a Nineteenth-Century Missionary Slogan', *Historical Journal* 28 (1985): 597–621.

evangelical periodicals and reports that form the basis for this book shed light on the way missionaries navigated various different traditions. In the missionaries' eyes, their theology was the best because it was vital and applied and their science was the most trustworthy because it was scriptural and tested by long-term experience in the field. Each of these forms of knowing was interrelated.

By locating negotiations between competing forms of practice in the South Pacific, the case may be made that the periphery is vital to understanding the formation of modern intellectual categories.[35] Though the South Pacific was geographically removed from London, it served as a test for forms of knowledge and conduct that were still in flux in the metropolis. In order to make this point it is necessary to move repeatedly between London and the Pacific. For example, the manner in which missionaries taught Pacific islanders science is comparable with how evangelicals at home taught poor children to read and write. Similarly, the agricultural improvement of Britain provided the ideology for missionary plantations. As will be explained, the rules adopted for dress by pious women at home were related to the supply of manufactured clothing to be used by poor orphans in the Pacific. The creation of the metropole is inextricable from the creation of colonies, and the creation of identities within the metropolitan populace may be related to the construction of distinctions between converts and unbelievers, civilised and depraved. With the deconstruction of geographical distance, it is possible to reconfigure the disciplinary boundaries of history. British history should not be seen as separate from Pacific history: what it meant to be British was defined against the Pacific, while the relationship of science and religion in the Pacific had implications in the metropole.

As a whole the book aims to highlight how science and religion worked in unison in the colonial setting. By writing, observing, collecting and displaying nature, missionaries used the environment as a source of symbols and revelation. The distinction between men of science and missionaries should be shed, because scientific speculation was seen to be the rightful preserve of the theologically minded before the professional vocation of the scientist was forged. Instead of writing a sanitised history of science and empire which focuses on great men such as Cook, it is the aim

---

[35] This is in keeping with recent trends in the historiography that link the metropolis with the colony. For some examples, see C. A. Bayly, *Imperial Meridian: The British Empire and the World 1780–1830* (London, 1989), Peter Cain and Anthony Hopkins, *British Imperialism*, 2 vols. (London, 1993), Felix Driver, *Geography Militant: Cultures of Exploration and Empire* (Oxford, 2001), Catherine Hall, *Civilising Subjects: Metropole and Colony in the English Imagination, 1830–1867* (Oxford, 2002), and John M. MacKenzie, *Propaganda and Empire: The Manipulation of British Public Opinion 1880–1960* (Manchester, 1984).

of this book to construct an account of knowledge from below. The missionaries' science could justify a range of activities from control and civilisation to conversion. What emerges from these claims is a more comprehensive view of how knowledge intervened in the contact and transformation of cultures.

1   The light of the sun: stimulus for mission

A celebratory game called 'Links and Ladders' was published in 1945 to mark the hundred and fiftieth anniversary of the London Missionary Society (figure 1.1). Intended to be played in the same manner as 'Snakes and Ladders', but without the theologically offensive associations of the serpent, 'Links and Ladders' provided supporters with a survey of the Society's history. Players were advised to cut out figures representing children from China, Papua, Madagascar, Africa, India and the South Seas to use as their pieces on the board. The starting point was marked 'Prayer Groups meeting all over the country' and each of the squares on the board symbolised a year in the life of the Society. When a player reached the foot of a ladder, for example the 'Abolition of Slavery in the British Empire and William Wilberforce' in 1807, they could move to the end of the ladder, in this case, 'India Opened to missionaries by Charter' in 1813. Similarly, if they came to the top of a link, for example 'John Williams murdered at Erromanga' in 1839, they were forced to move several squares backwards, in this case to 'John Williams sailed for the South Seas' in 1816.

By the twentieth century, the Society's history had therefore come to be widely celebrated by evangelical believers. Before proceeding any further it is necessary in effect to follow the players around the board of 'Links and Ladders' in order to understand the Society's operations and chronicle its important milestones. This will clarify the foundations from which the Society's South Pacific mission sprang. The Society was born in 1795, and cast itself as an organisation that brought together evangelicals from across the denominational spectrum. Its enthusiasm for mission was stoked by the notion that the time was right for the expansion of Christianity, and that believers stood at the door of the millennium. As the century passed, however, the Society became increasingly Congregational, partly as a consequence of other denominations setting up rival organisations for spreading the news of the gospel overseas.

The first section of this chapter will present a definition of evangelicalism, which will be useful in making sense of the Society. 'Links and

Ladders' illustrates how twentieth-century evangelicals hoped to redeem their time. Playing this game was a worthy occupation, when contrasted with secular amusements. The term 'New Advance' which appeared on the top left-hand corner denoted a successful appeal which by 1947 had raised two hundred thousand pounds: in addition to time, money could also be spent in a godly way to support the missionary enterprise, rather than personal pleasure.[1] The early nineteenth-century equivalents of these practices will be central to my definition of what it meant to be an evangelical.

Instead of prioritising the beliefs that evangelicals held, I hope to shed light on the daily routines which governed their lives, and which gave their faith a sense of assurance and hope. The use of time and money might serve as examples of such practices, but crucial to this book is the particular question of how evangelicals related to nature. Evangelical reflections on nature could take the form of daily meditation, regular preaching, scriptural exposition and Christian reasoning. Later in the chapter, I will investigate how theologies of nature came to their heyday in the nineteenth century, and how visions of improving nature motivated the founders of the Society. The evangelical appetite for interpreting nature in line with revelation needs to be located in the context of religious attitudes towards learning.

A particular issue that requires some care at the beginning of any study of missions is the nature of missionary relations with empire. 'Links and Ladders', for instance, makes a note of the date when missionaries were allowed access to India, and the date when slavery was abolished. While missionary links with colonialism were far from simple, as recent work has revealed, it is necessary to attend to the multiple forms of control – informal and formal, providential, commercial and secular –that could co-exist in the early nineteenth century. A strict definition of colonialism as political annexation sanctioned by the state cannot be applied to missionary work. Yet the triumphalism of 'Links and Ladders', as it celebrated the long history of the Society, draws attention to how Christian missionaries had, in effect, step by step, taken control of most of the world. This spiritual expansionism might have been distinct from state-led imperialism, and missionaries may have at times critiqued direct intervention; yet the rhetoric of evangelical missions, encompassing change and settlement, needs to be carefully studied. Was this a contestant form of colonialism that was separate from state control? The third section of the chapter will survey

---

[1] Norman Goodhall, *A History of the London Missionary Society, 1895–1945* (Oxford, 1954), 587.

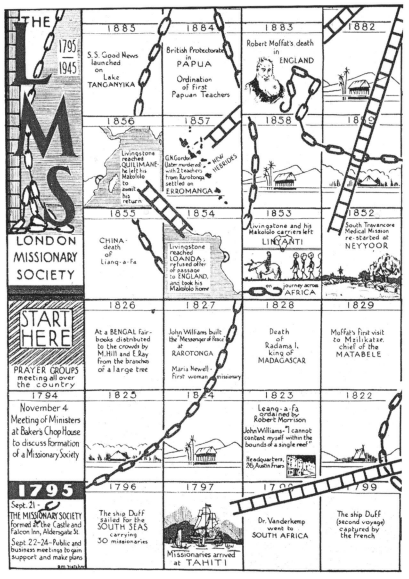

Figure 1.1: Inset from 'Links and Ladders', a game published to mark the hundred and fiftieth anniversary of the London Missionary Society in 1946. Some events from the history of the South Pacific mission are amongst those commemorated here: for example, the departure of the *Duff* in 1796 and the baptism of King Pomare in 1802. From Home Odds Box 14, CWM, SOAS.

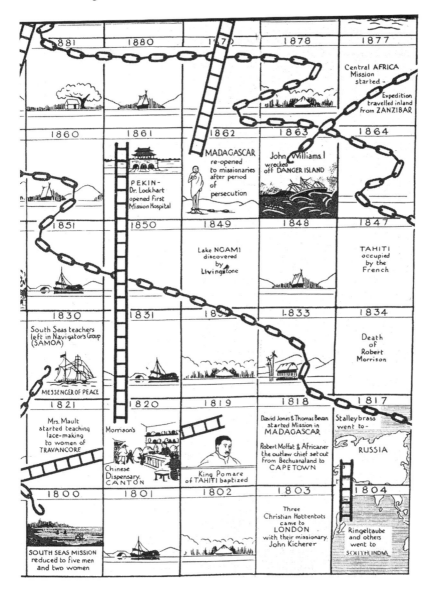

the historiography on this issue, and will come to some tentative conclusions with respect to the early nineteenth-century South Pacific mission.

While the London Missionary Society is in prime focus throughout this work, the setting-up of the *Evangelical Magazine* calls for some introduction. This widely read periodical served as the most significant route through which news of the Society's missionaries was disseminated. I will outline its provenance and aims, before using the periodical to consider the nature of the Society's subscribers. The claim that missionary organisations were bastions of the middle class has repeatedly been made. Yet the South Pacific mission had many working-class missionaries and its organisers took advice from renowned travellers and learned gentlemen. The question of how to place the Society in term of class composition therefore becomes a vexed one. Social mobility, however, might usefully serve as a distinctive feature of evangelical supporters of mission and their agents abroad. All of those who were associated with this mission saw it as an avenue through which they could enhance their standing. As with the question of colonialism, a healthy scepticism of reductionist answers must thus be entertained on the issue of class. But before moving to the contentious questions of the Society's relations with colonialism, learning and class hierarchies, I will begin by outlining its emergence, and placing it in the context of late eighteenth-century evangelicalism.

Evangelical emergings

The inaugural meeting of the London Missionary Society – held on 22, 23 and 24 September 1795 – became the talk of the metropolis. The manner in which the Independent minister, Revd David Bogue, and the Anglican, Revd John Eyre, rushed into each other's arms, when they met at Spa Field's Chapel in London, was said to epitomise the reconciliation of the established church with Dissent.[2] Bogue's sermon to the Society was strident on this note: 'We have now before us a pleasing spectacle, Christians of different denominations, although differing in points of church government united in forming a society for propagating the Gospel among the heathen. This is a new thing in the Christian church ... Behold us here assembled with one accord to attend the funeral of *bigotry*.'[3] Bogue's listeners responded with a shout.[4] The Society's Fundamental Principle – adopted in 1796 – ensured that inter-denominationalism was formally written into the structures of the organisation.[5] The Society's inter-denominational status was also stressed by its early title, which was simply 'The Missionary Society': only in 1818 was it to become 'The London Missionary Society'.

[2] Roger Martin, *Evangelicals United: Ecumenical Stirrings in Pre-Victorian Britain, 1795–1830* (London, 1983), 43.
[3] Lovett, *The History of the London Missionary Society*, 35–6.
[4] Martin, *Evangelicals United*, 43.
[5] Lovett, *The History of the London Missionary Society*, 49–50.

According to the plan adopted at this meeting, the sole object of the Society was to 'spread the knowledge of Christ among heathen and other unenlightened nations'.[6] Anyone who subscribed one guinea or more annually was a member and any minister whose congregation subscribed or collected fifty pounds annually was registered. General meetings were to be held annually in London on the second Wednesday in May, to choose directors, a secretary and collectors, and receive reports, audit accounts and deliberate on the progress of missionary work. Twenty-five directors were appointed at the first meeting; and it was decided that three-fifths and no more should reside in London so as to help with the regular transactions of the Society. This enthusiasm for foreign missions was characteristic of the time; the Society was preceded by the Baptist Missionary Society, which was founded in 1792, and followed closely by the Anglican evangelical Church Missionary Society, founded in 1799. The birth of three separate organisations in close succession might be explained by an exchange of ideas and personal friendships across denominational boundaries, amongst enthusiasts for mission.[7] These institutions were soon followed by other voluntary societies for improving hospitals and prisons, distributing Bibles, promoting education and abolishing the slave trade.[8] In order to come to terms with the proliferation of evangelical societies in the late eighteenth century, it is necessary first to understand the rise of evangelicalism.

The term 'evangelical' is not easy to define. The difficulty in coming to a precise meaning is compounded by the various fault-lines within the movement: distinctions between Arminians and Calvinists, Dissenters and establishmentarians, and post- and pre-millenarians flared up at various times in the late eighteenth and nineteenth centuries. Evangelicals were also very successful at influencing wider society; by the late eighteenth century they could be found amongst the working class, the middle class and the upper class. David Bebbington, however, provides a helpful set of characteristics that may be used with some caution to demarcate the boundaries of the term evangelical.[9] These are: conversionism, the belief that by the act of faith, and at the end of a process of sometimes intensive self-scrutiny and agonising, an individual could come to the certain standing of a believer; activism, the teaching that upon conversion believers should immerse themselves in serving the community and the 'heathen'

[6] Ibid., 30.
[7] Andrew Porter, *Religion Versus Empire? British Protestant Missionaries and Overseas Expansion, 1700–1914* (Manchester, 2004), 40–1.
[8] Mark Noll, *The Rise of Evangelicalism: The Age of Edwards, Whitefield and the Wesleys* (Leicester, 2004), 233.
[9] Bebbington, *Evangelicalism in Modern Britain*, 1–17.

world in urging others to convert; biblicalism, the aim held by evangelicals
to rely on the Bible in teaching, and to encourage its use in devotion; and
crucicentrism, meaning the centrality accorded to the doctrine of atonement as the fulcrum of evangelical preaching and worship. Boyd Hilton
explains that evangelicals fervently believed in vital religion; they often
used the phrase 'the religion of the heart' so as to identify their tradition.[10]
Their beliefs were said to be vital when contrasted to the ritual and
nominalism of formal religion in the Anglican church and in Roman
Catholicism. Britain's wars with Catholic France had a major part to
play in setting the social context for the emergence of evangelicalism.[11]

I will borrow these fundamental definitions of evangelicalism. However,
since the relation between nature and missions is at the focus of this work,
a specific aspect of evangelical identity will be the primary subject of
scrutiny. While emphasising the necessity of conversion and hard work,
and the Bible and its doctrine of atonement, evangelicals in doubt or far
away from affirming communities, such as the South Pacific missionaries,
needed reassurance. Observing nature was one way of finding such
strength; evangelicals came to terms with life and death, and the boundaries between civilised and 'heathen', in relation to nature. The way in
which believers used nature may be placed in the context of a range of
evangelical practices. The evangelical may be equated with an individual
who followed a set of daily rituals, alone and in the fellowship of believers.
These included reading, meditating, singing, conversing and praying.
Activities such as these drew on the material and the immediate to make
faith mature: the sight of friends, the contemplation of a political event
such as the French Revolution, prayers stimulated by news from the
mission field, the well-known chords of hymns sung on special occasions
in the past, and the contemplation of nature, could all strengthen belief.
Nature allowed faith to become real by linking the unseen spiritual realm
to the observed. It is not the contention of this work that nature was the
only way through which faith was materialised; but in the late eighteenth
and early nineteenth centuries, when the observation of nature was in
vogue, it constituted an important avenue through which evangelicals
could contemplate the hand of God.

The necessity of paying attention to the historical space where faith and
lived experience interact is borne out in the extant historiography.
Bebbington has pointed to the importance of a new notion of assurance
in late eighteenth-century evangelicalism: the ability to have complete
certainty in faith and salvation is tied, he argues, to the influence of the

---

[10] Hilton, *Age of Atonement*, 7–8.   [11] Noll, *The Rise of Evangelicalism*, 13.

Enlightenment on evangelicals. Preachers like Wesley could articulate such a strong faith because of what they borrowed from empiricist philosophy.[12] In the meanwhile, Boyd Hilton asks: 'Evangelicals professed to believe but could never quite be sure that they did so. Were they not Pharisees and hypocrites pretending to a faith which they had not?' Hilton emphasises that the evangelical movement contributed to the sense of anxiety and precariousness which prevailed at the time.[13] Two of the leading historians of evangelicalism therefore take assurance and doubt in turn to be characteristic of the movement. Instead of voting for one of these positions, I will take it as a given that confidence and anxiety worked side by side in the everyday experience of evangelicals. This is why a description of evangelical theology alone cannot give a comprehensive history; theology cannot be taken at face value. We need to combine an intellectual history of evangelicalism with an attention to the material artefacts and cultural practices that played an important role in supporting beliefs. This will prevent evangelical history becoming top-down with an undue emphasis on great figures and ideas. For ordinary men and women who called themselves evangelicals, belief could also have its moments of doubt. A definition of evangelicalism which emphasises everyday practices can come to terms with such contradictions.

This is not to say that there is no value in locating the birth of the Society in the terrain of theological developments. While in the sixteenth and seventeenth centuries the word evangelical could be used almost synonymously with Protestant, and as an opposite to Roman Catholic, by the later eighteenth century it had come to be associated with the revivals initiated by the Wesley brothers and George Whitefield in England and Jonathan Edwards in America.[14] But these evangelical leaders did not emerge out of nowhere: the Puritans of the seventeenth century bequeathed to evangelicals a stress on personal devotion and communion with God. In fact the rise of evangelicalism in the later eighteenth century might in part be explained by the passing from public memory of negative reminiscences of Puritan enthusiasm, where private religious inspiration excused people from observing ordinary laws and reasonable public duty, leading to disorder on the streets.[15] Eighteenth-century evangelicals also drew inspiration from continental pietism, and later missionary work cannot be understood outside this European context.[16] Networks of

---

[12] Bebbington, *Evangelicalism in Modern Britain*, 42ff.   [13] Hilton, *Age of Atonement*, 18.
[14] Noll, *The Rise of Evangelicalism*, 14–15.   [15] Ibid., 133.
[16] Andrew F. Walls, 'The Eighteenth-Century Protestant Missionary Awakening in its European Context', in *Christian Missions and the Enlightenment*, ed. Brian Stanley (Richmond, Surrey, 2001).

correspondence and personal friendship linked the continental pietists to John Wesley, Jonathan Edwards and the like. Mark Noll notes that though eighteenth-century evangelicals were the descendants of the Puritans and the pietists, they were not exactly similar to their forebears: 'Evangelicals stood very differently to the body politic than earlier Puritans; English-speaking evangelicals understood gospel religion against a different social background than did European pietists.'[17] Nevertheless the rise of evangelicalism might be pinned to the legacy of Puritanism and the influence of continental pietism; and it also drew strength in England from moves to reform the Anglican church, by returning it to primitive Christianity. The parents of the Wesleys, for example, were concerned that the established church imitate the faith and life of early believers.[18]

John Wesley's trip to Georgia in 1735, to minister to settlers and to preach to indigenous peoples, served as a decisive moment, both in his own life and in the rise of evangelicalism. On the eve of his departure he wrote that his chief motive in leaving Britain was the hope of saving his own soul. Wesley hoped that Georgia would be an idyllic place where he would find primitive religion; he would not be distracted by 'vain philosophy' or all that was 'luxurious, sensual, covetous, ambitious'.[19] When Wesley went on board, having convinced his brother and several other Oxford graduates to join him, he discovered that they were to travel together with Moravians, who were well known for their hard work in mission and who exemplified the practice of continental pietism. During the journey the Moravians had a profound influence on Wesley. They taught him German and he was happy to participate in their shipboard services. In conversation, one of them asked Wesley, 'Does the Spirit of God witness within your spirit that you are a child of God?' Wesley wrote: 'I was surprised, and knew not what to answer.' The Moravian asked him again, 'Do you know Jesus Christ?' When Wesley replied that he knew that Jesus was the Saviour of the world, the Moravian persisted in asking Wesley if he knew Jesus personally as his saviour. Wesley eventually said he did, but added in his diary: 'But I fear they were vain words.' These conversations with the Moravians confused Wesley as to the basis of his salvation, leading eventually to a move away from his high church belief in duty as the grounds for eternal life to a more experiential view of his relationship with God and divine grace as the foundation of salvation.

In Georgia, Wesley had a wretched time; by early August 1737 he was on his way back to England. Back at home George Whitefield had been

---

[17] Noll, *The Rise of Evangelicalism*, 59.   [18] Ibid., 60.   [19] Cited in ibid., 75.

converted in Oxford, and became a national sensation, preaching the necessity of faith in Jesus alone as the basis of Christian assurance. After more meetings with Moravians, and after a lengthy period of reflection, Wesley eventually came to place his faith in Jesus Christ in 1738. He wrote of a meeting he attended at Aldersgate, which probably resulted indirectly from the ministry of Whitefield: while the minister was 'describing the change which God works in the heart through faith in Christ, I felt my heart strangely warmed. I felt I did trust in Christ, Christ alone for salvation.'[20] Wesley now joined Whitefield as a preacher of the vital transformation of the heart; and lay societies sprang up everywhere for the spiritual nurture of young believers. By 1744 the first Annual Methodist Conference had been organised. While Wesley was adamant that no split from the Anglican church was necessary, the network of preachers and itinerants over which he came to take a lead had as its aim the rejuvenation of the established church. Early evangelicalism arose, therefore, as a movement within the establishment; only in the late century did it start to attract significant interest amongst Dissenters.[21] In the meanwhile, Whitefield was less enthusiastic about the structural organisation of his followers, though they did band together to form several societies. Later in the eighteenth century the chapels and the training school for preachers, established by Selina, Countess of Huntingdon, came to be associated with the Whitefield tradition.[22]

Even in the early 1740s, the seeds of debate between the followers of the Calvinist teachings of Whitefield and the Arminian teachings of Wesley had been sown. While this debate has often been emphasised as crucial in understanding evangelical history, it is important to point to how the opposing sides at times minimised their differences. For instance, Wesley wrote to John Newton in 1765 that his thoughts on justification were the same as those of Calvin, the hero of Wesley's opposition.[23] All of these evangelicals also held a common emphasis on itinerant preaching and the establishment of local societies, while taking a lax attitude to matters of discipline and norm in the Anglican church.[24] At issue was the doctrine of predestination and the relation between good works and salvation. The Methodists asserted the Arminian doctrine that salvation was available to everyone who believed and not just to those who were elected by God. Wesley therefore rejected outright the belief that some human beings are preordained for salvation, which was central to Whitefield's teaching. Wesley also railed against the Calvinist belief that converts might sin, and still be accepted by God because of the cross; Wesley held that as

[20] Cited in ibid., 89.   [21] Ibid., 125.   [22] Bebbington, *Evangelicalism in Modern Britain*, 29.
[23] Ibid., 27.   [24] Noll, *The Rise of Evangelicalism*, 114.

soon as a Christian sinned he ceased to be a believer. There was therefore no excuse for lax behaviour, and discipline was an important marker of belief for Methodists. In 1770, these differences erupted into a pamphlet war, initiated by the publication of the minutes of Wesley's annual conference of that year, which were interpreted as indicating that good works were a condition of salvation. Bebbington notes, however: 'Wesley seemed to be rejecting no less a doctrine than justification by faith. In reality he did not. Good works, according to Wesley, were not the way of justification, but they were essential to final salvation. So the "Calvinistic Controversy" of the 1770s that drove Methodism further apart from other Evangelicals was based in part on a misunderstanding.'[25]

With the passage of the eighteenth century there was a remarkable diversification in evangelicalism. The consolidation of evangelical presence within the Anglican church is exemplified, for instance, in the work of the converted slave trader John Newton; or in the beginnings of Charles Simeon's successful ministry in Cambridge; or for that matter by the iconic status of William Wilberforce, the MP who stood at the core of the Clapham Sect. But evangelical concerns were growing even faster outside the established churches. The relation between the Methodist Connexion and the Anglican church was always uncertain during Wesley's own lifetime; but after his death in 1791 his congregations moved towards Dissent. The difficulties with holding baptisms and participating in communion precipitated this separation. In the meanwhile, the descendants of George Whitefield's ministry had already separated from the Church of England, under the oversight of the Countess of Huntingdon. Evangelical belief was also mounting amongst Independents and Baptists. Even as evangelical thinking spread into such a variety of settings, alternative forms of organisation for religious expression became more popular.[26] Evangelicalism was also attracting a growing degree of attention amongst the middle classes, and the voluntary societies that burgeoned at the end of the century were particularly conducive venues for this group of believers. Robert Raikes' Sunday Schools movement is said to have provided the paradigm for this genre of evangelical society.[27]

It is in this context that the supposedly inter-denominational London Missionary Society sprang into existence. The Society's attempt to unite a diversity of denominations seems surprisingly distant from the eighteenth-century theological controversies between Calvinists and Arminians. This serves to outline how significantly the theological climate had changed by this period; by 1808 one Anglican clergyman claimed to have heard only

[25] Bebbington, *Evangelicalism in Modern Britain*, 28.   [26] Martin, *Evangelicals United*.
[27] Noll, *The Rise of Evangelicalism*, 232.

one sermon on predestination in twenty years.[28] By this time evangelicals were starting to move away from the Calvinist doctrine that God destined certain souls to hell. Instead there was an emphasis on human responsibility; damnation was said to result from a failure to respond to the gospel. In general there was disinclination to stress a strong view of God's control over human destiny. These shifts provided a bridge between rival theologies; and the term 'moderate Calvinism' might be applied to denote the changes. Moderate Calvinism is said to have been a typical product of the pragmatism of this period.[29] This middle ground between the legacies of Wesley and Whitefield was also an effective launch pad for evangelism. For if Christ had died for everyone, then everyone deserved the opportunity to come to their own decision regarding their salvation, and it was imperative that the message of Christianity be preached to all nations. All that was necessary for justification, or acceptance by God, was faith in the efficacy of the cross. It was then the hearer's responsibility to respond. Similarly, even if God elected his people, evangelicals could not know whom He had chosen, and they were thus obliged to spread the message as far as they possibly could.

The new wave of enthusiasm in mission was stimulated by these shifts in theology, and also by a growing dissatisfaction with patchy eighteenth-century attempts to preach the gospel in North America.[30] Wesley went to Georgia as a missionary attached to the Society for the Propagation of the Gospel in Foreign Parts (SPG), which was formed in 1701. This was a voluntary society with a decidedly establishment flavour. It arose out of high church Anglicanism and had as its aim the setting-up of officially sanctioned churches in North America, that would take a similar shape to the Anglican church in Britain. The SPG focused primarily on white settlers, though there were some haphazard efforts to reach indigenous peoples and slaves. Throughout the course of the century, it had limited success and its efforts were viewed with some disdain in Britain. Side by side with the SPG, Dissenters in North America also saw evangelism as a priority, but had even less success in moving beyond settlements. Moravians in the meanwhile, though well respected, led essentially isolated lives in small self-sufficient communities where quietism was valued. In the context of these endeavours and their lack of success there was a feeling that a re-evaluation was needed: no longer was the idea that missionaries should operate within the ambit of established settlements taken for granted.

---

[28] Bebbington, *Evangelicalism in Modern Britain*, 63.   [29] Ibid., 63ff.
[30] This is a summary of the strand of argument made by Porter, *Religion Versus Empire?*, chapter 1.

Uniting for mission?

The early documents of the London Missionary Society illustrate the arrival of this quickened interest in missions. There is in these documents the repeated sentiment that the 'time is right' for overseas evangelism. In the context of the revivals in Britain and America, the French Revolution and even the Lisbon earthquake, evangelicals firmly believed that the millennium would not be long in coming. All that was required in this context was a few well-worded publications, calling for the formation of missionary societies to spread the gospel overseas, to spur evangelicals into action.[31]

William Carey's *An Enquiry into the Obligation of Christians to Use Means for the Conversion of the Heathens* (1792) stands at the head of these. Carey urged his readers that the Great Commission was not restricted to the apostolic age, and went on to survey how the early church had pursued its evangelism. Characterising contemporary feeling, he dismissed eighteenth-century efforts at mission in a few words. Most striking, however, was the extensive table of all the nations of the world, arranged according to continent, and indicating the number of unbelievers.

> The inhabitants of the world according to this calculation, amount to about seven hundred and thirty-one millions; four hundred and twenty millions of whom are still in pagan darkness; an hundred and thirty millions the followers of Mahomet; an hundred millions catholics; forty-four millions protestants; thirty millions of the greek and armenian churches, and perhaps seven millions of jews.[32]

Carey had evidently extracted his estimate of population from contemporary travel accounts; in fact he acknowledged his reliance on the voyages of Captain James Cook.[33] In urging the formation of a missionary organisation he deployed a telling analogy with a trading company, comparing subscribers to shareholders.[34]

Melville Horne's *Letters on Missions: Addressed to the Protestant Ministers of British Churches* (1794) had a more direct impact on the formation of the Society. Horne had been employed as a chaplain of the Sierra Leone Company, which had been founded to see to the welfare of freed slaves from North America, by settling them in Freetown in Sierra Leone. When stationed in Sierra Leone, the enthusiastic Horne had soon

---

[31] See also Brian Stanley, *The Bible and the Flag: Protestant Missions and British Imperialism in the Nineteenth and Twentieth Centuries* (Leicester, 1990), 56.

[32] William Carey, *An Enquiry into the Obligation of Christians to Use Means for the Conversion of the Heathens* (London, 1792), 62.

[33] Cited in Stanley, *The Bible and the Flag*, 58.

[34] Porter, *Religion Versus Empire?*, 45.

been defeated by his isolation and his lack of language. He left Africa after a little more than a year. He took to heart the lesson of his experience: missionaries attached to companies such as he had been could expect limited success in evangelism. What was needed was a more comprehensive programme of missions that moved beyond settlements.[35] Haweis reviewed Horne's letters in the newly formed *Evangelical Magazine*, in November 1794; and this review was widely read.[36] Perhaps Horne's most important influence on the Society was in directing the body towards inter-denominationalism. He wrote: 'Let liberal Churchmen and conscientious Dissenters embrace with fraternal arms. Let the press groan no longer with our controversies and let the remembrance of petty interests we have contended for be buried in everlasting oblivion.'[37] That Horne could write like this is testimony to the spread of moderate Calvinism.

Carey's publication led the way for the formation of the 'Particular Baptist Society for Propagating the Gospel Amongst the Heathen' (later the Baptist Missionary Society). Amongst the readers of Carey's letters, however, was Revd David Bogue, who was to become another moving force in the direction of the Society. Bogue published in the *Evangelical Magazine* for September 1794 an article titled 'To the Evangelical Dissenters who practise Infant Baptism.' In the course of the article Bogue urged Dissenters who held to the doctrine of infant baptism to set up a Nonconformist missionary organisation to match that already established by those Dissenters who did not practise the rite. But, by November 1794, Bogue had also come to value an inter-denominational missionary effort over a narrowly denominational one, and he joined a meeting at Baker's Coffee House in London to plan the formation of the Society and sit on the first committee.

In the spring of 1794, the first meeting to pray and plan for the new missionary society was organised by the Anglican minister Revd John Eyre at the Dissenter's Library, Red Cross Street, London. The focus of this meeting was Horne's *Letters on Missions*, and a diverse group of ministers was in attendance: Revd Alexander Waugh, minister of Wells Street Congregational Church; Revd James Steven, Scots Presbyterian minister of Crown Court Chapel and Revd John Love, also a member of the Church of Scotland and minister of Artillery Street Chapel. These meetings became fortnightly occurrences and grew in size, eventually including Haweis and Bogue. At a meeting held in January 1795, Love was appointed to write a circular letter to evangelical ministers residing in

[35] Ibid., 47.   [36] Lovett, *The History of the London Missionary Society*, 11.
[37] Melville Horne, *Letters on Missions Addressed to the Protestant Ministers of the British Churches* (Bristol, 1794), 21.

or near London about the formation of a new missionary society. This
included news of a plan to hold the first general meeting in the summer of
1795. He again emphasised the inter-denominational basis of such a
society.[38] Revd George Burder of Coventry also drew up an address
which he submitted to the committee meeting at the Castle and Falcon;
this was circulated widely.[39]

This triumphant rhetoric of unity might be contrasted with the language
of the Calvinist–Arminian controversy of the late eighteenth century. Yet,
despite the new theological temper, the Society lacked denominational
comprehensiveness.[40] In actual fact, evangelical Baptists, Wesleyans and
Anglicans were thin on the ground. Baptists were the least likely to patronise the Society, because they already had their own organisation. The
Wesleyans continued to work towards a safer alternative Society that
would service their own camp. But most surprising by their absence from
the early proceedings of the Society were the Anglican evangelicals. This
group shared a common Calvinistic tradition with Independents and
Dissenting members of the Society, and yet their absence pointed to fears
kindled by the French Revolution. Dissenters had from the start been
warm supporters of the Revolution, believing that it would liberate
Protestant believers from the autocracy of the state. Yet Anglicans worried
that such sentiments characterised Dissent as bent on destroying the
church and state. Napoleon's excessive violence and the Terror soon
repulsed the Dissenters and caused a renunciation of their enthusiasm
for the Revolution. Yet their characterisation as rebels did not fade in
the Anglican memory until the second decade of the nineteenth century.

For these reasons, the London Missionary Society – despite being
surprisingly pan-evangelical when the controversies of the late eighteenth
century are considered – was not as widely supported as its founders had
hoped. It also had a strong Scottish connection. The newly formed missionary societies of Scotland in the late eighteenth century sent their
contributions on to the Society; and of the 475 missionaries appointed
by the Society between 1795 and 1845, 81 came from Scotland.[41] By the
second decade of the nineteenth century, the limited degree of denominational variety was definitely on the wane. The change in name from the
'Missionary Society' to the 'London Missionary Society' signified the
realisation that the organisation could no longer portray itself as denomi-
nationally diverse, because of an ever increasing Congregational dominance. Robert Steven, a Congregational lay director of the Society,
suggested that the name be changed because several other missionary

[38] Lovett, *The History of the London Missionary Society*, 16.   [39] Ibid., 20.
[40] Martin, *Evangelicals United*, 44.   [41] Stanley, *The Bible and the Flag*, 57.

societies had been formed, and because 'some confusion had arisen for want of a title more *distinctive* than that which was then adopted'.[42] By this time the founders of the Society had witnessed the establishment of the Church Missionary Society in 1799 and the formalisation of the Wesleyan Missionary Society in 1818.

A few incidents also made the Society acutely aware of its mostly Congregational base. One cause of resentment was the issue of collections. Since the Society had set itself up as pan-evangelical it felt obliged to collect funds from all denominations, yet Baptists and Wesleyans were aggrieved by this. In addition, Congregational supporters in the provinces urged that the Society's constitution be changed to reflect the denomination's creed. In 1818, Revd John Griffin, the Congregational minister in Portsea, wrote to the secretary of the Society that the denomination 'has now a magazine, it is said, of rising influence ... and some think that it should [now] have a distinct Society for missionary and general objects ... in order to counter-act the avowed principles of some other societies'.[43] The danger of Congregational revolt was avoided by the reconstitution of the Society as a denominational organisation. By 1823, the Society's Fundamental Principle had been modified to exclude Baptists from applying and soon Arminians were discouraged also. Ironically this repudiation of pan-evangelical ideals led, in the second decade of the nineteenth century, to improved relations between the various missionary societies, aided by the formation of a centralised committee in London which allowed the various secretaries to meet and discuss the needs of their respective organisations.

Theology or politics?

Explanations of the rise of missionary enthusiasm should take the spread of the newly moderate Calvinist theologies of the late eighteenth century seriously, even if the progression of the century saw mission organisations become more denominational. By the end of the eighteenth century, no longer could evangelicals sit complacently in the belief that the conversion of 'heathens' entailed no human responsibility. Stanley's seminal account of the emergence of mission has taken exactly this route. He writes: 'the only adequate explanation of the origins of the missionary societies is in terms of theological changes which were quite autonomous of develop-ments in imperial history'.[44] It follows, then, for Stanley that it is mean-ingless for missionary expansion to be linked simply to colonialism, or explicitly to Britain's imperial ambitions at the end of the century. This

---

[42] Martin, *Evangelicals United*, 72.   [43] Ibid., 73.   [44] Stanley, *The Bible and the Flag*, 59.

position is easily applied to the early history of the South Pacific mission. The islands were not the object of direct British control in the early nineteenth century. The tiny landmasses and negligible populations offered little to tempt empire-builders. After Cook's voyages a prolonged period of informal penetration followed: beachcombers, whalers, sandalwood traders and naturalists, with the occasional man-of-war, disturbed the authority of the Society's missionaries.

However, Stanley's argument about the distance between missionary work and colonialism has been vigorously called into question by Susan Thorne. Thorne argues that missionaries were often in the vanguard of the empire; and that religious motivations and humanitarian concerns were explicitly championed by many missionaries, not as an alternative to imperial control, but as the best means of securing it.[45] In the early nineteenth century, evangelicals moved away from focusing their missionary activities towards North American settlers and took on a concern for the local peoples of Asia, the Pacific and Africa. This shift is linked, Thorne urges, to new forms of imperialism brought into motion by the second British Empire.[46] The missionary dimension was crucial in neutralising British expansion by claiming divine sanction; especially at home where empire and the representation of 'heathen' peoples were twinned in popular imagination.[47] Mission supporters urged that the new terrain that was opened up to view was a providential call to evangelism. Thorne is quick to point out that missionary expansion was quite distinct from more secular forms of colonialism. The religious expansion espoused by evangelicals prioritised the introduction of the Bible over any other type of control. This is why evangelicals often critiqued the violence and godlessness of traders, military men and travellers abroad. But despite these differences, Thorne emphasises that missionary activity was a form of middle-class and working-class colonialism, which contested more elite visions of empire. At the core of Thorne's argument, then, is a view of multiple colonialisms in tension with each other and espoused by diverse segments of the British populace.

Even more recently, Andrew Porter's authoritative work has provided a definitive survey of missionaries' relations with state-led imperialism. Porter summarises his argument as follows:

Attitudes ranged from total indifference or harsh criticism of empire, through discomfort and toleration to enthusiastic support. The great majority of missionaries displayed a fitful interest in empire, giving it their temporary and often

---

[45] Susan Thorne, *Congregational Missions and the Making of an Imperial Culture in Nineteenth-Century England* (Stanford, Calif., 1999), 9.
[46] Ibid., 36.   [47] Ibid., 10.

grudging attention chiefly when it hindered evangelisation or might bring its authority to bear in a necessary defence of missions' past achievements or basic freedom to carry out their work.[48]

Porter is keen to restrict the place of empire in missionary ideology and to suggest that the evangelists' motivation came from millenarian thinking, revival and biblical interpretation. The empire seemed inconsequential when viewed in the light of these divine certainties. Furthermore, by tracing the links that Britain's Protestant missionaries cultivated with other societies from the continent and America, Porter hopes to show how missionary activity was carried out by a global band of supporters, rather than a narrowly national one. These qualifications are well supported. Yet Porter focuses his attention primarily on missionary relations with empire, rather than how missionary ideologies were appropriated by a godly populace at home, or how they were put into practice through engagements with local peoples. Even though a colonial discourse might not have been successfully transmitted by missionaries, local peoples often viewed their evangelists as colonists and authorities.[49]

While no easy generalisations may then be made about the relations between missions and colonialism, since the early nineteenth-century South Pacific mission is the subject of this work, the nature of that mission is worthy of attention here. Niel Gunson has explored the links between the South Pacific mission and colonialism in an early article.[50] Gunson's work has pointed to how the sending of the first missionaries to the region drew on colonial rhetoric. Haweis, for instance, wrote to Henry Dundas, the Home Secretary, that the South Pacific mission represented 'an English incipient Colony and every benefit resulting from the Civilization we hope to introduce must ultimately terminate in Britain'.[51] Missionaries in the islands encouraged unofficial use of the British flag; one missionary even presided at the coronation of a new monarch in Tahiti in 1824.[52] Coming from a Dissenting tradition, the South Pacific missionaries took as important a lack of interference in native government. But, despite this commitment, they took their role as advisers of the state seriously. South Pacific missionaries had a part, for instance, in instigating the revolution in Tahiti in 1808.[53] In the meanwhile, they actively formulated laws in the Pacific that put evangelical morals at

[48] Porter, *Religion Versus Empire?*, 323–4.
[49] For Porter's argument with respect to how indigenous peoples responded to missionary ideology see the conclusion of ibid.
[50] Niel Gunson, 'Missionary Interest in British Expansion in the South Pacific in the Nineteenth Century', *Journal of Religious History* 3 (1964): 296–313.
[51] Gunson, *Messengers of Grace*, 141.
[52] Ibid., 286.   [53] Ibid., 281.

the core of society. Such laws were put to public approval by the chiefs and people but it is clear that the missionaries were responsible for drafting them. On one occasion, for instance, a missionary complained of being 'surprised, grieved and vexed' at a law being formulated without his knowledge. The Tahitian Code, containing eighteen articles, was publicly approved on 12 May 1819; a similar code containing twenty-five articles was adopted for the Leeward Islands in the Society Group, Raiatea, Tahaa, Borabora and Maupiti on 12 May 1820.[54]

South Pacific missionaries also portrayed themselves as representatives of the British crown. The slippage between these two roles was such that the missionary Revd George Pritchard was appointed British Consul in Tahiti. Pritchard's appointment was not well received by his colleagues. One of them wrote: 'Never was I so ashamed to see a poor missionary in the tinsel of gold bouncing about and swaggering with a long sword by his side.'[55] But perhaps the most vital evidence for the relation between British representation and missionary work in the Pacific is the widespread assumption held by Pacific peoples that the evangelists were sent by the British monarch. Some aspects of the missionary's engagement with nature – which are at the focus of this work – were particularly potent visualisations of colonial control for the local populace. For instance, when an agricultural missionary attempted to stay longer in Tahiti, the king is said to have voiced his disapproval: 'he will go and report what long canes grow in Tahiti and then he says there will be ship loads of people come and make us titis, which is captives'.[56] Missionary work was not always or simply linked with British expansion. Indeed, by the second decade of the nineteenth century, evangelicals were keener on isolation from official British power, unless they felt threatened by French interests and Catholic missions. But with further European contact, trade and illicit recruitment of labour, missionaries started to require official sanction; a gun-boat then became a welcome sight. But in the early period, in the absence of extensive surveillance, the missionaries had a degree of independence perhaps unseen elsewhere, which allowed them to present themselves as authorities, at least to the local populace and to themselves.

Therefore there is benefit in applying Thorne's argument to the case of the South Pacific: instead of exploring the links between official colonialism and missions, it is valuable to attend to how mission texts point to an independent genre of control that existed side by side and in tension with political

---

[54] Ibid., 285.   [55] Ibid., 140.
[56] Letter dated August 9 1819, Folder 1/A, Incoming Letters from the South Seas, Box 3, Council for World Mission Archives (CWM), School of Oriental and African Studies (SOAS).

annexation. The language employed by missionaries – descriptions of the change from idolatry to Christianity; pleas for the need for settlements of Christianity; and metaphors of darkness and light – is symptomatic of their providential colonialism, particularly in relation to the environment. In addition to this the evangelists' insistent territorialism might exemplify their spiritual empire-building. The claiming of land for Christ's kingdom drew inspiration from the scriptural promise of the coming millennium, when all the nations would belong to the redeemer. In the South Pacific it was almost as if the missionaries were in a contest for the islands fought against traders, beachcombers and other travellers designated 'worldly sinners' who were polluting the region. In a document written to the directors of Bible and missionary institutions this opinion came to a fever pitch with the criticism of sailors whose 'vicious practices cannot fail to subvert and banish every virtuous feeling; – whose example only teaches them to sin as with a cart-rope and who are like a swarm of destructive locusts that eat up every green thing wherever they come'.[57] The early history of the mission attests to the evangelists' territoriality and their intense desire to outdo competitors in the islands. The first consignment of missionaries sent aboard the *Duff* in 1797 set up stations in Tahiti, Tonga and the Marquesas, though it was only the Tahitian mission that survived longer than two years. The Tongan islands were later taken under the control of the Wesleyan missionaries. Soon there were fraught discussions about how to divide up the Tongan and Samoan islands between the two societies. In the meanwhile the Church Missionary Society, under the patronage of Revd Samuel Marsden, pioneered work in New Zealand in 1814, and American evangelists set up a thriving station in Hawaii in 1820, with the help of Revd William Ellis. The search for new territories for the London Missionary Society took on a new impulse with the voyages of Revd John Williams, who explored the New Hebrides, New Caledonia and the Loyalty Islands. This expansionism went together with a desire to set up settlements, to educate, to separate 'saved from damned' and to usher in Christ's kingdom.[58]

In drawing attention to how missionary activity could count as a form of colonialism, distinct from political annexation, it is not my intention to present South Pacific missionaries as individuals in control of every situation. Just as secular political authorities faced resistance and revolt, South Pacific missionaries often found their plans distorted by renegade converts

---

[57] R. Ferguson, *Affecting Intelligence from the South Sea Islands: A Letter Addressed to the Directors and Friends of Bible and Missionary Institutions in Great Britain and America* (London, 1839), 3.

[58] For a more extensive account of the evangelisation of the South Pacific, see Gunson, *Messengers of Grace*.

who returned to practices which the evangelists had outlawed; heretical groups that mixed evangelical teaching with other doctrines; and the spread of nominal Christianity, as a form of religion practised by whole communities rather than the committed individuals that missionaries yearned for.[59] As an illustration of how missionaries in the South Pacific were rarely in control of events, it is well to attend to how the early confidence of the mission was quickly dissipated. The promoters of the mission had to re-evaluate their plans and to take account of the power and resistance of local peoples in the islands.

Soon after the first consignment of missionaries to the South Pacific left the shores of Britain, Haweis wrote to the Society's missionaries: '[If there is] an Otaheitian brother or sister joined to the Lord in one spirit, convey to them our kindest regard.'[60] His Calvinist idea that Pacific islanders were chosen by God was thus full of expectation. When the missionaries landed in Tahiti, they were able to see the people for themselves and were quick to lay aside Haweis' optimistic belief that conversions would be instantaneous. They commented, for example, on the 'wild disorderly behaviour' of the local priests, and their 'strong smell of cocoa-nut oil' which 'lessened the favourable opinion' with which they had arrived.[61] When the *Duff* was taking the second band of missionaries to the islands, disaster struck when it was captured by the French. While the crew were on their way to Rio de Janeiro they were taken hostage by the Portuguese. Soon the South Pacific mission was plagued by further trouble. The missionaries in the field, from the *Duff's* first consignment of labourers, were reduced to five men and women, when two missionaries were almost killed on Tahiti, and the majority fled aboard a ship named *Nautilus*.[62] It is clear, then, that the hopes for the South Pacific mission had gone awry; Haweis' early confidence was misplaced. At the annual general meeting of 1802, one speaker said:

If the sun be not yet risen, let us not thence infer that it will never rise; the morning star already appears, dispelling the gloom of night and cheering our hearts with all the expected blessings of approaching day ... The people do not possess all that simplicity of manners which we supposed ... but that precious seed of the kingdom will there be sown, and watered by the care and dew of Heaven.[63]

[59] Niel Gunson, 'An Account of the Mamaia or Visionary Heresy of Tahiti, 1826–1841', *Journal of Polynesian Society* 71 (1962): 209–43.
[60] Letter from Revd Thomas Haweis to the missionaries in the South Seas reprinted in the *Evangelical Magazine*, 1797, 510.
[61] W. Wilson, *A Missionary Voyage to the Southern Pacific Ocean Performed in the Years 1796, 1797, 1798 in the Ship Duff* (London, 1799), 56.
[62] *Evangelical Magazine*, 1799, 390.
[63] *Sermons and Report of the Missionary Society for 1802* (London, 1802), 43. The 'morning star' refers here to Jesus, and is probably a reference to Revelation 22: 16, the Authorised Version (all references to scriptural passages will be from this version).

In 1800, the *Royal Admiral* took twelve new missionaries from the London Missionary Society to the Pacific, with the aim of ascertaining the state of the mission.[64] Most commentators explained the mission's lack of success by pointing to the depravity of the islanders. The missionaries' 'increased acquaintance with the people had discovered a dreadful degree of moral turpitude generally prevailing among them, which has, no doubt, been much aggravated by the intercourse of wicked Europeans among them'.[65] 'These worthy missionaries are much entitled to our sympathy and prayers.'[66] '[T]he natural depravity of the human heart, and its enmity to the truth have been manifested: and these have shewn themselves either by a seeming assent to the doctrines of the gospel, while the affections remained unsanctified and the conduct unreformed.'[67] The early phases of the South Pacific mission therefore demonstrate that though the evangelists hoped to win the islands for Christ, they were far from achieving that ambition. It seemed that the local people held the upper hand. In the early anticipation of the mission's success no account was taken of indigenous agency.

This was why the early failure of the mission led directly to a more negative view of local peoples. There was thus a dramatic decline in the representation of islanders as 'noble savages' in missionary writings. This comes out clearly in Revd Matthew Wilks' sermon to the annual general meeting in 1811, where he critiques an individual who holds to the older tradition of the peaceable savage.

'Let them alone', said an eminent British physician to Mr. Eyre and me, when we solicited his pecuniary assistance, 'they are happy now, and you will disturb them.' So he wrapped it up. 'They are happy now!' and yet one of our missionaries at Tongataboo, also beheld a warrior draw his knife and cut off a slice of flesh from the arm of his captive, and eat it raw before them. 'They are happy now,' said this safe son of Esculapius, and yet another of our missionaries saw eight peaceable men seized, butchered, baked and eaten by these happy savages.[68]

But, strangely, it was only after the Pacific islanders were depicted as completely fallen that their conversions occurred. By 1815, the directors of the Society noted that fifty islanders could be considered as 'worshippers of Jehovah'. These people were said to be 'regular in their attendance on the means of instruction; that they are in the habit of retirement for secret prayer'.[69] By the next year the number was up to 'five or six

---

[64] Lovett, *The History of the London Missionary Society*, 65.
[65] *Sermons and Report of the Missionary Society for 1805* (London, 1805), 199.
[66] *Sermons and Report of the Missionary Society for 1806* (London, 1806), 4.
[67] *Sermons and Report of the Missionary Society for 1808* (London, 1808), 6.
[68] *Sermons and Report of the Missionary Society for 1812* (London, 1812), 58.
[69] *Sermons and Report of the Missionary Society for 1815* (London, 1815), 4.

hundred including most of the principal chiefs'.[70] And in 1817, 'the number of candidates for Christianity exceeds 1000 and ... idolatry has
received a universal shock and totters from its foundation throughout all
the islands'.[71] The logic had come full circle. Tahitians were now said to be
easily convinced of the truth of Christianity, not because of their nobility
but because of the depth of their barbarity. In 1816, a fresh band of
missionaries was despatched from London. With these new missionaries
the South Pacific mission was set on a successful course.

The successive waves of optimism and pessimism that marked the early
history of the South Pacific mission might be extrapolated to make a case
against reductionism. This was not a mission where confident plans could
lead to certain results: it therefore does not represent a form of colonialism
which went uncontested. In explaining the nature of the South Pacific
mission, the moderate Calvinism of the Society might usefully explain
why Haweis was so certain of conversions; yet the missionaries' aspirations
for territory need also to be seen as a form of spiritual expansionism.
Historical explanations of missions should not privilege theology or politics. In the meanwhile, the Society's relations with official colonialism
might be explored even while its activities might be cast as a separate genre
of providential colonialism. Speaking of missionaries as colonists should
not simplify our views of how they engaged in trade, or how they advocated civilisation and political annexation.

Nature's place

Some observers put the lack of success experienced by the early South
Pacific missionaries down to their inferior education. The views of Haweis,
who was responsible for the choice of the first evangelists, were: 'A plain
man, – with a good natural understanding, – well read in the Bible, – full of
faith, and of the Holy Ghost, – though he comes from the forge or the shop
would I own, in my view, as a missionary to the heathen, be infinitely
preferable to all the learning of the schools.'[72] This strand of thought was
soon called into question by Revd David Bogue who went on to establish
a Missionary Seminary in Gosport, where the outbound agents of the
Society were trained: this institution will be the subject of discussion in
the next chapter. But the views of men like Haweis have had a profound
effect on the historiography of evangelicalism and missions until quite
recently. The suggestion that learning and evangelical enthusiasm followed

---

[70] *Sermons and Report of the Missionary Society for 1816* (London, 1816), 3.
[71] *Sermons and Report of the Missionary Society for 1817* (London, 1817), 5.
[72] Cited in Lovett, *The History of the London Missionary Society*, 28.

distinct paths has traditionally seen evangelicalism cast as separate from the Enlightenment. Whilst Enlightenment thinkers stressed reason, it has been supposed that evangelicals followed intuitions and passions. In this context discussions of missionaries' attitudes to nature and science have seemed irrelevant.

Yet there were cogent links between the Enlightenment and evangelicalism at several levels. Obviously evangelicals derided the extreme scepticism of some Enlightenment thinkers, but they relied heavily on John Locke for the notion that true religion was determined not by formal authorities or traditions passed down through generations, but rather by knowledge available to all.[73] The individual could, through a process of step-by-step reasoning, move towards a relationship with God. Crucial in this were two forms of revelation: the Bible and nature. While the Bible was said to be a divinely inspired text revealing God's plan of salvation for humankind, nature was said to be intricately designed, pointing towards the existence of the Creator. Following the scientific method, evangelicals held that true religion could be put to the test. While these links suggest that Protestantism was recast in the mould of Enlightenment philosophy, it would be too simplistic to assume that all of evangelicalism's tenets were derived directly from the Enlightenment. Some of evangelicalism's doctrines had long traditions that preceded the Enlightenment. But it seems undeniable that these doctrines were reworked by the late eighteenth century. The peoples of the South Pacific, for instance, forced evangelicals to rethink some of their Enlightenment ideas. The missionaries often failed to convince their charges that they should feel the guilt of their sin and so to experience the vital change of conversion, because of the emphasis placed by the islanders on communities and tribes.[74] In the meanwhile, the islanders were observed and classified by the missionaries on an ethnological scheme that arose from new schools of learning.[75] The Enlightenment therefore profoundly shaped mission, even when the evangelists were working-class men of little education.

In this context a study of missionaries' views of science and the environment seems apposite. The tradition of natural theology experienced a resurgence in the mid-seventeenth century amongst natural philosophers, who hoped to show how their writings were reconcilable with piety. Robert Boyle, for instance, portrayed nature as God's temple and natural

---

[73] Bebbington, *Evangelicalism in Modern Britain*, 57; Noll, *The Rise of Evangelicalism*, 140–1.
[74] D. Bruce Hindmarsh, 'Patterns of Conversion in Early Evangelical History and Overseas Mission Experience', in *Christian Missions and the Enlightenment*, ed. Brian Stanley (Richmond, Surrey, 2001).
[75] Jane Samson, 'Ethnology and Theology: Nineteenth-Century Mission Dilemmas in the South Pacific', in *Christian Missions and the Enlightenment*.

philosophers as priests.[76] By the eighteenth century Isaac Newton's works had joined the canon of natural theology. Newton had the decoding of prophecy firmly in view in his work on astronomy; by engaging in science it was his belief that he could understand scripture; those who performed Newtonian demonstrations often claimed to be showing the powers placed by God in nature.[77] But the climax of the tradition came with the work of William Paley, whose *Natural Theology* (1802) became the classic. The popularity of Paley's work lay in its easy style, which allowed any reader to use common observations as a basis for an argument for the existence of God. Nineteenth-century texts that followed in Paley's wake deployed a similar style by piling up numerous examples to reach the summit of the certain knowledge of God's existence. Natural theological rhetoric appealed to the mind's eye as much as reason, by pointing to the aesthetic adaptations of nature: its coherence, order, harmony, unity and symmetry. Natural theologians also pointed to the sublime in nature in the hope of stimulating awe and reverence. The typical form of the argument was an analogical one: if the eye was as intricate as a mechanical contrivance, then why was it surprising that it had its maker too? Readers were confronted with a choice: it was within their terrain to decide whether the natural world was ordered or chaotic.[78] A feature of this genre was its popular appeal. From artisans to gentlemen, all could be edified by meditating on nature.

Typically it has been assumed that evangelicals were suspicious of natural theology, because it diverted attention from scripture as the sole authority of revelation. But this argument has now been superseded. Attention is being directed to theologies of nature – devotional beliefs about the character of God derived from nature – which could encompass and move beyond natural theology.[79] While natural theology had a demonstrative function in arguing for the existence of God from nature, a theology of nature by definition could depend on reason or revelation to consider God's relation to humankind demonstrated in nature, and could foster prayer, meditation and elevated piety. A theology of nature could therefore have a significant role after conversion in upholding beliefs. The hugely popular works of Thomas Dick, for instance, sought to present the middle and lower ranks of society with a thoroughly evangelical account of

[76] Astore, *Observing God*, 48.
[77] John Hedley Brooke, 'Religious Belief and the Content of the Sciences', *Osiris* 16 (2001), 10.
[78] Brooke and Cantor, *Reconstructing Nature*.
[79] Topham, 'Science, Natural Theology, and Evangelicalism in Early Nineteenth-Century Scotland'. The distinction between natural theology and the theology of nature was first made by John Hedley Brooke, 'Natural Theology from Boyle to Paley', in *New Interactions between Theology and Science*, ed. Clive Lawless (Milton Keynes, 1974), 8–9.

nature.[80] Dick intended that his works would teach moral lessons which would serve to advance the millennium and to prepare believers to explore God's creation in the afterlife. In effect his theology of nature was an attempt to prevent the secularisation of science and to show that proper studies of nature were those that were conducted by devout believers. Opposing the growing trend towards the professionalisation of science, Dick defined a new calibre of scientific practitioner named 'the Christian Philosopher' who would practise science as a subject intimately linked with his beliefs. The *Evangelical Magazine*, the bastion of the Society's support, applauded Dick's works. In the meanwhile organisations such as the Religious Tract Society, for which Dick wrote, set about promoting this emerging evangelical theology of nature by putting the newest technologies of print to work in publishing a range of authors.[81] There were a myriad of authors then, of whom Dick is one of the best known, who sought to popularise the study of nature as the bounden duty of evangelicals.

The extensive use of theologies of nature in the early nineteenth century points to interesting links between the Enlightenment and evangelicals. It suggests how popular science was amongst evangelicals: theological discourses on nature could contest the emerging genre of professionalised science partly because of their wide following. This was a genre of knowledge that could be practised by ministers and lay people alike. The use of natural metaphors by missionaries has already been noted in passing by several historians.[82] A set of articles written by a Thomas Lovegood in the *Evangelical Magazine* provide a good example of how believers, who were closely associated with the Society, could use nature.

Lovegood, who may have been a real person, or a mythical character in the mould of Christian in Bunyan's *A Pilgrim's Progress*, wrote to the editor of the *Evangelical Magazine*: 'I am Sir a mechanic, in a close part of London, where I have passed my life; and thro' the divine blessing on my industry can now venture to leave my shop occasionally.'[83] Lovegood was acquainted with the views of some authors who disapproved of any who 'venture to sip any of those streams which the worldly are encouraged to drink in copious draughts'. But knowing that his family 'longed for a holyday' and wishing to reward them for 'orderly conduct, industry and obedience', he decided to 'see the fields and the gardens, which bear testimony to God's faithfulness!' This idea came to him whilst listening

---

[80] Astore, *Observing God*. See chapter 2, for instance.   [81] Fyfe, *Science and Salvation*.
[82] Jean Comaroff and John Comaroff, *Of Revelation and Revolution: Christianity, Colonialism and Consciousness in South Africa* (Chicago, 1991), 80, and Hall, *Civilising Subjects*, 302.
[83] *Evangelical Magazine*, 1806, 212.

to his 'minister's sermon, which, in a sweet manner described the faithfulness of God to his promises from the works of Nature'.

After instructing his 'wife and little ones (who have all been taught to read) to search their Bibles for those passages of scripture, which mention trees, and flowers, and grass', the family set off into the provinces of nature. Lovegood wrote to the editor about three separate journeys: to the countryside of Essex, to the seashore and down the Thames. Whilst in Essex, having little knowledge of natural history, he felt unable to direct his family and 'asked a child, bred in those parts, to walk with [them], and tell [them] the names of the birds and flowers, which principally attracted the children's notice'. As soon as the natural object was named, a relevant scriptural passage was found and meditation commenced. On seeing some lilies, for example, 'my eldest boy eagerly examined, and said, "Our Lord has commanded us to examine the lilies how they grow" ... Who can tell what we felt, when turning to St Luke's Gospel, we pursued the passage, and read the gracious assurance that Solomon, in all his glory, was not arrayed like one of these.'[84] Whilst on the Thames, and when the sun was sighted rising over the river at dawn, Lovegood wrote: 'I ordered all my children to look towards the east, and, in my poor humble way took my Bible, and explained the darkness of the soul by nature, and how "the Sun of Righteousness arises with healing under his wings" and dispels the darkness of the human soul, and brings light and immortality to the mind, by the gospel.'[85] And again, 'my oldest girl pleased me, who, as we were near landing, saw a lovely tree, green and verdant; and clasping my hand and looking in my face, with irresistible sweetness she said, "The trees of the Lord are full of sap!"'[86]

A contributor to the *Evangelical Magazine* claimed, 'perhaps no study, except that of the sacred scriptures, is so well calculated to expand and elevate the intellectual faculties as that of Nature'.[87] Because of the 'wonderful analogy' between the created world and the spiritual world, there were important truths that believers could come upon through the practice of meditation.[88] 'Almost every object they see, when they are in a right frame of mind, leads their thoughts to Jesus, or tends to illustrate some scriptural truth or promise.'[89] Lovegood, for example, could

---

[84] From Luke 12: 27: 'Consider the lilies how they grow: they toil not, they spin not; and yet I say unto you, that Solomon in all his glory was not arrayed like one of these.'

[85] *Evangelical Magazine*, 1806, 359. This is a clear reference to Malachi 4: 2: 'But unto you that fear my name shall the Sun of righteousness arise with healing in his wings; and ye shall go forth, and grow up as calves of the stall.'

[86] Ibid. This is a reference to Psalm 104: 16: 'The trees of the LORD are full of sap; the cedars of Lebanon, which he hath planted.'

[87] Ibid., 1812, 340.   [88] Ibid., 1793, 24.   [89] Ibid.

compare the sun rising over the dark river to the light revealed to the human soul in the darkness of sin. This light came from the Sun of Righteousness, Jesus Christ, making this meditation a worthy one for an evangelical.

Natural metaphors could point the individual to his or her interior state, because they were easily understood and peculiarly arresting. Lovegood wrote, 'I understand our minister better, and feel great delight as I associate with his lively descriptions those days of recreation which pointed out to my view the works of creation.'[90] And again: 'A right sermon acts upon my mind as the blessed Sun does upon the pretty buds; it opens them, causes them to expand, and finally to bring forth fruit. So did this: I retired after service to a seat in a lovely grove by the sea-shore.'[91] Meditation was always framed by other practices, such as listening to sermons and reading the Bible. 'When I clasp my Bible to my breast', Lovegood wrote, 'I feel such a repository of choice promises garnishing all the works of creation, that I am constrained to remember the apostles' admonition, "Rejoice evermore."'[92] In understanding the tides, Lovegood wrote, 'I had with great pains put some philosophical notions about it into my head which I learned out of one of my son's books.'[93] The *Evangelical Magazine* thus fell in place alongside other artefacts of evangelical instruction such as the sermon, the lecture and the book, which all provided scientific training in how to observe nature.

Lovegood's narrations were accessible and interesting because readers could locate themselves in relation to him. Personal announcements of the state of Lovegood's soul were crucial in keeping this interest: 'Providence still blesses me in my "basket and my store;" and I persuade myself, your religious feelings will be gratified when I tell you that the Bible continues to guide my sober pursuits and necessary relaxations.'[94] He also commented on his material condition: 'forgive my fondness, Sir, whilst I tell you, when, in the scarcity of bread, my repining heart spoke its fears, how it was reproved and relieved by a little girl, who with ingenuousness of youth called upon me to remember how the young ravens, such as we found in the wood, were fed by God when they cried out to him'.[95] Lovegood found his meditations on nature particularly arresting because of his confinement in the city. In describing the sight of the sun he noted, 'we live in a very close and narrow street; and I had never seen the peculiar glories of such a scene'.[96] Lovegood wrote of his meditations: 'I rejoice in the enlargement

---

[90] Ibid., 1806, 214.   [91] Ibid., 1811, 214.   [92] Ibid., 1806, 360. From 1 Thessalonians 5: 16.
[93] Ibid., 1811, 213–14.   [94] Ibid., 212.
[95] Ibid., 1806, 213. This may refer either to Psalm 147: 9 or Luke 12: 27.
[96] Ibid., 1806, 359.

my mind feels upon a review of what I have seen!'[97] This expansion of the mind was intimately related to the proper relationship of man and God, with man as subject and God as ruler, and man as created and God as Creator. Lovegood wrote when he saw the sea: 'Has the wonderful Being who "holds these waters in the hollow of his hand," deigned to remember me in my low estate?'[98] Meditating on nature brought evangelicals to an understanding of human insignificance. The environment showed how greatly they needed to improve and how extensive the task of converting the world would be.

The London Missionary Society's reliance on a theology of nature is borne out clearly in a sermon presented to the inaugural meeting of the organisation by Revd John Hey of Bristol. The scriptural text from which he spoke was Ephesians 1: 10, which promised that God would in 'the fulness of times ... gather together in one all things in Christ, both which are in heaven, and which are on earth; even in him'.[99] This was taken to be a direct reference to the millennium, and Hey was adamant that his hearers stood at the doors of a new era, when the nations would turn to Christ. In the course of his sermon, Hey hoped to retell 'every moment of terrestrial existence, from the creation to the end of the world' in order to demon-strate the 'astonishing variety of occurrences which are comprised and connected in the universal providence of God'.[100] The setting-up of the Society and the choice of the Pacific would then appear as part of that predestined plan. For my purposes, what is striking is that Hey used so many images from nature to illustrate the work of Providence.

The centuries following the creation of the world were said to show how 'darkness had covered the earth, and gross darkness the people'. Though 'celestial rays' did shine upon a line of chosen people, the rest of the world remained under 'clouds of intellectual gloom'. The only revelation at hand to guide their experience was to be found in nature: 'they had just light sufficient to render their darkness visible'. At the appointed time, however, 'the refulgent SUN OF RIGHTEOUSNESS unveiled his hidden glories' and soon 'the dismal caverns of darkness which were lined with thickest folds of sullen darkness ... became irradiated with the splendours of heavenly day'.[101] With the arrival of Christ, the project of spiritual irrigation could begin once more. But the first shoots of spiritual progress were soon devoured by several 'beasts'. First on the scene were the Roman emperors, followed by Prophet Mohammed and 'about one hundred years after him, in the seventh century, that hydra-headed monster the Papal

---

[97] Ibid., 360.   [98] Ibid., 1811, 212.   [99] Ephesians 1: 10.
[100] *Sermons and Report of the Missionary Society for 1795* (London, 1795), 75.
[101] This was probably a reference to Malachi 4: 2.

beast took his rise, that beast that opposeth and exalteth himself, above all that is called God'. Again there was a 'lowering of clouds of ignorance, superstition, and barbarity' across the Christian world.[102]

The long battle between light and darkness had not come to its end. With the Reformation, these clouds of gloom were confronted by light, and truth once again 'began to shine in its native lustre and beauty'. According to Hey, by the time of the Reformation the church had arrived at last at the period ordained for the millennium. Now Hey's text could come to its fulfilment. In this, the 'fulness of times', the chief object was the unification of everything on heaven and earth in the body of Christ, the church. Vital to this process was the rejuvenation of nature:

> If we take a survey of the system of nature in general, we behold the red lightning gleaming through the vast expanse and menacing the inhabitants of the earth with fiery fury … So terrible and violent are the convulsions of nature sometimes, that it appears as if she meditated her own destruction. If we turn to the brutal tribes, we clearly perceive with what sanguinary gust, and savage ferocity many of them prey upon each other. If we contemplate beings of a higher order, beings that are distinguished by rational and immortal powers; what baneful and destructive quarrels have obtained among them?[103]

This chaos, Hey explained, resulted from humankind's sin. Sin had bestialised the civilised and destroyed the proper organisation of society. But the millennium provided the opportunity to reverse these effects. Transgression could now be cancelled and people could convert to Christian truth. As this occurred, every part of the habitable globe would be cultivated and occupied.[104] Nature would return to its proper function and state; and human beings would come into a relationship with the Deity. The extirpation of most of 'the noxious creatures' of the earth, and the domestication of any that remained, would follow.[105] The scriptural prophecy that the wolf and the lamb would dwell together would be fulfilled – not just at a symbolic level as human enemies united but also at a literal level – as nature itself was realigned.[106]

The next chapter contains a study of the organisation of sermons delivered at meetings of the missionary society. For the moment, however, Hey's sermon might serve as evidence of how a theology of nature informed missionary work, especially since this was one of the first sermons delivered to the Society. A theology of nature might also be traced in Haweis' article in the *Evangelical Magazine*, and his speech to the

---

[102] All quotes in this paragraph from *Sermons and Report of the Missionary Society for 1795*, 75–7.
[103] Ibid., 79.   [104] Ibid., 82.   [105] Ibid.
[106] The reference to the wolf and lamb arises from Isaiah 11: 6.

44 Nature and the Godly Empire

inaugural meeting, urging the choice of the Pacific islands as the first venue of mission work.

In the article which appeared two months before the inaugural meeting, Haweis urged that 'no other part of the heathen world affords so promising a field for Christian mission'.[107] In his very next sentence, Haweis explained how 'the temper of the people, the climate, the abundance of food, and easy collection of a number together for instruction' meant that the Pacific islands were 'fields ripe for harvest'.[108] There is also evidence of the pietist legacy in Haweis' article. He observed that the Moravians were putting their lives to the test in the 'frozen mountains of Greenland, and feeding on whales' flesh to carry the Gospel into the hut of the savage Eskimaux'.[109] Given their success in such a hard environment, would not the salubrious Pacific climate by its own virtues guarantee the success of the missionaries' labours? The island of Tahiti, for example, could 'realize the fable of the gardens of Hesperides'.[110] The weather was presented as perfect: 'the heat is tempered with those refreshing breezes which alternately blow to and fro from the land'. Haweis also described the vegetation of the islands in Edenic language: 'Nature has spontaneously provided a supply of food for the inhabitants in the trees that shade their habitations.' So luxurious was this provision that work was needless, just as it had been before the Deity cursed Adam and Eve.

The affability of the inhabitants of the South Pacific was said to be evident in their manners, which were described as 'mild and gentle'; in their emotions which were so tender that 'their sorrow for the loss of relations is written literally in tears of blood'; and in their language, which was described 'as more soft and full of vowels than elsewhere'.[111] Nature had made these people quite unlike the 'northern savage' who spoke with 'guttural roughness' or a 'Hottentot' who speaks with a clack that would be an insurmountable barrier to communication. They were also said to be distinct from the 'polished Chinese' who use 'an immense number of characters'. Haweis concluded that there was no other tribe inhabiting the earth that nature had prepared more appropriately for the reception of the gospel.

But Haweis had to be careful of stretching his argument too far. It was too easy to imply that nature had equipped the islanders well enough, making it unnecessary to send the revealed religion of scripture to them. This hesitance comes out, for instance, in his admission to the inaugural meeting: 'I am afraid to speak, what is recorded lest some should think

---

[107] *Evangelical Magazine*, 1795, 262.
[108] The image of harvesting was used several times in the gospels; see, for instance, John 4: 35.
[109] *Evangelical Magazine*, 1795, 262.   [110] Ibid., 264.   [111] Ibid., 266.

I were painting a fairy land.'[112] The portrayal of Pacific islanders as peaceable and leisured sat uneasily with the Society's belief that all human beings were sinful and that perfection was impossible. So Haweis noted: 'amidst these enchanting scenes, savage nature still feasts on the flesh of its prisoners – appeases its Gods with human sacrifices – whole societies of men and women live promiscuously'.[113] There were clearly limits to the uses of a theology of nature. But taken together with Hey's sermon and Lovegood's letters, Haweis' reasoning suggests the multiple uses of a theology of nature. A theology of nature could affect the choice of a region of the world for mission; it could stimulate reflection on the course of history that had led to the formation of a missionary society; and it could be used for personal meditation.

Printing mission

Both Lovegood's letters and Haweis' article appeared in the *Evangelical Magazine*. I will make extensive use of the *Evangelical Magazine* as a source in tracing the uses of a theology of nature in publicising the triumphs of the South Pacific mission. The *Evangelical Magazine* was launched in 1793 and appeared every month, selling for sixpence and having a circulation of eighteen to twenty thousand at its commencement.[114] It has been identified as 'the earliest of the second generation of religious magazines'.[115] While following the style of the very early *Gospel Magazine* (1766–84), it made innovations with such features as illustrations, and predated many of the smaller denominational magazines that appeared in the second quarter of the nineteenth century. It was published first by T. Chapman of 161 Fleet Street, and after 1801 by T. Williams of Stationers Court, Ludgate Street.[116] Revd John Eyre, an Anglican divine brought up in a Calvinist family, was the founding editor, holding this post until 1802, the year before his death.[117] Revd George Burder, an Independent minister, succeeded Eyre.[118] Both Eyre and Burder were also closely associated with the London Missionary Society.

---

[112] *Sermons and Report of the Missionary Society for 1795*, 168.   [113] Ibid., 12.

[114] *Evangelical Magazine*, Preface, 1808. There had been some discussion of extending the circulation to France. See Lovett, *The History of the London Missionary Society*, 95.

[115] Josef L. Altholz, *The Religious Press in Britain, 1760–1900* (New York, 1989), 44.

[116] By 1805 T. Chapman, was out of favour with evangelicals. There was a dispute over the publication of the missionary voyages to the South Seas. For this dispute, see the letters from T. Chapman dated 21 March 1805 and 6 April 1805, in Home Correspondence, Box 2, CWM, SOAS.

[117] The biographical details for Revd John Eyre appear in *Evangelical Magazine*, 1803, 225 ff.

[118] See Martin, *Evangelicals United*, 206. Burder had an interest in art, and took lessons in drawing from the line engraver Isaac Taylor.

Amongst the magazine's contributors, in the early years, were evangelicals from all camps, with the possible exception of Wesleyans.[119] Because
of these pan-evangelical beginnings it was possible for the magazine to
forge close ties with the Society. The breadth of denominational representation did not survive long: both organisations became increasingly
Congregational through the course of the century. One of the causes of
this change was a comment made by Haweis, who noted in the pages of
the periodical that the Baptist denomination was enlarging its numbers,
'not perhaps so much from the world, by awakenings of conscience in
new converts, as from different congregations of Dissenters and
Methodists'.[120] In response to this accusation, four trustees of the
Evangelical Magazine resigned and set up a rival publication, which
became the *Baptist Magazine*. This created a chain reaction, with other
denominations setting up their own magazines to supplement or replace
the *Evangelical Magazine*. Despite this loss of representation, the
Evangelical Magazine 'prospered and continued on its noncontroversial
theological and pietistic course'.[121] The genre of the *Evangelical Magazine*
continued to be cherished by all evangelicals, while its example was followed by many specialist periodicals.

In addition to the coming together of similar individuals, and a shared
trajectory of theological change, the links between the *Evangelical
Magazine* and the Society were trumpeted in the periodical's pages.
Soon after its foundation, the *Evangelical Magazine* was said to be the
'standard medium' through which the Society's news was published.[122]
Burder claimed that he had 'the satisfaction to believe that no publication
whatsoever [had] so powerfully contributed to the establishment and
prosperity of the missionary cause' as the periodical he edited.[123] The
Evangelical Magazine passed through 'nearly the whole' of the Society's
subscribers, making it inconceivable that anyone who read the magazine
remained uninterested in missions.[124] The magazine's foundation two
years before the Society might even have been interpreted as a divine sign
which showed that the support was in place to send missionaries overseas. Revd John Griffin, addressing the Society at one of its annual
meetings, claimed that 'the art of printing broke upon a dark world
with irresistible light, and like the sun, moved on in a majestic course,
dispelling ignorance from the mind, as that luminary drives before it the

[119] Ibid., 56.   [120] *Evangelical Magazine*, 1810, 506.
[121] Altholz, *The Religious Press in Britain*, 46.
[122] *Report of the London Missionary Society* 1797, 57.
[123] *Evangelical Magazine*, 1813, 265.
[124] *Report of the London Missionary Society*, 1798, iv.

darkness of the night, and fills both hemispheres with its beams'.[125]
Griffin continued that printing was the 'means of diffusing [knowledge] throughout the world'. Reading societies, tract societies and Sunday Schools had all contributed to this interest in knowledge, he claimed, but 'the establishment of missionary societies [was] the pre-eminent means of increasing it'.

The *Evangelical Magazine* was linked with mission in the field as much as at home. One missionary wrote home from the South Pacific concerning a parcel of letters he had received: 'Their contents we experienced refreshing, comforting and encouraging. Yea they were to us as "cold water to a thirsty soul!" ... We are in daily anxious expectation of the arrival of brother Hayward, hoping to receive by him Magazines &c.'[126] Often missionaries did not hear from Britain for two or three years at a time: therefore receiving regular copies of the *Evangelical Magazine* and other such periodicals served to fill them in on the news of the religious world and help them to persevere in faith. Since these magazines were gifts, they could also serve as physical testimonies of Christian love and remembrance. One South Pacific missionary wrote home, in a letter published in the *Evangelical Magazine*: 'we now earnestly entreat a continued interest in your prayers and request you will not fail to write to us by every opportunity that offers and regularly transmit us the Evangelical Magazine and missionary publications which we always find to have a tendency to quicken and refresh us'.[127] Another wrote: 'the magazines and other publications are always very acceptable presents'.[128] And again: 'we remain entirely ignorant of whom we are obligated, and consequently to whom our warmest thanks are due'.[129]

Meanwhile, in Britain, acknowledging those who had donated issues of the *Evangelical Magazine* was an important task. Names of donors appeared on the last page of the magazine, after an account of the sums donated by various auxiliary missionary societies to the main body. Despite the fact that the type used in these lists was about half the size of the normal type of the magazine, one correspondent wrote to the editor: 'every individual is desirous to know if his money reaches its destination.

---

[125] 'The signs of the times favourable to the cause of missions', a sermon preached before the London Missionary Society by the Revd John Griffin, Thursday 14 May 1807, in *Sermons of the London Missionary Society* (London, 1807), 102.

[126] Letter dated 9 April 1821, from G. Platt and W. Henry, Incoming Letters from the South Seas, Box 3, CWM, SOAS. The phrase 'cold water to a thirsty soul' arises from Proverbs 25: 25.

[127] *Evangelical Magazine* 1813, 474.

[128] Letter dated 24 August 1826 from D. Darling, Incoming Letters from the South Seas, Box 5, CWM, SOAS.

[129] Letter dated 20 May 1825 from G. Platt, ibid.

The first thing many look at is the list of subscribers and donors.'[130] Subscribers were gratified to find their names in print. Thomas Lovegood wrote: 'When my children have worked diligently, I generally reward them by letting them read the Evangelical Magazine aloud; and you cannot imagine how suprized and pleased they were, when they found their poor father's name.'[131] The lists of subscribers made examples of certain individuals, making them appear worthy evangelicals who had set their sights on the heavenly treasure as opposed to the earthly one.

Frontispieces of the magazine drew attention to the fact that the profits of the magazine were donated to the widows of gospel ministers. The particular sums that were allocated were also presented in the text. By subscribing to the *Evangelical Magazine* it was thus possible to improve the spiritual condition of widows and 'heathens'. But widows in turn were also urged to take part in this work of improvement by attempting to introduce their friends to the *Evangelical Magazine*. One widow wrote to the editor: 'It has been much impressed upon my mind of late, that if the widows who receive assistance from the Trustees, were all to exert themselves as they ought, a great increase to the sale of your valuable Magazine might thereby be effected. I found no difficulty upon trial of securing 12 new subscribers.'[132] Mutual improvement was therefore central to this periodical. Missionaries who received old copies were also expected to participate in this activity. They contributed pieces of information to the magazine, thereby improving the knowledge of the magazine's readers. Meanwhile, it was hoped that Pacific islanders would notice the magazine and other books being read by their missionaries, and by that example acquire the habit of reading. King Pomare of Tahiti, in a letter translated by the missionaries, wrote to Haweis:

I have sent you evil spirits (idols) which you sent me for, all of the large idols are consumed having been burned in the fire. There is only a little one that remains, the name of the little idol is Taroa ... Send me three books: one very large Bible, one good portable one, very small and one book of Geography.[133]

Haweis and the evangelicals at home were ecstatic. They dispatched the books without delay. Their joy lay in the fact that these networks of exchange had achieved the aim for which they had been set up: the improvement of each and every person who came into contact with the printed word. I will return to how the contents of the *Evangelical Magazine* were organised to foster this notion of development when I consider the

---

[130] *Evangelical Magazine*, 1829, 548.   [131] Ibid., 1806, 358.   [132] Ibid., 1841, 28.
[133] Letter dated 1 January 1820 from Pomare, Incoming Letters from the South Seas, Box 3, CWM, SOAS.

relation between a theology of nature and evangelical education in the next chapter.

Improving classes

The association between the reading audience of the *Evangelical Magazine* and the Society's supporters might at first imply that mission enthusiasts were mostly middle-class men and women. The new evangelical organisations that burgeoned at the end of the eighteenth century have, for example, been linked with middle-class values of improvement and a desire to infiltrate rather than overthrow traditional forms of social structure.[134] Yet it is difficult to define the Society simply as middle-class. For instance, the Society had links with the upper classes: Sir Joseph Banks's patronage of the organisation will be discussed in chapter 3; and the Countess of Huntingdon's help in the early moves towards the formation of the organisation are also noteworthy.[135] When Revd John Williams published his best-selling *A Narrative of Missionary Enterprises* (1837), which served as an early marker of the successes of the Society, he was pleased at the degree of attention excited by renowned philosophers, philanthropists and men of science. In a letter to Lord Brougham, with which he enclosed a copy of his book, Williams wrote: 'My Lord I venerate science; but the voyages of Parry, Ross and all their predecessors, to all benevolent purposes, have been "the baseless fabric of vision" for they have left the wretched Esquimaux as ignorant and wretched as they found them.'[136] Williams desired to link his explorations with those of men of science, while critiquing the godlessness of those very voyagers.

There was also a significant degree of working-class and artisan support for the Society. The letter that one subscriber wrote, in providing six spades, nine hammers and 4,000 nails for the equipment of the first voyage of the *Duff*, was printed in the *Evangelical Magazine*, so as to exemplify how evangelicals were expected to provide donations to the out-bound missionaries. The author noted:

I am a poor man ... I have sent the goods for the use of the beloved brethren, now going to the South Seas ... And glad shall I be to hear of our Lord Jesus Christ making use of the ministers of God, to break the hearts of sinners. May his Spirit water them, and nourish them up in the faith is the prayer of a well-wisher to Sion.[137]

[134] Noll, *The Rise of Evangelicalism*, 233.
[135] See, for instance, Stephen Orchard, 'The Origins of the Missionary Society', *Journal of the United Reformed Church History Society* 24 (1996): 440–8.
[136] Prout, *Memoirs of the Rev. John Williams*, 459.
[137] *Evangelical Magazine*, 1796, 293.

In the meanwhile, the first band of missionaries sent out on the *Duff* were mostly from the working classes:

Four only were ordained ministers: James Fleet Cover, John Eyre, John Jefferson, and Thomas Lewis. Of these Cover and Eyre were married, the wife of the latter, though he was only twenty eight being sixty four years old! The remaining twenty six were Henry Bicknell, carpenter; Daniel Bowell, shopkeeper; Benjamin Broomhall, harness maker; John Buchanan, tailor; James Cooper, shoemaker; John Cock, carpenter; William Crook, gentleman's servant; Samuel Clode, gardener; John A. Gillham, surgeon; Peter Hodges, blacksmith; William Henry, carpenter; John Harris, cooper; Edward Hudden, butcher; Samuel Harper, cotton manufacturer; Rowland Hassell, weaver; Seth Kelso, weaver; Edward Main, tailor; Isaac Nobb, hatter; Henry Nott, bricklayer; Francis Oakes, shoemaker; James Puckey, carpenter; William Puckey, carpenter; William Smith, linen draper; William Shelley, cabinet maker; George Veeson, bricklayer; James Wilkinson, carpenter.[138]

The class status of the Society is therefore far from simple. Evangelicals derided sloth and alcoholism, but they also eschewed luxury and worldliness. While these two positions could lead to criticisms of both the working classes and the upper classes, these critiques did not restrict links between the Society and these groups. John Comaroff writes that the Society's missionaries who went to South Africa, 'came from the interstices of a class structure undergoing reconstruction; many of them ... were caught uneasily between a displaced peasantry, an expanding proletariat, and the lower reaches of the rising British bourgeoisie'.[139] Caught in the processes of a transforming society, those associated with the Society sought after greater things. Working-class men and women saw the opportunities provided by the mission station as a route to join the greater middle class; while properly middle-class ministers hoped to push themselves further by organising voyages overseas and corresponding with respected gentlemen on the virtues of particular regions for mission. Being linked with preaching the gospel overseas gave supporters new knowledge and attachments that could promote their social position.

Writing specifically about the South Pacific, Niel Gunson notes that this band of evangelists fought hard to leave their working-class roots behind them; their past served as a place of contrast. By education and ordination they hoped to better themselves and prove their worthiness to the middle-class badge; having got to the islands they built themselves English houses and had tea with the king and queen while being waited on

---

[138] Lovett, *The History of the London Missionary Society*, 127.
[139] John Comaroff, 'Images of Empire, Contests of Conscience: Models of Colonial Domination in South Africa', in *Tensions of Empire: Colonial Cultures in a Bourgeois World*, ed. Laura Stoler (Berkeley, 1997), 166.

by servants.[140] Gunson also points to the importance of a shift in the composition of the South Pacific mission by the end of the 1830s. The older missionaries referred to the new missionaries who came at this time as 'gentlemen missionaries'. By this time the recruitment policy of the Society had moved beyond Haweis' optimistic idea that people with little education would make the best missionaries. The committee that called for the establishment of Bogue's Missionary Seminary recommended that 'a year should elapse, from the date of their acceptance to their actual entrance on the work itself, in order that their characters may be more fully ascertained, their minds more enlarged by appropriate instruction, and their stability more satisfactorily proved'.[141] As the century progressed, therefore, the South Pacific missionaries seemed to come with more qualifications and from more respected backgrounds.

The biography of Revd John Williams, who came to epitomise the mission, may serve as a good example of social mobility in the South Pacific mission.[142] Williams is typical of many of the South Pacific missionaries in having an urban upbringing and being trained as an artisan. He was born in Tottenham in 1796, and at the age of fourteen was made an apprentice in metal-work. His early biographer writes of how, by the age of eighteen, Williams' evangelical mother and friends looked with sorrow at his wayward behaviour: he had given up attending church on the Sabbath and had taken up the company of some irreligious young men.[143] Williams was eventually converted in January 1814, in the Old Whitefield Chapel, near the City Road. On that night Williams had been lounging outside a tavern, waiting for some friends to appear, when he had been noticed by a friend of the family. She dragged him to church.[144] 'From that hour', Williams wrote later, 'my blind eyes were open and I beheld wondrous things out of God's laws.'[145] As characteristic for a prospective missionary, Williams quickly enrolled himself in a class for serious youth at the London Tabernacle, where difficult subjects were considered every week, for mutual improvement. The Tabernacle came under the ministry of Revd Matthew Wilks, a guiding force of the London Missionary Society. The congregation had its own Auxiliary Missionary Society. At one of the meetings of this Society Williams came to the idea that he would become a missionary. Wilks took Williams under his instruction and the young man soon became a preacher.[146] Williams' social mobility had begun and the life of the tavern had been left behind.

---

[140] Gunson, *Messengers of Grace*, 31–4, 134.   [141] Ibid., 68.
[142] The details of his biography that follow are, unless stated otherwise, extracted from Prout, *Memoirs of the Rev. John Williams*.
[143] Ibid., 11.   [144] Ibid., 17–18.   [145] Ibid., 18.   [146] Ibid., 27–31.

By July 1816, Williams had applied to the directors of the Society; they decided to send him without further training to the South Pacific. He reached Moorea, in the Windward set of the Society Islands, on 17 November 1817. Shortly after his arrival, he was transferred to the Leeward Islands. He went to Huahine to assist with a new mission, and eventually to the island of Raiatea, on 11 September 1818. Before his arrival Christianity had become the national religion of Raiatea, but there was said to be a lack of moral transformation. Since Williams saw a close link between industry, civilisation and conversion, he urged the Raiateans to build a respectable European settlement. Williams himself built a house, replete with French sashes and Venetian blinds, tables and chairs, a yard for English poultry, and a plot with English vegetables.[147] In his habitation he therefore visualised his newfound status. He noted: 'It was my determination, when I left England to have as respectable a dwelling-house as I could erect; for the missionary does not go to barbarise himself.'[148] He was never content in his station and always longed to expand the reaches of Christianity and further his own career. He later wrote, in perhaps his most famous sentence: 'For my own part, I cannot content myself within the limits of a single reef.'[149] For the rest of his life he never thought of himself as restricted to one station, as did other missionaries. He cast himself more as a roving evangelist. Ambition was central to his sense of self.

Williams and his wife were first plagued by elephantiasis in their early years on Raiatea. Whilst in Sydney recovering, Williams decided to purchase a vessel called the *Endeavour*, which was to be the means of increasing intercourse with other countries. After returning to Raiatea on the *Endeavour*, via New Zealand, he set off again, on 4 July 1823, for Aitutaki in the Cook Islands. Happy at the sight of the island's transformation, and pleased with the work of the teachers he had left there, he was intrigued by accounts of an island called Rarotonga, now in the Cook Islands, which did not feature on the map. His voyage in search of that island later became the staple of many early twentieth-century Sunday School books.[150] His claim to be the discoverer of Rarotonga was later contested.[151] This voyage came to be the first in a series of explorations into new terrain for which Williams became renowned. It seemed that he wished to cast himself as an explorer as much as a missionary. Exemplifying the ambitions of the missionary class, Williams noted: 'Had I a ship at my command, not an island in the Pacific but should (God permitting) be visited.'[152] On his return to Raiatea, the censures of

---

[147] Ibid., 70.   [148] Ibid.   [149] See, for instance, the frontispiece of ibid.   [150] Ibid., 182.
[151] Ibid., 185.   [152] Ibid., 227.

the directors awaited him. They disapproved of his purchase of the *Endeavour*, claiming that a missionary should not concern himself with commerce.[153] Williams was forced to sell the vessel and remained in Raiatea for three years. This episode suggests again how his personal goals and desire for social mobility conflicted with metropolitan agendas.

Hard work was essential to Williams' social aggrandisement. Whilst on Rarotonga, waiting for a vessel to take him back to Raiatea, Williams again saw the necessity of a ship for the progress of mission work. As none was expected, Williams set to the task of building a vessel, which he called the *Messenger of Peace*. In a feat that aroused much admiration, he made the cordage, the sails, the substitutes for nails, oakum, pitch and paint, the anchors and the rudder, from the simple tools of a pickaxe, an adze and a hoe.[154] On 24 May 1830, he set off on his next major voyage, pioneering the way into the Samoan islands. After being well received, he deposited some teachers on those islands and returned to Rarotonga where there was much to keep him busy. A violent storm destroyed much of Rarotonga, which he helped rebuild; he translated more of the Bible into the island's language and attempted to stem the tide of alcoholism on Raiatea. He was finally able to get himself away to visit Samoa again on 11 October 1832. He was greeted warmly. At Sapapali'i, the ladies performed a 'heavenly dance' for Williams. They sang:

> Now our land is saved, and evil practices have ceased.
> How we feel for the lotu! Come! let us sleep and dream of Viriamu.[155]

Viriamu, as Williams was called in Samoan, was no doubt ecstatic, but it was stories such as this last one that aroused the suspicions of his colleagues and the directors, who believed that Williams was making a name for himself, without expanding the realms of Christianity. Williams' standing amongst the islanders is also demonstrated by this account.

In order for Mrs Williams to recover from illness, and also to accelerate the publication of the Bible in Rarotongan, Williams returned to England shortly after this Samoan voyage, arriving in London on 12 June 1834.[156] He captivated audiences around the country with descriptions of the spread of the gospel. With the help of his increased following, Williams was able to purchase the *Camden* as a permanent missionary ship for the islands. A farewell ceremony was held for him on 4 April 1838. His fellow passengers on the *Camden* complained that he had filled the ship with goods for the use of his son who was hoping to become a businessman. In a telling comment on Williams' social aspirations they noted: 'He says, "The vessel is my own to take where I please." Do you consider Mr and

[153] Ibid., 192.   [154] Ibid., 258–9.   [155] Ibid. 379.   [156] Ibid. 407 ff.

Mrs Williams real friends to the cause or to their own interest only? I fear England has spoiled them – they are now going to heaven with Dukes and Lords &c.'[157] On returning to the islands, Williams made his new home, at Fasitoouata, in the Samoan Islands, amongst a tribe that was seen to be the most despised in the region. Travelling on to the Cook and Society Islands from there, Williams again set himself towards new territory in the New Hebrides. Calling at Apia in the Samoan islands, Williams headed to Rotuma, and then to Tana, where he was well received, though he was unable to communicate the purpose of his visit. On 18 November 1839 he was martyred, and I will study his death in greater detail in chapter 3.

But Williams' trajectory, from an apprentice in metal-work to a household name in the metropolis, illustrates the attractions of a missionary career. In one of many books written in his honour, it was said: 'John Williams will be venerated as one of the most illustrious Fathers of the New Era – as one of the royal line of Stephen and Antipas, and other martyrs of our God.' Williams' life demonstrates one of the salient features of the missionary class: they were not socially static. Even though the vast majority of his colleagues never met the fame that Williams did, they shared with him the desire to improve their lot and to move from their humble backgrounds higher and higher up the social ladder. Williams of course was supremely successful in this and set them a model example. In the meanwhile, throughout his career in the Pacific, Williams hoped to transmit these values of industry and improvement to the islanders. He urged them to build, read and work hard, just as he had done; and to leave behind them alcohol and sloth. There was in this injunction both identification and differentiation.

This appetite for social advancement explains why missionaries like Williams were so interested in science and keen on reporting their observations of natural phenomena. With the shift in the social background of the missionary in the 1830s, the confidence with which speculations on science were entertained was enhanced. For instance, Revd William Henry, who had been a carpenter and itinerant preacher before sailing on board the *Duff* in 1796, had a very difficult life, but had time to write on natural history. He was one of the few missionaries to remain after the majority of those sent aboard the *Duff* fled for their lives. Henry wrote on coral formation:

The reefs of these islands & of the others in these seas were most probably formed by large quantities of broken coral being rolled by the sea towards them, in some places going nearer, & in others farther from them as it met with hindrances: and on

---

[157] Quoted in Daws, *A Dream of Islands*, 61.

these bodies of coral, other coral growing and being thrown down by the agitation of the sea from the storms, and on that other coral growing, then falling & more growing upon that, & so on until the reefs reached the surface of the sea; and the whole being cemented by a kind of calcine or limy substance, produced by a coral insect & mixed with other substances becoming one mass.[158]

In the meantime, Revd John Williams, who was amongst the new batch of missionaries, used 'carbonate of lime' to describe the growth of coral instead of Henry's 'a kind of calcine or limy substance'.[159] Williams categorised the islands and presented figures and observations in his best-selling *A Narrative of Missionary Enterprise* (1837), whilst Henry spoke of broken coral being rolled by the sea. Williams then displayed more scientific training and expertise. The South Pacific missionaries were interested in science because of their social mobility, and their success in improving themselves was displayed in how they commented on science.

Conclusion

When Revd Thomas Haweis addressed those gathered at the inaugural meeting of the London Missionary Society, he noted: 'Every partition wall is broken down, and every heart big with expectation, that the time approaches when the great Redeemer of lost souls will receive the Heathen for his inheritance, and the uttermost parts of the world for his possession.'[160] Haweis' triumphant statement makes sense in the light of the fading memory of the evangelical controversies of the eighteenth century. A new framework of theology – which has been called moderate Calvinism – set the context for inter-denominational endeavours such as the formation of the Society. The patrons of the Society believed that they were following a providential call in preaching the gospel abroad. Haweis himself echoes a post-millenarian line here: he urges the need to preach the message of Christianity to all the nations before the return of Christ. It is easy to privilege theological context in reading Haweis' proclamation, but these words might as easily be read as colonial. Words such as 'inheritance' and 'possession' which feature here suggest how evangelicals envisioned their campaign using language that was shared with other colonists; in fact Haweis spoke of a 'colony' in writing to Dundas. Missionary activity must be seen as a form of spiritual expansionism and

---

[158] Gunson, 'British Missionaries and their Contribution to Science in the Pacific Islands', 268.

[159] John Williams, *A Narrative of Missionary Enterprises* (London, 1837), chapter 1.

[160] *Sermons and Report of the Missionary Society for 1795*, 161.

ownership. Might it be labelled providential colonialism, to suggest its distinction from state-led imperialism?

Haweis singlehandedly persuaded the members of the Society that the South Pacific should be chosen as the first region for missionary work. He deployed a theology of nature in order to make the case. The islanders were said to be prepared by nature for the reception of the gospel: their characters, their manners and even their speech was said to be quite unlike other 'heathens'. Since Captain Cook had opened the region to the gaze of Europeans, Haweis held that his contemporaries were bequeathed with the spiritual responsibility of transporting the gospel to the shores of the Pacific Ocean. The islanders were expected to convert quickly and prove that the first experiment in mission could be repeated elsewhere. Haweis noted, using agricultural language: 'We have a field wholly uncultivated but the soil is fit for seed, and the climate genial, and coming first, we have everything in our favour, and may without dispute or opposition, inculcate the true knowledge of God our Saviour.'[161]

Haweis was not unusual in relying on natural historical imagery in coming to an idea of divine purpose. In this chapter I have outlined the roots of natural theology and the particular version of theological contemplation of nature approved by nineteenth-century evangelicals. In seeking to engage with nature, evangelicals believed that true science had to be twinned with an exposition of scripture, and that the best science should be readily accessible to all believers. Evangelical natural history therefore counts as a popular science that challenged more elite versions of knowledge. The relation between evangelical theologies of nature and gentlemanly science seems similar to that between missionary expansion and state-led imperialism. On both counts religious believers were aiming to forge a type of activity that they held to be a more credible and godly alternative in response to the secularisation of knowledge and politics. The confidence with which evangelicals responded to the new science suggests that they must be placed firmly within the orbit of Enlightenment philosophy, without being seen as peripheral.

The Society's formation and the sending of missionaries to the Pacific attracted a remarkable degree of popular attention. The *Evangelical Magazine*, which had close ties to the Society, publicised these events. This periodical served as an organ through which evangelicals could learn how to regulate their daily lives, by keeping abreast of Christian news and using their leisure profitably. While the relation between the periodical and the missionary organisation might at first lead to the assumption that

[161] Ibid., 172.

evangelical enthusiasts of mission were middle-class, in fact closer inspection serves to complicate the question of class status. The first band of missionaries to the South Pacific were mostly from the working classes. But having got to the Pacific, they quickly asserted their improved standing by building respectable homes, socialising with the nobility of the islands and writing on science. Social aggrandisement was one reason for choosing to be a missionary. In London, in the meanwhile, Haweis cultivated the friendship of such figures as Sir Joseph Banks and Captain Bligh, as I will show in chapter 3. Across the board, then, amongst both missionaries and promoters of the Society's mission, the project of sending the Word overseas could provide the opportunity for social advancement.

This chapter has presented a predominantly metropolitan perspective, while emphasising major figures such as Haweis and Williams. But if the injunction that has been presented here is to be followed – that more attention should be paid to the lived experience of evangelicalism – it is necessary now to focus our attention elsewhere. In the chapters that follow the manner in which missionaries used theologies of nature, and how that set of beliefs permeated their everyday lives, will be discussed. By spiritualising nature missionaries hoped to show their learning, and to bring the Pacific islands into the reaches of the civilised world. As my first point of attention I will now turn to how theological ideas of nature were implicated in the education imparted to out-bound missionaries, and the instruction given by missionaries to islanders. Central to my analysis of missionary pedagogy is the claim that metropolitan theologies of nature were reconstructed in the islands, in the process of meditation, reading, preaching and writing. The implication, then, is that attention might duly be paid to the manner in which ideas about nature were received by islanders.

Having surveyed the theological climate of Britain, the emergence of missionary enthusiasm and the resurgence of natural theology, we are ready to launch our own voyage to the Pacific in order to visit the sites at which missionaries and islanders conversed, sometimes at cross-purposes. The school serves as one of the foremost sites where this happened. By starting my study with how natural history is linked with education, it is also possible to discuss how missionaries were trained for their life overseas, alongside an analysis of how islanders were taught.

Despite being a gentleman's servant before taking up his position as one of
the first missionaries to arrive on the *Duff*, Revd William Pascoe Crook
became the mission's most ardent educationalist. 'Education is to mankind what culture is to vegetables', Crook noted. 'If this is neglected the
Garden is overrun with noxious weeds; if that is forgotten the manners of
men degenerate into vice and profaneness.'[1] At the first school that he
oversaw in New South Wales, Crook taught the children under his care to
read and write, in addition to instructing them in the skills of book-
keeping, geometry, trigonometry, mensuration, navigation, surveying
and gauging. As these arts were learnt, Crook envisaged the development
of the mind in analogous terms to the processes of agriculture.
Agriculturalists were, however, a separate class of missionary in the
South Pacific, segregated from those who were assigned the sacred duty
of teaching the Bible like Crook, and associated instead with other missionaries whose main responsibilities were printing or hat-making. So
Crook continued: 'As far therefore, as the reasonable creature excels the
vegetable, so far does education surpass agriculture. Shall a man therefore,
attend with utmost diligence to the improvement of his ground, and
neglect this far more important concern, the instruction of his offspring?'

The Society's missionaries to the Pacific were keen on education. Since
conversion was thought to depend on their charges' ability to understand
the Bible, literacy was held to be vital to evangelism. From scripture,
evangelicals also believed that there was a special responsibility to teach
the young in the ways of God, so that they would grow up to transform
their communities. Children, and especially orphans, were thought to
deserve particular protection given their vulnerability.[2] The practices
that arose from literacy – reading, writing, preaching and meditating –
were central to the definition of the evangelical. The inculcation of these

---

[1] Cited in Gunson, *Messengers of Grace*, from *Sydney Gazette*, 19 August 1804.
[2] For an explanation of why children should receive special attention, see George Pritchard,
   The Missionary's Reward, or the Success of the Gospel in the Pacific (London, 1844), 128.

practices, and the strict rules that surrounded them, occupied a crucial place in the training of both missionaries and their converts.

Pierre Bourdieu writes: 'Among all the solutions put forward throughout history to the problem of the transmission of power and privileges, there scarcely exists one that is better concealed ... than the solution which the educational system provides by contributing to the structure of class relations and by concealing by an apparently neutral attitude that it fills this function.'[3] The efficiency of education as a means of social reproduction is demonstrated by the many missionary schools that continue to dominate post-colonial societies. Yet only passing attention has been paid to the didactic element of the civilising mission by historians.[4] While social theorists are keen to see the school as a site of discipline, indigenous peoples were able to appropriate missionary education in order to suit their own agendas.[5] From the perspective of local peoples, the setting-up of schools could easily be a means of deriving the benefits of the 'white man's goods'. Access to education could also provide the capacity for peoples from lowly castes or from dominated factions to isolate their histories and identities and attempt to subvert traditional hierarchies. There is therefore a new-found attention to strategies of appropriation in the history of missionary education.[6] These shifts in the historiography have a direct impact on my study of how a theology of nature is implicated in evangelical education.

While the tradition of spiritualising nature saw a resurgence in England, it already had a long history in the Pacific. Therefore, when Pacific islanders were taught natural history, they did not passively accept. They used the alphabet, which they repeated endlessly, as a prayer. They were depicted on one occasion chewing an incoming parcel of correspondence. While evangelicals in London adopted biblical themes in their sermons, using conceptions of rain to suggest the workings of the Spirit, Pacific islanders preached sermons that drew on crabs, coral trees and sea serpents. Missionaries entrusted with the task of education attempted in vain

---

[3] Pierre Bourdieu, 'Cultural Reproduction and Social Reproduction', in *Power and Ideology in Education*, ed. A. H. Halsey and Jerome Karabel (New York, 1977), 87–8. For the social theory of education, see also Pierre Bourdieu, *Reproduction in Education, Society and Culture* (London, 1970).

[4] J. A. Mangan, 'Introduction', in *Benefits Bestowed: Education and British Imperialism*, ed. J. A. Mangan (Manchester, 1998).

[5] For a short summary of how missionary education could be taken up, see Porter, *Religion Versus Empire?* 317–19.

[6] See, for example, Dick Kooiman, 'The Gospel of Coffee: Mission, Education and Employment in Travencore', in *Conversion, Competition and Conflict: Essays on the Role of Religion in Asia*, ed. Dick Kooiman, Otto van den Muijzenberg and Peter van der Veer (Amsterdam, 1984).

to control rebellious children who paid no attention to their instructions about reading and writing.

The parameters of what it meant to read, write, meditate and converse changed as much as what was communicated in the process of education.[7] In Brian Simon's words, 'education becomes and is best seen as a site of struggle'.[8] In order to support this claim, this chapter will move through several vehicles of education in order: schools, periodicals, missionary training institutes and missionary meetings. To appreciate how knowledge was transmitted and reconstructed, it is also vital to travel back and forth between London and the Pacific, as I will do in the course of this chapter. By analysing how missionaries were trained alongside how converts were taught, it is possible to discuss the making of the teacher and the taught person side by side.

In focusing attention on the relationship between nature and education, I also hope to show how a natural history of the development of the mind was central to evangelical attitudes to education.[9] Evangelicals played an important role in defining popular education in the late eighteenth and early nineteenth centuries.[10] Traditionally, the religious catechistical style of education has been aligned with mechanism because it drew inspiration from the organisation and discipline of the factory.[11] In urging instead that evangelical instruction was closely linked with nature, this chapter will question the established narrative.

The development of science education bears this argument out. In the teaching of science, nature is said to have acted as teacher, and catechised

---

[7] In making this claim the chapter engages with recent work at the intersection of the history of science and the history of the book. Starting points for book history/history of science are: Marina Frasca-Spada and Nicholas Jardine, eds., *Books and the Sciences in History* (Cambridge, 2000), Adrian Johns, *The Nature of the Book: Print Knowledge in the Making* (Chicago, 1998), James Secord, *Victorian Sensation: The Extraordinary Publication, Reception, and Secret Authorship of Vestiges of the Natural History of Creation* (Chicago, 2000), Jonathan Topham, 'Scientific Publishing and the Reading of Science in Nineteenth-Century Britain: A Historiographical Survey and Guide to Sources', *Studies in History and Philosophy of Science* 31A (2000): 559–612.

[8] Brian Simon, 'The History of Education: Its Importance for Understanding', in *The State and Educational Change: Essays in the History of Education and Pedagogy*, ed. Brian Simon (London, 1994), 14.

[9] For the doctrine of progress and its religious association, see David Spadafora, *The Idea of Progress in Eighteenth-Century Britain* (New Haven, Conn. and London, 1990).

[10] See the now outdated John McLeish, *Evangelical Religion and Popular Education: A Modern Interpretation* (London, 1969). This work deals with a slightly earlier period and has as its aim the interpretation of evangelical education in line with Marxist, anthropological and Freudian theories. See also Paul Sangster, *Pity My Simplicity: The Evangelical Revival and the Religious Education of Children 1738–1800* (London, 1963).

[11] Alan Richardson, *Literature, Education and Romanticism: Reading as Social Practice 1780–1832* (Cambridge, 1994).

students asked questions of nature and received answers in her clear undisputed voice.[12] In this mode of viewing, nature embodied instruction, as it was thought to provide a parallel ordering to relationships in society.[13] But nature was not only teacher; it was also the gauge of improvement. When Pacific islanders were educated by missionaries, natural historical creatures could be taken to characterise industry or idleness, and believers were urged to contemplate how they fitted a scale of maturing spirituality. By serving as a model of development, and providing lessons for pedagogy, nature complemented the machine as a metaphor for didactic practice.

Nature was inscribed rather than opposed by this new style of education; it took an important place in defining the content and procedures of evangelical education. Since both converts and missionaries were educated and trained before being put to other tasks, attitudes to natural improvement were implicated in the crystallisation of religious identity. It is appropriate, then, to begin a study of missionary views of natural history with the subject of education.

Learning letters

In 1808, a Tahitian called Tapeoe wrote to his king, Otoo: 'I am in School in England which place I like very much and live very happy.'[14] After arriving in the country, Tapeoe had been put under the protection of the London Missionary Society. He continued: 'I shall feel myself much obliged to you if you will have the goodness to make a School for Missionaries to teach the boys to read and write and to believe and worship the God of Heaven and not your wooden Gods.' The former king of Tahiti, Pomare, had written several letters to the directors of the Society,

---

[12] Eugenia Roldan Vera, 'Useful Knowledge for Export', in *Books and the Sciences in History*, ed. Marina Frasca-Spada and Nicholas Jardine (Cambridge, 2000), 340–1.

[13] Steven Shapin and Barry Barnes, 'Science, Nature and Control: Interpreting Mechanics' Institutes', *Social Studies of Science* 7 (1997) 36. Other accounts of popular science education in the early nineteenth century include James Secord, 'Newton in the Nursery: Tom Telescope and the Philosophy of Tops and Balls, 1761–1838', *History of Science* 23 (1985): 127–51, Topham, 'Science and Popular Education in the 1830s: The Role of the Bridgewater Treaties'. See also Topham's doctoral thesis, '"An Infinite Variety of Arguments": The Bridgewater Treatises and British Natural Theology in the 1830s' (Ph.D. dissertation, University of Lancaster, 1993). For surveys of the subject, see David Layton, *Science for the People* (London, 1973). For the later mechanics' institutes, see J. F. C. Harrison, *Learning and Living 1790–1960: A Study in the History of the English Adult Education Movement* (London, 1961) and E. Royle, 'Mechanics' Institutes and the Working Classes, 1840–1860', *Historical Journal* 14 (1971): 305–21.

[14] Undated letter from Tapeoe to his king, Incoming Letters from the South Seas, Box 3, CWM, SOAS.

and these had been crucial to the establishment of a cordial relationship. The directors, however, were more dubious about their connection with Otoo. Making Tapeoe write to Otoo was an attempt to win the monarch's favour. It was hoped that the islander's flowing hand would show how civilisation came with conversion, and that by these means Otoo would come to the considered view that promoting missionary education was best for Tahiti.

When he was in London, Tapeoe came to the attention of Joseph Lancaster. Rote learning was an essential characteristic of the Lancasterian system. The Borough School, which Lancaster established in 1798 as his first experiment, was divided into small classes, each under the care of a monitor. Flat desks covered with a thin layer of sand were used for the early exercises in writing. Sheets taken from a spelling book and pasted onto boards were placed before each class and the teacher pointed to the words until each was spelt.[15] Joseph Fox, a close friend of Lancaster's, observed that Lancaster's method of learning involved 'the repetition of the same word many times' so as to 'rivet it firmly in the memory'.[16] Lancaster himself noted: 'Now *the frequent recurring of one idea*, if simple and definite, is alone sufficient to impress it on the memory, without sitting down to learn it as a task; and in the method of tuition just described every boy is obliged to repeat it, at least three times.'[17] Strict rules were therefore crucial to Lancaster's methodology.

In the mission field also, strict rules governed the education imparted to islanders. Revd George Pritchard, the missionary who went on to become British Consul to Tahiti, wrote of how children were taught in school by rote. 'They are taught the alphabet by singing and marching to the tune called "Cottage."' Concepts of arithmetic were also imparted by the use of verse. 'One little fellow will put up his hand as high as he can reach and sing out, "This is perpendicular". A second will put out his hand on a level before him, saying, "This is horizontal".'[18] Pritchard's description of a school run by a Mrs Coan in Hilo exemplifies the rigidity of this education. Twenty girls from seven to ten years were under Coan's instruction. The children's weekly food was supplied by the people in the surrounding area;

---

[15] For a starting point for Lancasterian education see Joyce Taylor, *Joseph Lancaster: The Poor Child's Friend: Educating the Poor in the Early Nineteenth Century* (West Wickham, Kent, 1996). For a more sophisticated interpretation, see the much older, Michalina Vaughan and Margaret Scotford Archer, *Social Conflict and Educational Change in England and France 1789–1848* (Cambridge, 1971).

[16] Joseph Fox, *A Comparative View of the Plans of Education as Detailed in the Publications of Dr. Bell and Mr. Lancaster*, 2nd edn (London, 1809), 18.

[17] Joseph Lancaster, *Improvements in Education as It Respects the Industrious Classes of the Community* (London, 1803), 73.

[18] Pritchard, *The Missionary's Reward*, 129.

the country around the mission settlement was divided into five sections
and each took their turn in supplying the weekly provisions.[19] The children
were clothed in a cheap cotton fabric, which together with furniture,
books, cards, maps and stationery were provided by Coan.[20] Next to the
school building was a garden containing exotic trees. In order to inculcate
practical skills, the girls were entrusted with the responsibility of tending
this garden. In equivalent schools elsewhere boys were taught to be black-
smiths, tailors and shoemakers.[21] Precise rules were put into place as to
how the garden should be tended: 'The garden is surrounded and inter-
sected by gravelled walks, and divided into little sections, each pupil being
responsible for the neatness and good order of one section, while all unite
in keeping the walks and common pleasure grounds in good taste.'
Pritchard added nonchalantly, in concluding his description of Coan's
school, that the hours of sleeping, eating, labour, recreation, study and
devotion were all closely defined.[22]

Despite the rule-bound nature of schools such as this, it was possible for
Pacific islanders to reinvent the meaning of reading and writing. Vanessa
Smith, in a wonderful discussion, pays attention to how islanders in
Hawaii, under the instruction of American missionaries, used alphabets,
books and writing to express status. Otto von Kotzebue, a visiting Russian
captain on an astronomical tour, on entering the residence of Queen
Ka'ahumanu, observed that the stairs were full of children, adults and
even old people of both sexes, who were 'reading from spelling-books, and
writing on slates'. He carried on: 'Some of the old people appeared to have
joined the assembly rather for example's sake, than from a desire to learn,
as they were studying with an affection of extreme diligence, books held
upside down.'[23] On Rarotonga, Revd Aaron Buzacott recorded the tale
of how Pacific islanders used the alphabet that they had been taught
by the Society's missionaries as a prayer.[24] The amusing account was
retold of how an elderly couple were visited one night by a cat. The cat's
peculiar mew drew their attention to the door of their dwelling, and, it
being pitch dark, they saw what they described as two balls of fire.
'The wife began to remonstrate with her husband for having anything to
do with the new religion; for, without her consent, and contrary to her
wishes, he had attended the daily instructions.' She implored him to use
the prayers that the missionaries had taught to send the monster away.
'Tiaki began most earnestly to cry, "*B a, ba; b e, be; b i, bi; b o, bo*".'

---

[19] Ibid., 142.   [20] Ibid.   [21] Ibid., 129.
[22] Ibid., 143.   [23] Cited in Smith, *Literary Culture and the Pacific*, 73.
[24] Smith notes that we need to be wary in reading this anecdote naively as it presents Pacific
islanders 'in a comically infantilised relationship to written language'. From ibid., 2.

The cat disappeared, leaving the aged couple impressed at the powers of the alphabet.[25] The use of the alphabet as a prayer to chase away a cat seems a long way from how missionaries hoped that the education they imparted would be used.

The islanders did not, however, hold a monopoly over the reinvention of the practices of learning. Despite all their pretensions to careful surveillance and control, evangelicals in London also moulded the arte-facts that emerged from the civilising mission of the Pacific to suit their own agendas. In the eyes of the directors of the Society, a letter could become a curiosity. For instance, when Pomare had written to the directors, his letter had been redefined as an object of display in the metropolis. 'This will be read, and a Fac Simile distributed, which will no doubt produce such satisfaction, as affording a pleasing symptom of advance-ment towards civilisation; and as probably introductory to the reading of the Scriptures.'[26] Pomare's letter, like Tapeoe's, was replicable: it could be passed on to others as an indicator of the king's conformity to a practice that was crucial to the constitution of a convert. His letter was not hidden in the archive like the dozens of letters written by their missionaries, complaining about their conditions and the lack of resources; it was displayed and made public. Indeed there seems to have been little difference between these letters and articles of commerce, such as specimens, masks and 'idols', as is borne out by another exchange of words. The Governor of New South Wales told the South Pacific missionary Revd William Henry that he was 'highly pleased' on seeing some other letters written by Pomare and requested that they be sent immediately to the directors of the Society. Henry could not comply with this wish: 'I had promised them to the Governor's Secretary, John Thomas Campbell Esq. a gentleman to whom I was under peculiar obligations, who wished to send them to some friends as literary curiosity.'[27]

Repetition was crucial to the making of letters like this one. The *Evangelical Magazine* for 1808 described the manner in which Pomare *wrote* his letter to the directors: 'His letter was first written in the Taheitian [sic] language, very fairly, It was then translated by the Missionaries into English; which translation was copied by the King. From the last of these a fac simile (or exact imitation stroke for stroke) has been engraved; and several hundred copies were gratuitously distributed among the members of this meeting.'[28] The copying and rewriting

---

[25] Cited in ibid.
[26] *Sermons and Report of the London Missionary Society 1808* (London, 1808), 8.
[27] *Sermons and Report of the Missionary Society for 1812* (London, 1812), 36.
[28] *Evangelical Magazine*, 1808, 263.

involved in writing letters explains the nature of the mistakes made by Tapeoe in his spelling. Tapeoe's word 'pospr' was changed to 'prosper', while another hand corrected the errors in the sentence: 'Sire, I shall be to heayr Majesty is in good health. When I have learnt to read well I shall, return to Otaheiti to learn the boys myslf, but I am afraid that will be anothr year or more.' 'Heayr' was changed to 'hear'; 'myslf' to 'myself' and 'anothr' to 'another'. At each of these stages of writing, it was possible for islanders and missionaries to change the meaning of what was written; and the fact that the act of writing involved so many steps opened more room for reinterpretations of what constituted writing.

In the Pacific, missionaries deployed catechistic strategies to convey information to their charges. In a typical report from Tahiti, Revd J. Orsmond noted that, at the annual missionary meeting in 1837, the local children had repeated large portions of scripture. He wrote: 'Three printed catechisms were repeated by memory by at least 300 children . . . I was pleased to hear six parties, or the children of six stations in separate bodies, each asked separately and each in rotation making prompt replies to the questions of the catechists.'[29] These methods of teaching came in for fierce criticism from some visitors to mission stations. Kotzebue wrote, for instance, of what he saw at a school-house. 'I had not waited long before the pupils of both sexes entered. They were not lively children, nor youths, whom ardour for the acquisition of knowledge led to the seat of instruction, but adults and aged persons, who crept slowly in with downcast looks, and prayer-books under their arms.' When they were assembled, a psalm was sung; one islander then read a chapter from the Bible, after which they sang. 'Another psalm, another chapter, and another prayer were sung and said; again and again, as I understood, a fresh performer repeated the wearisome exercise; but my patience was exhausted, and, at the second course, with depressed spirits and painful expressions, I left the assembly.'[30]

The missionaries were aware of how supporters of the mission responded negatively to reports like this. Pritchard wrote, for instance, of how the evangelists attempted, by the means of catechism, not merely to get their charges to commit to memory a large quantity of information, but also to lead them to understand what they learnt.[31] Orsmond, however, was less optimistic. 'I want the children to see with their own eyes', he noted, 'yet

---

[29] Letter dated September 26 1837, from J. Orsmond, Incoming Letters, Box 11, CWM, SOAS.

[30] O. von Kotzebue, *A New Voyage around the World in the Years 1823, 24, 25 and 26* (London, 1830), 202.

[31] Pritchard, *The Missionary's Reward*, 150.

I have not been able to find an argument sufficiently weighty.' 'Indeed every habit of the natives militates against the increase of knowledge.' Orsmond continued that even though chiefs made laws making attendance at schools compulsory, the 'heart is unchanged'.[32] Orsmond held, then, that despite the adoption of new methods, Pacific islanders would resist the process of education.

There was a paradox at the heart of evangelical education. On the one hand, in the Pacific and in London supporters and teachers believed that reading and writing, and also the inculcation of practical skills such as gardening, could be tightly defined. Rules and catechisms were deployed for education. Yet both evangelicals and islanders stretched the boundaries of the practices of education in the process of learning. Letters could become curiosities and the alphabet could become a prayer. The strategy of repetition, which was crucial to evangelical education, may have facilitated rather than prevented such reinventions. The rigidity of this education, meanwhile, denied islanders any real opportunity to learn.

Lancasterian education

Lancaster's system of teaching – which encapsulated rigid rules – was extremely popular amongst the Society's agents in the Pacific in the early years of the mission. Two features of this system are useful in explaining how it came to be applied in the islands. Firstly, debate about whether to educate the poor merged with how to educate colonial populations in the formulation of early nineteenth-century education. Further, both Lancaster and his opponent, Bell, saw the value of science education for the improvement of the mind, and deployed natural analogies to visualise their methods.

The directors of the Society encouraged missionaries to adopt Lancaster's scheme, so that they ensured that they were in the forefront of reforms in education.[33] This enthusiasm is explained by Lancaster's association with Nonconformity. Andrew Bell, who devised a rival system of learning, was an ordained minister of the Church of England and his system came to be associated with the National School Society, which sought to ensure that all education for poor children came under the scrutiny of the established church.[34] It is unsurprising, therefore, that the

---

[32] Letter dated September 26 1837, from J. Orsmond, Incoming Letters, Box 11, CWM, SOAS.

[33] Gunson, *Messengers of Grace*, 238.

[34] For the Lancaster–Bell dispute, see their entries in the *Dictionary of National Biography*. Also Richardson, *Literature, Education and Romanticism*.

Society hoped that their evangelists would apply Lancaster's proposals. In practice, however, Lancaster's ideas were adapted to suit local conditions. Referring to Lancaster's suggestion that mature students could act as teachers, Revd Charles Barff wrote: 'We do follow the Lancasterian plans as nearly as we can profit – we have an abundance of teachers and have no need on that account to adopt some plans recommended by Mr. Lancaster.'[35] The lack of equipment such as globes, slates and alphabet wheels also impeded the exact replication of Lancaster's methods.[36] Revd John Williams wrote, for instance: 'Our schools are attended with as much spirit as ever. The children's school conducted as near as the want of slates, rewards &c. will allow, on the Lancasterian plan. It consists of upwards of 250 boys and girls, for whom we solicit a supply of slates, pictures &c for rewards, also a supply of slates for the adult school.'[37] Missionaries in the field therefore followed a hybrid form of teaching that was dissimilar from the systems of both Joseph Lancaster and Andrew Bell.[38]

Back in London, Lancaster's fame rose to meteoric proportions. After his interview with the king in July 1805, George III promised his patronage and added his name to the list of subscribers to Lancaster's pamphlet. The interview concluded with the famous sentence: 'It is my wish that every poor child in my dominions should be taught to read the Bible.'[39] Captain Gronow, one of the 'dandies of the Regency', wrote that Lancaster had henceforth been lionised.[40] A few years after his lionisation, Lancaster and his friends found themselves in the heat of a battle to assert his priority in inventing the monitorial system of education. Though Lancaster's schools

[35] Letter dated 7 June 1821, from Revd C. Barff, Incoming Letters from the South Seas, Box 2, CWM, SOAS.
[36] Gunson, *Messengers of Grace*, 238.
[37] Letter dated 8 June 1821, from Revd J. Williams and L. Threkeld. Incoming Letters from the South Seas, Box 3, CWM, SOAS. For other comments with respect to the adoption of Lancasterian education, see letter dated 20 July 1826 from Revd T. Jones, Incoming letters from the South Seas, Box 5, ibid.; letter dated 26 June 1822 from Revd G. Platt, Incoming Letters from the South Seas, Box 3, ibid.
[38] Other early nineteenth-century colonial educational institutions also seemed to have followed a hybrid form of teaching which was borrowed equally from Bell and Lancaster. See Philip McCann, 'The Newfoundland School Society 1823–55: Missionary Enterprise or Cultural Imperialism?', in *Benefits Bestowed: Education and British Imperialism*, ed. J. A. Mangan (Manchester, 1998). The point that Lancasterian schools rarely followed the scheme proposed by their founder has been made by Harold Silver, *Education as History: Interpreting Nineteenth and Twentieth Century Education* (London, 1983), 19.
[39] The British and Foreign Bible Society, which was closely associated with Lancasterian education, distributed two and a half million copies of the Bible between 1804 and 1809. From Richard Altick, *The English Common Reader: A Social History of the Mass Reading Public, 1800–1900* (Chicago, 1957), 70, 74–5.
[40] See *Educational Record*, 1911, 241. For more on the custom of lionisation, see Secord, *Victorian Sensation*, 178–9.

followed a very similar method of instruction to Bell's schools, there were a larger number of students in Lancaster's classes and he used a different set of texts. Bell taught reading, writing, arithmetic, grammar, book-keeping, geography, geometry, mensuration, navigation and astronomy; Lancaster's published system only included reading, writing and arithmetic. Lancaster held to the principle that the poor should all be educated so that they learnt subordination; Bell urged that the education given to poor children should be restricted. Both systems used students as monitors to ensure that while teaching his fellows the monitor had his own lessons reinforced. Since the hierarchy was fluid, every boy could aspire to be a monitor, and a monitor could, by forgetting his lessons, revert to pupil status. School teachers were freed to attend to problems of discipline.[41]

Joseph Fox, one of Lancaster's friends, in his published defence of Lancaster's scheme of education, set out the differences between the two schemes. Fox observed that Bell had established his first school in Madras, 'for children of a low description, called *half-cast*'. The students were instructed in the alphabet, and asked to spell and add on the sand. He continued: 'there can be no doubt but that many boys educated in the Asylum, must have made great proficiency, and have been able to fill important places under the Presidency; and it is no wonder that one of them, William Smith, had the capacity to exhibit a number of philosophical experiments before Tippoo Sultan'.[42] That Bell had taught Indians was crucial in Fox's criticism of Bell's stance on the poor. Fox reproduced Bell's offending statement:

It is not supposed that the children of the poor be educated in an expensive manner, *or even taught to write and cipher*. Utopian schemes for the universal diffusion of knowledge, would soon realize the fable of the belly and the other members of the body, and confuse that distinction of ranks and classes of society, on which the general welfare hinges, and the happiness of the lower order, no less than that of the higher depends.[43]

Fox continued, 'Strange language indeed to be addressed to the sons of England, when the *half-cast* children of Madras were qualified to fill the most important offices of society, and one of them to become a lecturer on

---

[41] By 1819 there were 4,167 'endowed schools' in England, including about 700 traditional grammar schools with 165,433 pupils; 14,282 'unendowed schools', from 'dame schools' to Dissenting academies, with 478,849 pupils, and for the children of the poor; 5,162 Sunday Schools with 452,817 pupils. From Richardson, *Literature, Education and Romanticism*, 45. For the statistics of literacy, see also W. B. Stephens, *Education in Britain 1750–1914* (Basingstoke, 1998).

[42] Fox, *A Comparative View of the Plans of Education as Detailed in the Publications of Dr. Bell and Mr. Lancaster*, 10.

[43] Ibid., 38.

Experimental Philosophy to Tippoo Sultan!'[44] It was impossible to debate the merits of educating the poor without coming to some conclusions on the issue of colonial education.[45]

Just as the debate about colonial tutelage was inextricably linked with the question of whether to educate the poor, these issues merged easily with discussions of the connection between criminality and education. The middling classes lived in fear of literate criminals.[46] In the meantime, Lancaster's method was also exported to Ireland. The *Evangelical Magazine*, in praising Lancaster's system of education, noted that 'WE are glad to find that schools, on the Lancasterian Plan (so well adapted to the instruction of the Irish peasantry) are established in several parts of Ireland.'[47] Just as Bell's system was first formulated in Madras, Lancaster's system itself had colonial origins: he had first entertained the idea of teaching as a vocation when conceiving of a journey to Jamaica, to 'teach the poor blacks the word of God'.[48] In another instance of how vocabularies could move between each of these sites of learning, Robert Raikes, the guiding force of the Sunday School movement, wrote that it was his purpose to take 'little heathens' off the street to be instructed in 'reading, and in the Church catechism'.[49] The notions of improvement associated with education crossed race and class: the poor at home, Irish peasants, urban criminals and 'heathens' abroad were comparable. This is why the improvement of the Society's missionaries and Pacific converts operated on the same premise. Lancaster's system of schooling was as applicable in the Pacific as in London.

The type of improvement envisaged by both Bell and Lancaster was scientific. Science played a vital role in the monitorial system, as demonstrated by the prominence given to the experiments performed before the Tipu Sultan. One of Bell's supporters published a pamphlet urging that Bell's system could be improved and extended so as to instruct the rising generation of the middle and higher classes of society in science. 'Knowledge is latent power', he noted, in concern that the appreciation of 'useful science' had advanced in 'gigantic strides' amongst the lower classes of society. In the meanwhile, the classical education received by the middle and higher classes of society, he bemoaned, was less useful. In this

---

[44] Ibid., 39.
[45] This point has also been made by Richardson, *Literature, Education and Romanticism*, 96–7.
[46] Patrick Brantlinger, 'How Oliver Twist Learnt to Read and What He Read', in *Culture and Education in Victorian England*, ed. Pauline Fletcher and Patrick Scott (London and Toronto, 1990).
[47] *Evangelical Magazine*, 1812, 73.   [48] *Dictionary of National Biography*.
[49] Richardson, *Literature, Education and Romanticism*, 66.

way the working classes were said to be coming to 'physical power' by means of their new-found education in science. The urgency of providing science for the elites was clear.[50]

The principles of natural history were occasionally employed in explaining Bell and Lancaster's educational methods: pupils' minds were envisioned in organic terms and the development of intellect was seen to be similar to how an embryo moves to full form. Bell wrote, 'Young minds are pliant and flexible – Like melted wax, they are ready to receive any impression. Like the tender twig they are easy to be bent in any direction.'[51] He continued: 'The fruits and flowers of our fields and gardens are multiplied and improved with great skill and labour, but the immortal spirits of our youths are suffered to languish and perish forever for want of due culture and Christian education'.[52] Lancaster wrote: 'The mental powers of boys are similar to those of men; but in embryo. – The same stimulus that animates men to action, will have a proportionate effect on juvenile minds.'[53]

In the meanwhile Pritchard wrote of the missionary schools in the Pacific:

These schools are as so many nurseries for the church of Christ ... In these institutions the seed of the kingdom springs up; the tender plants are here sheltered from chilling blasts, which would nip the buds of early piety, and are watered with the dew of heaven, until they shoot up as trees of righteousness, at a suitable age are transplanted into the sacred enclosure, the church, the soil of which is congenial to their nature, and favourable to their growth, where they will flourish and bring forth fruit, till at last they are removed to the Paradise above.[54]

These natural historical metaphors appeared frequently in descriptions of schools. The language associated with education in London, therefore, affected the orchestration of teaching in the islands. The usefulness of these images of nature arose from the perfect platform they provided for articulating notions of intellectual and spiritual development. A scientific mode of conceiving of the progress of the mind was close to evangelical views of nature.

---

[50] Anon., *Observations Upon the Practicability and Importance of Applying Some of the Principles of Dr. Bell's System to the Education in Useful Science of the Sons of Those in the Middle and Higher Classes of Society* (London, 1823).

[51] Andrew Bell, *Extracts of a Sermon on the Education of the Poor, under an Appropriate System, Preached at St. Mary's Lambeth, 28 June 1807* (London, 1807). The comparison of the mind with melted wax appears also in the Lockeian philosophy of education. See Richardson, *Literature, Education and Romanticism*, 13.

[52] Bell, *Extracts of a Sermon on the Education of the Poor*, 17.

[53] Lancaster, *Improvements in Education as It Respects the Industrious Classes of the Community*, 18.

[54] Pritchard, *The Missionary's Reward*, 158.

Revd David Bogue, one of the Society's prime movers, and its chief advocate of education for missionaries, in addressing the promoters of a Protestant Dissenting Grammar School in the parish of Hendon, Middlesex, said: 'A boy at school, sitting down to learn a lesson in Virgil, with his grammar and his dictionary by his side, presents an object by no means beneath the notice of a philosopher.' Bogue encouraged his listeners to use a scientific mode of observation in considering a student's development. He continued his description thus: 'Invention, judgement, memory are called into exercise: to make out his task, they must often be exerted with patient attention and perseverance: and it is only after repeated trials, that he succeeds.'[55] At one point of his discourse, Bogue illustrated the expansion of the mind by referring to nature's processes. The 'teacher of science', he said, 'by patient cultivation of the youthful mind', will 'open to it a new field of improvement and pleasure, extend its views and augment its sagacity and acuteness'.[56]

Through these means of education, Bogue asserted, the entire course of a society could be changed. 'A well-educated youth carries no small portion of knowledge with him into society: he increases it from year to year; he diffuses it among his friends and acquaintances.'[57] By the very act of educating one youth, public opinion might be given a 'decisive opinion in favour of everything that is good'. In this manner, by 'conversation, by prayer, by writing, the purity of the gospel is maintained, error is confuted, youth preserved from the snares of life, and the society to which they belong preserved in peace, while the enemies of religion are, by their christian deportment and powerful reasoning, put to shame'.[58] Education was then not just about the development of individuals – it was also about the transformation of communities.

Instruction in practice

The Missionary Seminary instituted in Gosport, under Bogue's tutorship, was designed to provide this type of education. The idea for such a seminary was first proposed by Bogue in 1794.[59] Numbers at the seminary varied considerably and were most often between eight and fifteen.

---

[55] David Bogue, *The Nature and Importance of a Good Education, a Sermon Preached before the Promoters of the Protestant Dissenters' Grammar School, Lately Opened at Mill Hill in the Parish of Hendon, Middlesex* (London, 1808), 10.
[56] Ibid., 25.   [57] Ibid., 17–18.   [58] Ibid., 21.
[59] See *Sermons and Report of the Missionary Society for 1795*, vi. For another early call for a Missionary Seminary, see *Evangelical Magazine*, 1799, 212. Before taking up his position at the seminary, Bogue had served as tutor at a theological seminary at Gosport, which sent out trained young men for ministry in the Independent Communion.

Bogue's teaching encompassed preaching, reading, meditating and conversing. The rules surrounding this institution may easily be compared to those that governed missionary schools in the Pacific. A typical working day consisted of the following pattern:

1. Rise at six
2. Devotion
3. Theological lectures till ten
4. Languages till lecture hour
5. After dinner relaxation
6. Subsidiary studies till half past six
7. Theological lectures till half past eight
8. After that sermons, plans &c and devotion
9. Retire to rest at eleven.[60]

Bogue commended this pattern to his students, saying that its variety would 'bring considerable relief and relaxation to the mind'.[61] On alternate Sundays, students were expected to preach in neighbouring villages. Refusal to do so, according to Bogue, would offend the ministers in charge of those congregations which in turn would probably mean that 'subscriptions to the Society might in many instances be withdrawn'.[62] The importance of these engagements had thus as much to do with the obligations that they entailed as with the preparation they provided for candidates.

Bogue gave his students a total of four hundred lectures, covering a range of subjects from rhetoric and preaching to astronomy and geography.[63] These, by his own admission, though they brought 'the substance of the subject into more narrow focus', provided a brief sketch of a huge range of topics. Despite this admission, Bogue expected that the lectures would 'strongly impress the heart' and 'engage the attention much'.[64] Bogue's voice, 'though not musical, was not unpleasing and was sufficiently powerful to fill the largest building without effort. He retained so little of his northern accent, he might have been mistaken.'[65] His students adorned themselves in Latin caps in lessons.[66] They were also accustomed

[60] Eighth Lecture 'Rules for the distribution and improvement of time.' Lectures on the Pastoral Office transcribed by J. Lowndes, L 14/8, Dr Williams' Library, London (hereafter DWL), 528.
[61] Ibid., 530.
[62] Report of the deputation appointed to visit the Missionary Seminary at Gosport, March 1817, in Home Correspondence, Box 3, SOAS.
[63] See ibid.
[64] Second Lecture 'On the means by which the branches of knowledge necessary for the ministry may be acquired.' Lectures on the Pastoral Office, L 14/8, DWL.
[65] James Bennett, *The Memoirs of the Rev. David Bogue* (London, 1827), 418.
[66] First Lecture 'To students entering the Seminary.' Lectures on the Pastoral Office, L 14/8, DWL.

'to sit at his feet and behold him in the professor's chair' and felt some restraint in his company.[67]

Bogue encouraged his students to come to him with any questions and to form friendships with each other that would facilitate healthy conversation. They were advised to show 'brotherly affection' to each other and to 'guard the heart against envy and contempt' while showing 'due regard to each other's character'.[68] These conversations could take place in the student lodgings. These were neither luxurious nor spacious; the students received just forty pounds per annum for board and lodging.[69] Those who attended the seminary were scattered in different houses around the town.

According to Bogue, healthy conversation 'much sharpens the mind' and 'serves to give clear ideas of subjects'. However, 'confident pretenders to knowledge are apt to impose on hearers' and the danger of being misled in conversation was great. Bogue warned his students that when a conversation gets heated, a participant gets angry, takes sides and resists changing his position. This was one reason why numbers were limited in lodgings: if there were too many candidates in one house this would not create suitable conditions for healthy conversations. Bogue warned: 'do not engross too much of the conversation', a failing that would not occur if numbers were limited.[70]

At each lecture Bogue recommended books for his students to read. When lecturing on astronomy he set 'Derham, Walker, Pemberton, Gregory, Herschell and Ferguson'.[71] He hoped to 'preserve students from desultory reading' and provide them 'with a comprehensive scheme of study'.[72] Bogue's reading practices clearly played an influential role in forming those of his students. We are told that his 'reading, though vast was not greedy and indiscriminate, nor hasty and barren'.[73] While reading, Bogue instructed his students to make the 'best man' on the subject their personal tutor and then compare authors on the same subject. He also

---

[67] Bennett, *The Memoirs of the Rev. David Bogue*, 390.
[68] Sixth Lecture 'On the Proper Behaviour of a student.' Lectures on the Pastoral Office, L 14/8, DWL, 510.
[69] Deputation appointed to visit the Missionary Seminary at Gosport March 1817. Home Correspondence, Box 3, CWM, SOAS.
[70] Sixth Lecture 'On the Proper Behaviour of a student.' Lectures on the Pastoral Office, L 14/8, DWL, 518.
[71] First Lecture 'On some general remarks.' Lectures on Missionary Work, in L 14/9, DWL, 522.
[72] Third Lecture 'On the business of the Seminary.' Lectures on the Pastoral Office L 14/8, DWL, 492.
[73] Bennett, *The Memoirs of the Rev. David Bogue*, 410.

advised: 'after reading meditation is both necessary and effectual for fixing it in the mind in its order and parts'.[74]

At his lectures, Bogue insisted that his students write down 'the best remarks of the best authors' which in turn would provide 'a valuable treasure for future years'.[75] Two sets of transcribed notes from the Missionary Seminary are extant, which give the opportunity for some comparative analysis.[76] The skeleton of the lecture was transcribed in exactly the same manner by both pupils. A considerable part of the evenings was occupied in the task of transcribing these notes: 'not much less than two hours every day'.[77] It is likely that students made rough notes during the course of the lecture which they then rewrote into elegant quarto volumes of manuscript.[78] This process of writing and re-writing could take a meditative form, and demonstrates again the suggestion that repetition was central to early nineteenth-century education.

Just as Lancasterian education was adopted in the Pacific in teaching local people how to read and write, Bogue's lectures on missionary work were translated into Tahitian and used in the training of missionaries from Tahiti to other islands. In 1831 Revd George Pritchard wrote of a seminary where local people were taught to be missionaries. He noted that each student was instructed in reading, writing and arithmetic, while taking with him to his station, in manuscript, 'a course of lectures in Jewish Antiquities, a course on the scriptures, and a course in Missionary lectures'.[79] One of the first graduates from Bogue's seminary, Revd John Orsmond, seems to have cherished the instruction he received at the seminary as a badge of his improved status. Rather amusingly, on his way out to the Pacific, he read out Bogue's lectures to impress his respectability on his hosts in Sydney.[80] The rules that governed the seminary, like those surrounding the missionary school, were crucial in the making of the evangelical. Reading, writing, preaching, conversing and meditating were interrelated. Bogue warned his pupils: 'When a student confines himself to any of these he will considerably impede his improvement.'[81]

---

[74] Second Lecture 'On the means by which the branches of knowledge necessary for the ministry may be acquired.' Lectures on the Pastoral Office, L 14/8, DWL, 481.
[75] Third Lecture 'On the business of the seminary.' Ibid., 492.
[76] These notes were taken by J. Lowndes and I. or J. Elliot.
[77] Report of the Deputation appointed to visit the Missionary Seminary at Gosport.
[78] Ibid.   [79] Gunson, *Messengers of Grace*, 323.   [80] Ibid., 69.
[81] Second Lecture 'On the means by which the branches of knowledge necessary for the ministry may be acquired.' Lectures on the Pastoral Office, L 14/8, DWL.

Sciences of the mind

In understanding the form and function of Bogue's lectures on science, it is important to keep the argument about the definition of multiple practices firmly in mind. Bogue was as concerned with note-taking as reading, conversation, meditation, preaching and clothing. The sciences were important for all of these activities.

Bogue's scientific lectures ranged from astronomy and geography to explanations of the formation of the world. He held that missionaries required an understanding of science because they would have to preach from appealing to 'the word of God', 'the reason and the light of nature and conscience', and 'from principles which they [the unconverted] hold in their religion'.[82] In a separate lecture, Bogue instructed missionaries to set up schools where reading, writing, singing, arithmetic, geography and the history of the world would be taught. 'The barbarous state of the people', he contended 'render all kinds of knowledge very needful.'[83] In addition to aiding conversion, teaching science would then also accelerate the progress of the civilising mission.

Various classes of peoples were said to require different types of science. According to J. Lowndes' transcript of Bogue's lecture:

What employments are most suitable and have usually been adapted
1. Among all nations
    1 Teaching useful knowledge
    2 Medical science. Luke the beloved physician
    3 Gardening and agriculture
2. Among civilised nations
    1 Useful science. Mathematics, Natural Philosophy, Geography and Chemistry
    2 Some of the more ingenious arts ... Watchmaking ...
3. Among barbarous nations
    1 Agriculture
    2 Common arts. Carpenter, Mason, Blacksmith, Weaver &c.[84]

Bogue advised missionaries to have some books on science and language in their libraries.[85] He instructed those leaving the seminary to spend time studying those parts of 'literature which are subservient to theological and biblical knowledge and highly useful to the minister'. Bogue included all types of knowledge that would increase the minister's understanding of the

---

[82] Fourth Lecture 'On Preaching II.' Lectures on Missionary Work transcribed by J. Lowndes, L 14/9, DWL, 35.
[83] Twelfth Lecture 'On Setting up Schools.' Ibid., 103.
[84] Twenty-fourth Lecture, 'Blending other Employments with Missionary Labours.' Ibid., 241.
[85] Appendix 5, 'Of the Studies of a Missionary.' Ibid., 330.

Bible under this rubric: languages and history, as well as the sciences.
Under sciences Bogue listed the following:

2. Sciences
1 Logic. Watt's Logic. Dunkin. Lock on the human understanding
2 Moral Philosophy. Hutchinson, Paley, Grove. Mamis translated from the
  French
3 Natural Philosophy. Ferguson, Adams, Walker.
4 Some part of the mathematic if there is a taste for them.
5 General principle of law, and the law of England. Blacestone.[86]

A close study of the transcribed notes suggests that Bogue followed a
question-and-answer format in his science lectures, rather similar to catechistic teaching. On the subject of comets:

Query 1st: Are we to suppose they were scorched with heat when they approached
        the sun and frozen with cold when they recede from it?
Answ. The Atmosphere may render it equal.
Query 2nd: Can they have any light from the Sun when they are at a great distance
        from him?
Answ. They may have as much as when they are near.[87]

Numbers also played a role here. The emphasis on numerical facts was
evident in the definition of astronomy as 'that which relates to the stars.
A mixed mathematical science, teaching the knowledge of the celestial
bodies, their magnitudes, motions, distances, periods, eclipses and
orders'.[88] The prominence of numbers in evangelical teaching might be
related to the practice of meditation. As missionary candidates reasoned
with the vastness of a figure, they were persuaded that the God whom they
worshipped was in control of their destinies, because He had created so
large a universe.

II Of the stars
1. What number is visible to the naked eye? 1000. How many by glasses? By
Flamsteed 3000. These are called Telescopic stars from their being invisible without
the help of a telescope. Dr. Herschell by his late improvement in telescopes had
discovered that the number of fixed stars is great beyond all conception. In the
milky way he has seen in one quarter of an hour 116000 stars pass through his

[86] 'A Lecture as an Appendix to those on the Pastoral Office.' Lectures on the Pastoral Office,
    L 14/10, DWL, 462.
[87] First Lecture 'Some General Remarks.' Lectures on Missionary Work transcribed by
    J. Londes, L 14/9, DWL, 368.
[88] Ibid., 351.

telescope, the field view of which was only 15 apparitions. He computed the whole number to be 75 000 000.[89]

In the Pacific, questions about science often arose in conversations, in sermons, and in the readings prescribed to students. An early tract used in teaching in Hawaii demonstrates the prominence of natural historical images.[90] Revd Charles Pitman reported:

Several questions were stated respecting the sun, moon, earth, stars &c which to the people are difficult to explain. When I told them that the sun was a fixed body and that the earth revolved around it they could not believe that to be a fact – and had a long conversation among themselves about it, making various remarks, suppositions &c if what I said to them were true.[91]

It was vital that a knowledge of nature was imparted to out-bound missionaries, so as to facilitate these exchanges in the field. In the Pacific, while talking about nature, it was hoped that missionaries would dissuade islanders from animism, and direct them towards rational theology. Different sciences were associated with different stages of development, while the typologies of natural history provided a means of conceiving how the mind and character developed and societies changed.

Nature as gauge

This science of development also comes to the fore in the *Evangelical Magazine*. This periodical might be interpreted as a site of religious education for metropolitan supporters of mission. The issue for 1800, for example, presented subscribers with a spiritual experiment (figure 2.1).[92] A barometer appeared on one of its pages as a gauge of improvement. The zero point of this instrument was marked 'indifference'. Subscribers were invited to scrutinise themselves by 'perusing' this scale from its middle. Had they experienced a 'concern for the soul?' If they answered 'yes' they were permitted to ascend the scale to plus four and attempt the next test. If they answered 'no' they were obliged to descend and ask themselves whether 'private prayer' was 'frequently omitted'. A positive answer to this second question entailed a further drop. When they finally gauged their spiritual pressure they had an idea of how they might 'progress' in 'sin' or 'grace'. The goal for true evangelicals was plus seventy. This point

[89] Ibid., 353.
[90] See Anon, *Kumumua* (Honolulu, 1846), 14. (This text is at the British Library.)
[91] Revd Charles Pitman, Entry for Monday 30 August 1828, South Sea Journals, Box 6, CWM, SOAS.
[92] *Evangelical Magazine*, 1800, 526.

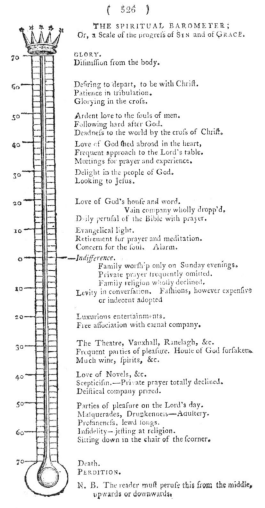

(526)

THE SPIRITUAL BAROMETER;
Or, a Scale of the progress of SIN and of GRACE.

GLORY.
Dismission from the body.

Desiring to depart, to be with Christ.
Patience in tribulation.
Glorying in the crofs.

Ardent love to the fouls of men.
Following hard after God.
Deadnefs to the world by the crofs of Chrift.

Love of God fhed abroad in the heart,
Frequent approach to the Lord's table.
Meetings for prayer and experience.

Delight in the people of God.
Looking to Jefus.

Love of God's houfe and word.
        Vain company wholly dropp'd.
Daily perufal of the Bible with prayer.

Evangelical light.
Retirement for prayer and meditation.
Concern for the foul.   Alarm.

—Indifference.
        Family worfhip only on Sunday evenings.
        Private prayer frequently omitted.
        Family religion wholly declined.
Levity in converfation.   Fafhions, however expenfive
        or indecent adopted

Luxurious entertainments.
Free affociation with carnal company.

The Theatre, Vauxhall, Ranelagh, &c.
Frequent parties of pleafure. Houfe of God forfaken.
Much wine, fpirits, &c.

Love of Novels, &c.
Scepticifin.—Private prayer totally declined.
Deiftical company prized.

Parties of pleafure on the Lord's day.
Mafquerades, Drunkennefs—Adultery.
Profanenefs, lewd fongs.
Infidelity—jefting at religion.
Sitting down in the chair of the fcorner.

Death.
PERDITION.

N. B. The reader muft perufe this from the middle,
        upwards or downwards.

Figure 2.1: 'The Spiritual Barometer.' From the *Evangelical Magazine* 1800, 526. Subscribers were expected to use the barometer to ascertain their own spiritual standing. The careful calibration of this instrument exemplifies the centrality of practices of measurement to the pattern of spiritual faith.

was marked 'glory' and 'dismission from the body'. Conversely, minus seventy read 'death' and 'perdition'.

The barometer demonstrates how a multiplicity of practices worked in unison in materialising belief. Reading served as a vital indicator of the state of the soul. Plus fifteen equated with 'daily perusal of the Bible with prayer'. On the negative scale at forty the barometer read 'love of novels'. The barometer showed the importance of meditation at plus six, which read 'retirement for prayer and meditation', and also at plus fourteen, plus forty-six and minus six. The practice of adopting 'fashions, however expensive or indecent' was criticised at minus twelve, while 'the love of God shed abroad in the heart' appeared as a description of charity at plus forty. The importance of attending meetings to listen to others and to encourage believers through prayer appeared on the scale at plus thirty-four.

Each of these activities when taken together could define the outward appearance of evangelicalism. The barometer also neatly summarises believers' criticism of both luxury and sloth; it attacks both the worldly upper classes and the slovenly working classes. At the foot of the spiritual barometer just before death appear the words: 'masquerades, drunkenness, adultery'; 'profaneness, lewd songs'; 'infidelity – jesting at religion' and 'sitting down in the chair of the scorner'. The barometer shows how the education of all the senses, and the learning of a variety of bodily practices, could present these various groups with the opportunity to escape their idleness and improve.

The barometer speaks then about the possibilities and urgency of spiritual improvement. Two natural historical articles in the *Evangelical Magazine* for 1803 reveal how this doctrine of development was linked with nature. Taken together, these two articles, on the beaver and the sloth, characterised the difference between industry and idleness; believers were urged to imitate the former. Both articles were accompanied by engravings, which were recycled from Buffon's *Natural History*[93] (figures 2.2 and 2.3). By paying close attention to these images, and to the text that accompanied them, it is possible to see how nature mediated in evangelical notions of the refinement of the self.

Unlike Buffon's sloth, the *Evangelical Magazine*'s sloth is presented as an inert creature: it is shown clinging to the branches of a tree with outstretched arms. The beaver, on the other hand, is actively searching for a means of moving from its spot. The subscriber is denied eye contact with the sloth, though it looks directly forward, for its eyes are not visible. In the course of the text the writer claims that they are 'sluggishly half closing' and 'sleepy eyes'. The beaver's eyes, though not directed at the

---

[93] The analysis refers to plates 13 and 39 in Louis Leclerc Buffon, *Histoire Naturelle* (London, 1792). The sloth is referred to as the Adult Ai. The images used in the *Evangelical Magazine* were not exact replicas, but were modified to emphasise certain features. For the interpretation of images, see Patricia Anderson, *The Printed Image and the Transformation of Popular Culture* (Oxford, 1991), 44.

terrible train of destroyers ; and, among these, how formidable are the names of Fevers, Coughs, and Consumptions ! Added together, these alone amount to 7283 : more than one-third of the whole number deceased.

6. The aggregate sum, how vast!—Solemn thought ! nearly 20,000 inhabitants of one city, swept away in the course of twelve months ! That is more than one departing every half hour in the year : 20,000 have given up the ghost ; — and where are they ? Fixed, unalterably fixed, in their eternal state, — the subjects of bliss or woe, — happy or miserable for ever.

7. O inhabitants of the highly-favoured metropolis, your privileges far exceed those of any city upon earth ! Know then, your gracious day ; and consider the things that belong to your peace, lest they be soon hidden from your eyes.

8. Many, probably, who read this paper, may die in the present year. Prepare, therefore, reader, to meet thy God ; and when death arrives, may he be found the minister of mercy, ushering thy soul into the glorious presence of our exalted Redeemer ! To him, the destroyer of death, be endless praises ! Amen.

THE NATURAL HISTORY OF THE SLOTH:

WITH REFLECTIONS.

THE God of nature, abundant in wisdom, seems to have formed the Sloth, with a design to represent to us, in a strong light, the odious and despicable vice which gives to the animal its name.—It is the most sluggish, and the most defenceless of all animals ; and has, of all others, the least appearance of any thing living. Its body is short ; its head is small ; and it has scarce any tail. The Eastern Sloth (for this of which we now speak is a native of America) has no tail at all. Its fur is very long and thick, and has less the appearance of hair than that of any other animal ; and from this, as well as the colour of the fur, which is a greyish green, the creature appears, on the bough of a tree, when seen there, rather as an excrescence, or a cluster of moss, than as a living animal. It is in size,

Figure 2.2: An engraving of the sloth. From the *Evangelical Magazine*, 1803, 69. This sleepy-eyed creature personified the biblical character of the slothful fool.

(158)

THE NATURAL HISTORY OF THE BEAVER *,
WITH REFLEXIONS.

HAVING, in a preceding Magazine (for February) drawn the picture of that ugly vice, Idleness, from the Natural History of the Sloth,—in this I shall attempt to delineate Christian Diligence, from the Natural History of the Beaver: an animal, in almost every respect, the reverse of the former.

The sacred writers often send us to the brute creation for lessons of wisdom and of virtue: " Go to the ant, thou sluggard !" is the advice of Solomon ; and for the same reason we may say, " Go to the beaver ;" — many of whose habits are not dissimilar to the ant's.

The beaver is a native of most of the northern parts of Europe and of Asia, but is most plentiful in North America ; and there is reason to believe, that they were formerly found in Wales, particularly in Cardiganshire. The general length of this animal is about three feet ; and its form may be judged of by the above cut. Its front teeth are very strong ; and it lives chiefly on the bark and leaves of trees. Its hair is very fine, glossy, and of a chesnut brown, sometimes nearly black ; and is an important article in the manufacture of hats, &c.

The natural sagacity of this animal is very remarkable, especially in its social habits ; living in an economy very similar to human society, and superior to what we sometimes see in the savage part of the human species. Capt. G. Cartwright, who resided fourteen years on the coast of Labrador, paid particular attention to them, and gives the substance of the following account : —

" The beavers live in general in associated communities, of two or three hundred ; inhabiting dwellings which they raise to the height of six or eight feet above the water. They select, if possible, a large pond, and raise their houses on piles, forming them either of a circular or oval shape, with arched tops,— which give them, on the outside, the appearance of a dome,

* See Buffon's Nat. Hist. and Bingley's Animal Biography, vol. 2.

Figure 2.3: An engraving of the beaver. From the *Evangelical Magazine*, 1803, 158. This industrious creature symbolised the wise Christian to readers of the periodical.

reader, are clearly discernible. The sloth and the beaver are shown to be very different with regard to their habitations too. We are told that the sloth 'rarely chuses to change its place – never, but when compelled by absolute necessity'.[94] The beaver, on the other hand, in choosing an abode, shows 'sagacity and intelligence . . . intention and memory . . . nearly equal to that of some part of the human race'.[95]

The writer tells us that the sloth eats 'not only the leaves, but the buds, and the very bark all the way as it goes, leaving only a dead branch'.[96] There is decay and death where the sloth is: it has the 'least appearance of any living thing'.[97] On the other hand, the appearance of a stream beside the beaver is said to be characteristic of its habitat, and conveys the idea of life and vivacity. The face of the sloth is dark, whilst the only part of the beaver that is kept free of colouring is its face. This is again a revision of Buffon's images: there the beaver had a dark face and the sloth's face was free from colour. The modification of Buffon's image is in keeping with the text of the article in the *Evangelical Magazine*, where we are told that the sloth's 'face hath much of the monkey aspect though greatly more unpleasing'.[98]

Other contrasts are accentuated in the picture. The colouring and place-ment of the creatures is significant. The beaver is placed parallel to the line of the page while the sloth is at an angle. The sloth is depicted in its woodcut clinging on to a branch which curves into the page. It is coloured irregularly whilst most of the lines used in the colouring of the beaver are straight. Revealingly, we are told that the beaver is tidy and efficient. Indeed, the figure of the beaver in the periodical is leaner than its figure in Buffon's *Natural History*. In the *Evangelical Magazine*, the hump on the beaver's back is symmetrical and its outline is smooth and shapely. The sloth's body has a rugged outline. This again conforms to the writer's description of the sloth as 'shapeless to view'.[99]

Contrasts such as this were easily manufactured in the genre of a period-ical, as readers could, and were expected to, compare successive issues and their contents. At the start of the article on the beaver the reader was told: 'HAVING in a preceding Magazine [for February] drawn the picture of that ugly vice of Idleness from the Natural History of the Sloth – in this I shall attempt to delineate Christian Diligence from the Natural History of the Beaver: an animal in almost every respect, the reverse of the former.'[100] Subscribers attached specific meanings to articles in relation to others that appeared alongside them; this characteristic of the periodical was extre-mely useful for evangelical typologies. The beaver was compared with the charitable evangelical who gave his or her resources away with enthusiasm

[94] *Evangelical Magazine*, 1803, 70.   [95] Ibid., 159.   [96] Ibid., 70.   [97] Ibid., 69.
[98] Ibid., 70.   [99] Ibid.   [100] Ibid., 156.

and foresight, while the sloth signified the evangelical who wasted his or her time in indolence.[101]

The sloth is described thus: 'This contemptible lump of matter well represents to us the man who lives only to eat and to drink; to indulge his appetite, to feast his flesh, to doze away his life in sleepy inactivity, and to consume himself (his nobler self, his soul) and his substance, in wretched indolence, and bodily indulgences.'[102] The beaver, on the other hand, is compared with the human whose soul has been discovered. This is the human who has achieved the full potential of his or her frame. The writer slips into talking of the beaver as 'he' not 'it' half-way through the article. 'What an admirable lesson is here of Christian watchfulness and Christian diligence! What zeal, what activity, what caution, do these sagacious animals discover!'[103]

The human who lived like a sloth, then, was presented as naturally depraved, while the individual who lived like the beaver was said to show improving spirituality. These articles on the beaver and the sloth presented readers with the opportunity to scrutinise themselves and consider how they might improve, and were characteristic of the genre of evangelical meditations on nature. The beaver typified a narrative of conversion, while the sloth, like the fallen man, described a story of damnation. The beaver depicted the individual who made the best use of his or her natural environment while the sloth denoted the individual who had stooped to natural depravity.

The anthropomorphism of these accounts made it easy for them to be applied in characterising the progress of believers. While I do not want to suggest that Pacific islanders were compared directly with beavers and sloths, typologies like that exemplified by this pair of articles were used by missionaries to contrast the industrious student with the islanders who whiled away their time in indolence. In Jane Warren's *The Morning Star*, an engraving depicts eight islanders eating a parcel of mail. Vanessa Smith discusses the story that accompanied the print. When one of the missionaries heard that a parcel of mail had arrived at a distant island, he imagined that it might contain some correspondence for him, and therefore desired to procure the packet. But to his amazement he discovered: 'The mail had been put on shore, but the savages opened it, and supposing the letters and paper to be some kind of food,

[101] For anthropomorphism, see Bernard Lightman, '"The Voices of Nature": Popularising Victorian Science', in *Victorian Science in Context*, ed. Bernard Lightman (Chicago and London, 1990).

[102] *Evangelical Magazine*, 1803, 72. The stereotype of the 'slothful man' appears repeatedly in the book of Proverbs: see, for instance, 19: 15, 26: 13–14.

[103] *Evangelical Magazine*, 1803, 160. The 'wise man' appears also in Proverbs 21: 22, 24: 5.

had *eaten the greater portion of them*! A few whole ones and some frag-
ments only remained, and for those he was obliged to pay. It is not stated
whether the natives found the "boki" to be a palatable diet.'[104] The
islanders are represented here as unable to differentiate between food
for the body and food for the soul. They appear to be lazy and more
concerned with their appetites than their minds.

Smith suggests that a different story is demonstrated in an engraving
from within a chapel, showing Revd Buzacott presenting prizes to children
belonging to his day school and Sunday School in 1853.[105] Images of the
interior of mission schools were common and were expected to trumpet the
achievements of missionaries so as to appease the demands of the directorate and their subscribers. In another image which appeared in the
Missionary Sketches for 1858, for instance, the viewer is presented with a
missionary superintending children reading. Here there is none of the sloth
found in the print of Pacific islanders eating mail; instead there is a proper
attention to text, as the girls under the eye of the missionary attentively
read from their books (figure 2.4). Stories of Pacific islanders' eager
appropriation of texts suggested that they conformed to the characteristics
that were associated with good converts.

Revd William Ellis recalled an islander in Huahine whose house had
burnt down and was considerably injured in attempting to save some of his
property. 'I told him I was sorry for his misfortunes. True, said he, It is
some work to build a house; but though I have lost my house, I have saved
my book – pulling at the same time a copy of one of the Gospels out of his
bosom and exhibiting it with great satisfaction.'[106] On another occasion,
when Revd John Williams was overturned with some local people in a
rough sea, they left the missionary to his own devices, until they had
ensured that some translated scriptures were dry and safe: 'when they
had spread their wet Bibles in the sun they returned and assisted him, for
whom they have the most lively regard'.[107]

Accounts such as these serve as the opposite of the story of the islanders who ate the mail. Taken together they point to the importance of
typologies in the missionaries' civilising mission; the behaviour of islanders prior to education and conversion was always set in stark contrast to
that upon conversion.

[104] Smith, *Literary Culture and the Pacific*, 237–8.   [105] Ibid., 237.
[106] Anon., *Polynesia or Christianity in the Islands of the South Seas* (Dublin, 1828), 102.
[107] Ibid., 98.

No. CLIX.—APRIL, 1858.

Missionary Sketches

FOR THE USE OF THE WEEKLY AND MONTHLY SUBSCRIBERS TO
THE LONDON MISSIONARY SOCIETY.

JUVENILE ANNIVERSARY AT HUAHINE.

Figure 2.4: 'Juvenile Anniversary at Huahine.' From *Missionary Sketches for 1858*. A missionary monitors the reading of a class of girls, while several adults and male students observe their progress. The use of repetition as a means of instruction was common in missionary schools.

Rules gone awry

Despite this rhetoric of progress, teaching Pacific islanders proved to be a frustrating enterprise. Failure rather than success often awaited missionaries who applied themselves to the task of teaching. Just as the early century saw an enthusiasm for Lancasterian education, by the 1840s the Infant School system had become the newest fashion in teaching in the islands. In July 1838, Revd John Williams visited the mission stations on the Cape of Good Hope and was impressed with the usefulness of this educational scheme. 'I was sorely grieved', he wrote, 'that no one of our members knew anything of the system.'[108] Ebenezer Buchanan, a son of one of the founders of this method of teaching, on meeting Williams and hearing of the work of the South Pacific mission, volunteered to accompany him back to the islands. Williams immediately employed him for five years, and Buchanan found himself in Samoa in 1838. Buchanan was given the task of training both missionaries and serious converts in the Infant School system, so that they in turn could set up schools that adopted this scheme. Williams, in the meantime, urged the directors 'to give every missionary a thorough knowledge in the infant school system'.[109] He even went to the extent of stating that a knowledge of how to run a school was preferable to all the training imparted to missionaries in colleges and seminaries.

In the Pacific, Buchanan faced severe trials; his experience may be used to suggest the fallibility of British modes of teaching. His biography also speaks of the necessity of destabilising the rhetoric of change – from illiterate savage to educated convert – which was discussed in the previous section. In Samoa, in his first year Buchanan established twelve schools on the island of Upolu and about twelve on Savai'i.[110] His wife busied herself in teaching girls and women reading, writing and sewing.[111] He wrote to the directors: 'For the first quarter ending March 1838 our labours were very arduous having to acquire the Samoan language to attend also to the schools and the sick.' The other missionaries sent Buchanan sixty islanders for training in the Infant School system. Buchanan did his best to comply with their wishes and accompanied his trainees to various villages where the islanders were stationed as teachers. There was a great demand for teaching. For instance, on the large island of Sapapali'i Buchanan reported that there were nearly 200 children, 100 youths and 100 young men and women desirous of instruction.[112] This made for a busy life. Buchanan described his daily routine at Sapapali'i thus:

I held first an infant school to which all were admitted, but were differently employed, the older part of them being occupied in writing, while the younger were exercising, reading, counting, spelling &c. Before closing the school (which commonly lasted from half past eight A.M. till half past ten) the whole were collected, learned a verse from scripture in Samoan, and went through

[108] Letter dated 18 July 1838, from Revd J. Williams, Incoming Letters from the South Seas, Box 11, CWM, SOAS.
[109] Ibid.   [110] Gunson, *Messengers of Grace*, 242.
[111] Letter dated 26 October 1839 from Ebenezer Buchanan, Incoming Letters from the South Seas Box 12, CWM, SOAS.
[112] Letter dated 25 October 1841 from Ebenezer Buchanan, Incoming Letters from the South Seas, Box 14.

conversationally some portion of scripture history. We then sang and prayed and dismissed till 11 o'clock when the boys and girls with those of the young men and women who could spare the time assembled again. They read the first eight chapters of the gospel according to St. John in English ... This class and those that met in the afternoon learned also the first four rules of arithmetic, writing, scripture history, natural history, geography and astronomy.[113]

This hectic schedule may at first indicate Buchanan's success. For instance, he noted with pride how an islander called Malachi stationed in Solosolo held morning and evening adult schools for reading which were well attended, an infant school with the assistance of two youths who had been trained by Buchanan and a daily writing school for adults and children. In addition to this, Malachi preached twice on Sundays and held catechistical exercises.[114] Buchanan's ingenuity was also displayed in how he made the equipment he required for teaching from raw material found in the islands, when supplies sent by the directors were delayed. Buchanan summarised the importance of his labours on Samoa in writing that teachers were leaving from Samoa annually for the islands to the westward that were yet to be reached for the gospel.[115] Despite all of these signs of success, Buchanan was dispirited by his time in Samoa. He noted of the local people: 'The material I have to work on is as rough as the rak in the forest. Who would attempt to build a noble vessel of such without tools?'[116]

In 1841, keeping with the original arrangement made with Williams, Buchanan was transferred to Tahiti. If his experience in Samoa had been exhausting, he was a failure in Tahiti. He was received coolly by the older missionaries and he took the boys' boarding school at Papara under his control. This school was intended for the sons of chiefs and those who showed especial talent and piety; it was also used for mixed-blood children.[117] Buchanan complained vehemently about the discipline of the children enrolled at this school. He laid some of the blame at the feet of their parents, writing of the 'entire neglect of domestic arrangements among the parents – The children go sometimes till mid day and not infrequently till evening without a morsel of food.' He wrote in disgust of the children's attitudes towards sex and alcohol. 'Being brought up without parental control they are no sooner able to provide for themselves than the boys join what is called the tute auri (rusty iron) class. They spend most of their time in the bush preparing drink which intoxicates them.'[118]

[113] Ibid.   [114] Ibid.   [115] Letter dated 10 February 1841 from Ebenezer Buchanan, ibid.
[116] Letter dated 25 October 1841 from Ebenezer Buchanan, ibid.
[117] Gunson, *Messengers of Grace*, 243.
[118] Letter dated 29 August 1842, from Ebenzer Buchanan, Incoming Letters from the South Seas, Box 15, CWM, SOAS.

This state of affairs angered Buchanan, as there was no scope for enfor-
cing rules. He wrote in disappointment of how the children's lack of control
had impeded progress in learning. In geography he had made a start by
drawing a large map of Tahiti, with which his charges were becoming
familiar. They could also point out and name most of the countries in
Europe. 'In astronomy we have gone no further than naming the planets
and learning the number of days in their years and a few other particulars
respecting them and the solar system.'[119] In practice, then, Buchanan's time
in Tahiti – and even Samoa – speaks of how the rhetoric of improvement
associated with missionary schools was often destabilised in practice.

While in company

This language of improvement, which motivated Buchanan, and which
could so easily draw lessons from nature and science, is also evident in the
last site of education that I will consider: the missionary meeting. For an
out-bound missionary, the opportunity to attend the Society's annual
general meetings was a remarkable privilege. These meetings served as a
spur to action and created a strong sense of community. Revd Matthew
Wilks, in addressing the Society at such a meeting, went so far as to say
that it was the most 'solemn' experience 'this side of eternity'.[120] A
number of varied individuals were brought together by these annual
assemblies.[121] Those who attended from remote parts found that the best
seats at the chapels were taken by members of the local congregation, who
did not give way to visitors. One visitor wrote to the *Evangelical Magazine*:
'I beg to complain of the inattention shewn at some places to strangers, in
not seating and accommodating them as far as convenient; and appeal to
those concerned whether if the persons were invited to their houses instead
of their churches, they would not act differently.'[122] Listening to a sermon
therefore necessitated a hierarchy of seating determined by evangelical
norms of charity.

The practice of preaching was also regulated. John Campbell, who
spoke before the Society in 1808, confirmed that he would preach, but
asked the directors to refrain from publishing the text of his sermon. 'I rely
with confidence on the pledge you have given me that this circumstance
will not be made known to others than the clergymen you alluded to.'
He also made sure that the directors had his credentials right by adding a

---

[119] Letter dated 3 December 1842, from Ebenezer Buchanan, ibid.
[120] *Sermons and Report of the Missionary Society for 1812* (London, 1812), 51.
[121] *Sermons and Report of the Missionary Society for 1816* (London, 1816), 56.
[122] *Evangelical Magazine*, 1798, 153.

footnote to his letter which read: 'John Campbell D.D. one of the ministers of the Tolbooth Church, Edinburgh and Secretary of the Society in Scotland for Propagating Christian Knowledge.'[123] R. P. Allen, who was asked to speak in the same year as Campbell, wrote to the directors accepting the invitation saying, 'I have scarcely enjoyed an hour's composure of mind since I read your letter – I have really been searching for excuses ... I think I am compelled to say (though I say it with a trembling Heart) I will endeavour to say something on the solemn occasion.'[124]

In preparing themselves to address the annual meeting, speakers could turn to a rich store of manuals and lectures on good preaching. At the Missionary Seminary, Bogue lectured on the subject of how to address special gatherings. On such occasions, he advised that 'the preacher is not under the necessity of paying strict attention to his text which is proper on ordinary occasions. It is quite enough if the discourse is founded on the text.'[125] More generally, in relation to preaching, Bogue urged that sermons should 'be easily remembered, and be so simple, that everyone is ready to think he would have fallen upon it himself'.[126] Speakers were instructed to view the subject 'in its various relations' by dwelling on it at length. 'This will happily diversify it, and the same leading thoughts will have distinguishing and agreeable peculiarities, and the whole subject will appear one.'[127]

Revd John Hyatt's sermon to the annual general meeting of the London Missionary Society in 1815 suggests how these rules worked in practice. Hyatt used Isaiah 55: 10–11 as his text.[128] In explaining the meaning of this passage, Hyatt portrayed nature as bounteous:

The earth produces innumerable blessings for our use, not one of which could be produced without rain. We enjoy the fruits of the rain in the bread we eat – the beverage we drink – the clothing we wear. The earth feeds the creatures by whose flesh we are nourished, and by whose wool we are warmed. Who can gaze upon the beautiful face of nature at the present season, and not admire the effects of 'the rain that cometh down from heaven'?[129]

---

[123] Letter dated 28 March 1800 to Revd George Burder in Home Correspondence, Box 2, CWM, SOAS.

[124] Letter dated 31 March 1808 from R. P. Allen to the directors, ibid.

[125] Fifteenth Lecture, 'On Preaching.' Lectures on the Pastoral Office, transcribed by J. Lowndes, L 14/8, DWL.

[126] Seventh Lecture, 'Thoughts on General Method.' ibid., 64.

[127] Sixth Lecture, 'General Observations on Preaching.' ibid., 56.

[128] This passage is said to record the words of the God of Israel: 'For as the rain cometh down, and the snow from heaven, and returneth not thither, but watereth the earth, and maketh it bring forth and bud, that it may give seed to the sower, and bread to the eater: So shall my word be that goeth forth out of my mouth: it shall not return unto me void, but it shall accomplish that which I please, and it shall prosper in the thing whereto I sent it.' Isaiah 55: 10–11.

[129] *Sermons and Report of the Missionary Society for 1815* (London, 1815), 45–6.

Nature appears here as abundant with fruit and visually pleasing. Yet the cause of this abundance is traced back to heaven. Hyatt continued, 'The gospel transforms mankind that were the counterparts of Satan, into a lovely image of the Son of God. Odiousness is exchanged for beauty – injuriousness gives place to utility – the hateful fruits of the flesh, are supplanted by the admirable fruits of the Spirit.'[130] Visible changes in nature illustrated the transformations wrought by the grace of heaven. 'In sovereign mercy God sent his word to some parts of it, and turned the wilderness into a fruitful field, and made the desert rejoice and blossom as the rose.'[131] With these words Hyatt entertained his audience with aesthetically pleasing images derived from scripture.

Conforming to Bogue's advice about the diversification of a theme, Hyatt did not restrict himself to the verses from Isaiah in establishing the efficacy of rain. He expanded his discussion to other passages in scripture concerning prophets praying for rain and psalmists longing for their thirst to be quenched. Hyatt asserted that God alone could orchestrate changes in nature; but he assured his audience that God would work at the right time. Quoting scripture, he asserted: 'While the earth remaineth, seed time and harvest, cold and heat, and summer and winter, and day and night, shall not cease.'[132] Similarly, 'The gospel *must* prosper and effect what its eternal author hath proposed. Its success cannot possibly be prevented.'[133] Nature, following God's timing, worked at best efficiency. 'The great and glorious Governor of the universe doth nothing in vain – *all* his works praise him ... We are not astonished at the efficiency of the rain when we consider the power by which it is employed.'[134] And again: 'God sends not the gospel to any place in vain: 'it shall prosper in the thing whereto I sent it'.'[135] In adopting these natural metaphors Hyatt ensured that his hearers would feel that they could have come upon these truths themselves – the very advice given by Bogue.

It is clear, then, that strict rules were deployed in organising sermons. Nature in the meanwhile could provide a ready source of illustration. The preparation of the heart by the Spirit and the dissemination of the word by men could be compared to the processes of natural growth: planting, cultivation, watering and harvesting. The transformations at each of

---

[130] Ibid., 46. The 'works of the flesh' and the 'fruit of the Spirit' appear in Ephesians 5.
[131] *Sermons and Report of the Missionary Society for 1815*, 40. This image arises from Isaiah 32: 15: 'Until the spirit be poured upon us from on high, and the wilderness be a fruitful field, and the fruitful field be counted for a forest.'
[132] *Sermons and Report of the Missionary Society for 1815*, 44. This is a quotation from Genesis 8: 22.
[133] *Sermons and Report of the Missionary Society for 1815*.
[134] Ibid., 43.   [135] Ibid.

these stages could illustrate the doctrines of evangelisation, conversion and sanctification. 'The wilderness is turned into a blooming paradise. The indolent become industrious – the revengeful, become kind and affection-ate – the licentious, become chaste – the proud become humble – the covetous become liberal.'[136]

Nature as teacher

Just as Pacific islanders reinvented the practices and artefacts of education, they also reconstructed this language of nature evident in evangelical periodicals and meetings. Upon conversion islanders preached sermons that drew on nature but that operated in distinctive styles. Despite the strict rules that defined an activity such as preaching, it was still possible for local peoples to appropriate and reinvent these practices.

Just as the metropolitan Society had annual meetings and branch insti-tutions in the provinces called auxiliaries, so also did the islanders set up auxiliary missionary societies in each of the stations. At the annual meeting of the Raiatean Auxiliary Society on 8 May 1822, a convert made this speech in Revd John Williams' presence:

Friends let us contribute with zeal in the heart and what we do let us do with prudence and skill. What are the means to kill the sea-serpent? Strike him in the middle, and he will not die; but strike him on the head, and he cannot live; so in all we do let us aim at the root and be active there.[137]

At another auxiliary meeting, Taataori addressed the meeting saying:

God has made great lights, the sun and the moon and placed them in the heavens; and for what has he placed them there? To push away darkness. So the Missionary Society, it is like a Great Light; its object is to push away the darkness and wickedness of the world, and to teach all the way of salvation by Jesus Christ.[138]

Another islander visualised the connection between auxiliary societies and the metropolitan organ in natural historical terms: 'Where come the great waters? Is it not from the small streams that flow into them? I have been thinking that the Missionary Society in Britain is like the great water, and that such little societies as ours are like little streams. Let there be many little streams.'[139]

Comments such as these were rarely recorded in early missionary dis-course. Much later in the century, however, Revd Wyatt Gill put together a

---

[136] Ibid., 46.   [137] Anon., *Polynesia or Christianity in the Islands of the South Seas*, 48.
[138] Ibid., 34.   [139] Prout, *Memoirs of the Rev. John Williams*, 94.

compilation of natural historical anecdotes which he had heard throughout his stay in the Pacific.

We poor sinners are like the *titi* – a foolish bird – hiding away in the dark and
noisome haunts of sin. Jesus is ever calling, and seeking to allure us out of that
darkness, and bring us into his glorious light of day. But, alas! we do not all, like the
titi, respond to His call, and fly to Him. Would that all the poor *titis* (sinners) come
to Jesus![140]

'Were we', added Teava, 'as willing to part with our favourite sins as this
mali'o crab is with its defiled limbs, there would be little doubt of our
reaching heaven. This is what the Lord means by our cutting off our right
hand and casting it from us.'[141] Gill noted, 'I once heard a native preacher
compare the most imperishable coral tree to God as the tree of life, and
mankind to the caterpillars which feed upon His bounty. He urged his
countrymen to imitate the caterpillar in never abandoning the parent tree,
where only it can live and grow.'[142] A final example, from this huge archive:
'Young cocoa-nuts thrown down from the crown of the palm, crack, and the
milk is sure to be spilt. Not so full grown nuts, which invariably come to the
ground unharmed.' 'So', said Ezekiela, 'it is with professors. Immature
Christians are easily turned aside by temptations and persecutions; whereas
mature faith remains steadfast under the severest trials.'[143]

These theological conceptions of nature did not result from the simple
diffusion of themes present in missionary sermons in London. Gill wrote,
for example, 'a native orator cannot open his lips save in parable, song or
proverb. These embody well-known facts in natural history.'[144] The fact
that there is a significant difference between theological conceptions of
rain and biblical truths illustrated by crabs need not be stressed. Such
distinctions have to be related to local geographies. The islanders' reinvention of the evangelical theology of nature must also be related to pre-
Christian cultures. For example, the titi bird is said to have had a special
significance. Wyatt Gill noted, 'The Titi burrows its nest in the mountain
side. During the period of incubation it is easily caught by the hand, or by
plaintively imitating its cry. Accordingly in Tahitian dialect a slave or
conquered person is called a Titi because the conquered took refuge in
the mountains where they were easily captured and slain.'[145] Pacific islanders had a long-standing tradition of anthropomorphising and deifying
nature. Indeed, the close relationship that they shared with nature is

[140] W. W. Gill, *Life in the Southern Isles or Scenes and Incidents in the South Pacific and New Guinea* (London, 1876), 136.
[141] Ibid., 127.   [142] Ibid.   [143] Ibid., 77.   [144] Ibid., chapter 1.   [145] Ibid., 33.

evident even in the names they ascribed to such birds as titis: the creature's sound could in this case become a signifier.

While the natural historical stories that missionaries and converts told each other demonstrate that there were striking parallels between the theology of missionary sermons in London and in the Pacific, local reinventions should not be forgotten. The process of learning is after all one of struggle and exchange.

Conclusions

Michel Foucault has called the monitorial system of schooling 'a machine for learning, in which each pupil, each level and each moment, if correctly combined, were permanently utilized in the general process of teaching'.[146] Social theorists are keen to locate the creation of the lone individual and the capitalist consumer in schools and universities. Yet often, like Foucault, they see this process of social production as a mechanised one. For them the invention of the bourgeois self is a myth, at the heart of which is the fact that all individuals are exact replicas of others that have arisen out of the mechanical processes of social reproduction. In these accounts nature is absent, because nature is seen as the realm of creativity which is controlled by the machine. Yet this chapter has served as a corrective to these histories of education and the self. It has shown that organicism was central to evangelical attitudes to teaching in the early nineteenth century. Didactic methods were said to correspond to natural processes of development, and nature itself was seen to be a source of lessons and a gauge of improvement.

In this chapter I have sought to highlight the care with which evangelicals defined activities which were central to the life of faith, even as I have shown how these practices were reinvented in use by missionaries and converts. The simplistic notion of a relationship of power between the teacher and convert needs to be shed. The theologies of nature evident in the missionary schools, the *Evangelical Magazine*, the Missionary Seminary and the missionary meetings were not consumed passively, either by the evangelists or by the Pacific islanders. Both missionaries and converts engaged in a dialogic process of exchange, where lessons were reconstructed and methods changed. An emphasis on observation and control, therefore, diverts attention from resistance and reconstruction.

Evangelical education in the Pacific and in London was essentially about improvement. Underlying this idea of progress was the notion that islanders could become like evangelicals. Step by step they could be

---

[146] Michel Foucault, *Discipline and Punish: The Birth of the Prison*, trans. Alan Sheridan (Harmondsworth, 1979), 165.

changed from being slothful to industrious; from being ignorant of the value of text to being respectful of books. The Missionary Seminary might thus be compared with the missionary schools in the Pacific: careful rules governed a diversity of practices, from meditation and conversation to writing and reading. The *Evangelical Magazine*, meanwhile, acted as an organ of spiritual improvement for its metropolitan audience. Despite this rhetoric of transformation, however, the experience of Ebenezer Buchanan shows how the reality of the evangelical mission was far from what was claimed.

When discussing the typological contrast between the beaver and the sloth, alongside that between the children who attended to their lessons and the islanders who ate their mail, I hinted that the intended transformation of the illiterate 'savage' to educated convert corresponded to a movement from a state of nature to a state of self-control. The next chapter will demonstrate how a growing awareness of the self could be forged in relation to nature in this way.

3   The seed of the soul: conversion illustrated by nature

For the vast majority of South Pacific missionaries, their primary aim was not the education of their charges, but rather their conversion. Natural husbandry was often combined with conversion in religious publications.[1] James Fisher, in a book entitled *A Spring-Day* (1808), wrote: 'How shall the field of the heart be kept? The answer is, By giving it to the care of the great Husbandman.'[2] Using a woodcut showing a sower at work, Fisher noted that, at conversion, 'the hard and stony heart, that would have intercepted the growth of the heavenly seed, is taken out, together with a great deal of the weeds of sin and corruption'.[3] Upon conversion, he continued, 'the field of the heart must be carefully kept from the inroads of sin and Satan, else these, worse than beasts of prey will soon destroy the crop of grace'.[4] A good crop would only arise if the seed was covered with soil and, similarly, 'the good seed of the word must be as it were covered up, and hid deep in the heart'.[5]

This chapter will discuss the relationship between the South Pacific missionaries' ideology of natural improvement and the process of conversion. Just as the growth of the mind, brought about by schooling, was likened to a natural process, the discovery and nurture of the soul could also be illustrated by a metaphor extracted from the environment. When missionaries adopted this mode of speech, they followed a tradition common amongst explorers, improvers and naturalists. Travellers in search of curiosities and new knowledge routinely likened local peoples, and especially those from the Pacific islands, to natural historical beings in the late eighteenth and early nineteenth centuries.[6] Debate revolved around the

---

[1] For the relationship between husbandry and spiritual growth, see John Flavell, *Husbandry Spiritualized: Or the Heavenly Use of Earthly Things*, ed. Revd C. Bradley (London, 1822; first printed 1699) and Richard Pearsall, *Contemplations on the Ocean, the Harvest, Sickness and the Last Judgement* (London, 1802).

[2] James Fisher, *A Spring-Day: Or Contemplations on Several Occurrences Which Naturally Strike the Eye in That Delightful Season* (Edinburgh, 1808), 109.

[3] Ibid., 100.   [4] Ibid., 108.   [5] Ibid., 99.

[6] See, for instance, David Bindman, *Ape to Apollo: Aesthetics and the Idea of Race in the 18th Century* (London, 2002).

question of how to distinguish the various peoples of the world – in terms of physiognomy as well as civilisation – and how those same peoples were related to the biblical tribes.

It is important to state that missionaries did not equate their charges to natural historical specimens, but they adopted a visual language of nature in speaking of their converts.[7] This mode of speech was scriptural and provided evangelicals with a stadial scheme which could be of use in articulating the step-by-step process that conversion was thought to entail. The use of this language was sufficient to allow Sir Joseph Banks, the eminent man of science, to patronise the Society. Banks's religious commitments are difficult to classify, but it is certain that he did not subscribe to the doctrine of the justification of sinners by faith alone.[8] He urged that good deeds must be crucial in the eyes of the Deity. Banks arranged for the Society's departing missionaries to be given free passage on government vessels, offered advice on the publication of the travel narrative of the *Duff*, and discouraged the Society from sending women to that region.[9]

Historians have provided numerous studies of early nineteenth-century cultivation and collecting, but the religious dimensions of these processes have often been ignored.[10] The imperial rule of nature involved the naming, classification and exchange of live plants. Missionaries also gave their converts new names, classified them as saved or lost and sent them for instruction elsewhere. Natural historical collecting brought a network of people into contact with each other: artisans associated with gentlemen, for instance. Missionaries were also participants in a network: they sent

---

[7] For the distinction between the human and the animal, see Erica Fudge, Ruth Gilbert and Susan Wiseman, eds., *At the Borders of the Human: Beasts, Bodies and Natural Philosophy in the Early Modern Period* (Basingstoke, 1999).

[8] See Gascoigne, *Joseph Banks and the English Enlightenment*, 42.

[9] For Banks's assistance with the passage of the missionaries, see Sir Joseph Banks to Revd George Burder, 13 January 1810, Dawson Turner Correspondence (hereafter DTC), Natural History Museum, London (hereafter NHM), Banks Archive Identifier (hereafter BAI): HLC951030/008.03810. For Banks's advice on the publication of the travel narrative, see Sir Joseph Banks to Revd Thomas Haweis, 6 May 1799, British Library, BAI: HLC951101/045.03799. For Banks's insistence on women not being sent to the South Pacific, see Sir Joseph Banks to Revd Thomas Haweis, 28 September 1799, Sutro Library California (hereafter SLC), BAI: JSB941103/014.03799.

[10] For studies of improvement and cultivation in the late eighteenth century, see Simon Schaffer, 'The Earth's Fertility as a Social Fact in Early Modern Britain', in *Nature and Society in Historical Context*, ed. Bo Gustafsson, Roy Porter and Mikulas Teich (Cambridge, 1997), and Simon Schaffer, 'Field Trials, the State of Nature and the British Colonial Predicament' (manuscript). For the culture of improvement surrounding Joseph Banks, see Gascoigne, *Joseph Banks and the English Enlightenment* and Gascoigne, *Science in the Service of Empire*. For studies of collecting in natural history, see Nicholas Jardine, James Secord and Emma Spary, eds., *The Cultures of Natural History* (Cambridge, 1995) and Roger Cardinal and John Elsner, eds., *The Cultures of Collecting* (London, 1994).

Pacific islanders to their directors in London who attempted to convert these souls for their God.

The theological doctrine of sanctification – the belief that once saved a believer would with time acquire certain gifts and perform good works as a proof of faith – could be compared with a natural historical process, as could conversion. The life of the believer, from sin to grace, could therefore mirror organic growth. This was why non-believers could be described as beastly, while those who had come into a relationship with the Deity, after being born of the Holy Spirit, were truly human. Pacific islanders were said to have revolted against the divine image by resorting to cannibalism, infanticide and idleness. Missionaries hoped to renew the islanders' awareness of their souls, and bring them into a relationship with the Deity in order to resurrect the fallen order of creation.

My discussion of the relationship between natural and religious improvement will begin with an analysis of Sir Joseph Banks's patronage of the Society. I will then consider how evangelicals defined what counted as good use of a theology of nature, in illustrating the process of conversion. The second half of this chapter will move to the question of how these metaphors were employed in interpreting the spiritual progress made by Pacific islanders brought back to London. These islanders were put on display rather like natural historical specimens and the last section will consider the strategies of display adopted by evangelicals. Studying the display of the islanders is important because evangelical missionaries, like all other collectors, established their own identities through their collections. They reassured themselves that their evangelism was succeeding. Their attempts at conversion became the outworking of a desire of self-replication, in dress, speech and action. If missionaries' collections of souls served as a mirror, we can trace their likeness in the looking glass and come to an understanding of who they were.[11]

Improving humanity

On 28 April 1789, the first act of the mutineers on the *Bounty* was to throw overboard the breadfruit trees that had restricted their lodgings on the vessel. Sir Joseph Banks had redesigned the ship so that it could hold seven hundred and fifty pots; the plants were to be taken to the Caribbean and planted there so as to feed colonial slaves. Captain William Bligh had treasured the plants, because they signified his connection with Banks, which in turn marked his ascendancy amongst the elite. A line from Bligh's

[11] See Susan Pearce, *On Collecting: An Investigation into Collecting in the European Tradition* (London, 1994), 254.

pen aptly demonstrates his doting: 'I looked at [the plants] with delight every day of my life.'[12]

Tending these plants was not easy. Banks's instructions were legendary for their detail. He told David Nelson, the *Bounty*'s botanist and gardener: 'one day or even one hour's negligence may at any period be the means of destroying all the trees and plants which may have been collected; and from such a cause the whole of the undertaking will prove not only useless to the public, but also to yourself'.[13] The *Bounty*'s crew were probably as lethargic in caring for plants as other sailors were. Often shipments of live plants were killed when they were left unprotected on deck during storms, or without water or ventilation. Lazy sailors may well have been in mind, a few decades later, when Wardian cases were invented. These required no watering whilst at sea: they were designed so that the moisture released by transpiration could be reabsorbed.[14]

Historians who focus on the transportation of dead specimens often lose the concern of Banks for live plants. Banks's patronage of the Royal Horticultural Society, which was founded in 1804, serves as another example of this.[15] The Society's *Transactions* noted: 'Highly is the society indebted to the zeal, and the abilities of some individuals belonging to it; among whom it will be pardonable to name that distinguished promoter of everything that is good and useful in the sciences and the arts, SIR JOSEPH BANKS.'[16] The description of Banks as a promoter of what is 'good and useful' is revealing. It was this Enlightenment agenda of use that lay behind his patronage of the Royal Horticultural Society.

One example, from his contributions to the Society's *Transactions*, illustrates his methods of improvement. In 1791 Banks procured some seeds of the *Zizania aquatica* from Canada, which he sowed in Spring Grove, near Hounslow. These seeds grew and produced strong plants, which ripened and produced seeds, which in turn produced other plants.

In this manner the plants proceeded, springing up every year from the seeds of the preceding one every year becoming visibly stronger and larger, and rising from

[12] See Greg Dening, *Mr Bligh's Bad Language, Passion, Power and Theatre on the Bounty* (Cambridge, 1992), this quote cited 81.
[13] Cited in Nigel Hepper, ed., *Plant Hunting for Kew* (London, 1989), 3.
[14] For Wardian cases see David Allen, *The Naturalist in Britain: A Social History* (Harmondsworth, 1978), 134.
[15] For the relationship between Banks and the Royal Horticultural Society, see Brent Elliot, 'The Promotion of Horticulture', in *Sir Joseph Banks: A Global Perspective*, ed. G. L. Lucas et al. (London, 1994). Banks was also involved with the Joint Stock Farming Society, which hoped to reinvigorate rural life in the Highlands of Scotland. See Sir John Sinclair, *Proposals for Establishing by Subscription, a Joint Stock Farming Society for Ascertaining the Principles of Agricultural Improvement* (London, 1799).
[16] *Transactions of the Horticultural Society* 2, 1817, ii–iii.

deeper parts of the pond, till the last year, 1804, when several of the plants were six feet in height, and the whole pond was in every part covered with them as thick as wheat grows on a well managed field.[17]

Through a successive process of growth and maturation, Banks had accomplished the goal of improving the *Zizania aquatica*.

Banks also explained how straw could be laid under strawberry plants, thereby protecting the roots from the sun; how the American cranberry tree could be grown in British soil if there was a good supply of fresh water, and how the fig tree could produce a second annual crop if the whole tree were surrounded by a glass case. His successful cultivation of the orchid in Britain was graphically illustrated in the *Botanical Register*. The use of a 'cylindrical wicker basket'[18] was said to allow the plant to flourish. He was also deeply concerned with the spread of insects and diseases and published a tract on the blight that threatened corn. Here he stated that the 'origin of this evil' was 'the pores which exist also on the leaves ... at the bottom of the hollows to which they lead, they germinate and push their minute roots ... into the cellular texture beyond the bark, where they draw their nourishment, by intercepting the sap that was intended by nature for the nutriment of grain'.[19]

In describing how the blight could be contained, Banks described the laws put in place by the Deity: 'Providence, however, careful of the creatures it has created has benevolently provided against the too expansive multiplication of any species of being; was it otherwise, the minute plants and animals, enemies against which man has the fewest means of defence, would increase to an inordinate extent.'[20] When Banks wrote of the spread of the apple tree insect, and how it could be stopped, his reliance on the outworking of the divine laws of balance and order was again evident: 'It is contrary to the usual course of nature that every created entity should be wholly destroyed by another, nature will, therefore, no doubt provide some remedy.'[21] That remedy, of course, was Banks.

Nature and God therefore dictated Banks's project of cultivation, improvement and nourishment. This was a project that spanned the globe from Tahiti to the Caribbean, and from Canada to Britain. It explains why Banks was such an ardent supporter and friend of the Society. The evangelicals were also interested in the cultivation, improvement and nourishment of the created realms: they sent out a number of

[17] *Transactions of the Horticultural Society* 1, 1812, 22–4.
[18] *Botanical Register*, 1817, tab. 220.
[19] Joseph Banks, *A Short Account of the Cause of Disease in Corn Called by Farmers the Blight, the Mildew and the Rust* (London, 1815), 403–4.
[20] Ibid., 406.   [21] *Transactions of the Horticultural Society* 2, 1817, 167.

missionaries with the specific duty of acting as agriculturalists and used a visual language of agriculture in articulating how unconverted 'savages' could be raised from their uncivilised situation. The connection is exemplified in the manner in which the Society introduced itself to Banks: central to the first meeting was no other than Captain Bligh.[22]

John Gascoigne has suggested that Banks used the Society to further his imperial concerns.[23] Gascoigne also documents how Banks was a fervent opponent of clerical meddling in any intellectual matter, seeing religion more as an enlightened project which should concern itself with ethics and reason as opposed to doctrine and revelation. These conclusions may be extended to a reading of Banks's correspondence with Revd Thomas Haweis.

The repeated phrase that Haweis used in corresponding with Banks was the 'interest of humanity'. 'I flatter myself we are united, & wish the greatest possible Happiness & fullest relief from Misery to all Mankind.'[24] 'These facts cry aloud to the Ear of Humanity, & but to mention them will excite every compassionate feeling of your Heart ... Be assured I have but one object the good of Mankind.'[25] 'I hope no friend to Humanity will withhold their Approbation of such conduct. I am sure you, Sir will be pleased with it.'[26] 'I will not trouble you with the details, assured that you will interest yourself for Mankind, for whose Benefit all our efforts are directed.'[27]

The evangelical belief in the sufficiency of faith and grace was, however, antithetical to Banks. This was why he wrote to Haweis:

Tho you & I certainly differ in opinion respecting the things we Each deem necessary for Salvation yet under a firm belief in the Boundless mercy of God I have no doubt that all men who Strive to their utmost according to their Consciences to do what they think good in his Sight will find favor in His

---

[22] Revd Thomas Haweis to Sir Joseph Banks, June (?) 1791, SLC, BAI: HBC930718/001.03791.
[23] Gascoigne, *Joseph Banks and the English Enlightenment*, 42, Gascoigne, *Science in the Service of Empire*, 185. For an earlier debate about the 'paradox' of this correspondence, see Niel Gunson, 'Co-operation without Paradox: A Reply to Dr Strauss', *Historical Studies Australia and New Zealand* 11 (1963–5) and W.P. Strauss, 'Paradoxical Co-operation: Sir Joseph Banks and the London Missionary Society', ibid.
[24] Revd Thomas Haweis to Sir Joseph Banks, 12 September 1798, SLC, BAI: JSB941102/012.03798.
[25] Revd Thomas Haweis to Sir Joseph Banks, 14 September 1799, SLC, BAI: JSB941102/013.03798.
[26] Revd Thomas Haweis to Sir Joseph Banks, 26 January 1798, SLC, BAI: JSB941103/004.03799.
[27] Revd Thomas Haweis to Sir Joseph Banks, 25 March 1799, SLC, BAI: JSB941103/005.03799.

Judgement & under this persuasion I ... express my satisfaction at the attempt of your Society to illuminate the dark paths of our pagan Brethren.[28]

While Haweis saw faith as essential to salvation, he urged holiness as a worthy indicator of faith, and sanctification as crucial. As an Anglican minister with Methodist sympathies he could thus accommodate Banks's concern for good works with a belief in justification by faith, and could write of the missionary societies' operations in terms of human improvement. The relationship between the Society and Banks therefore required more negotiation than that between the Society and Joseph Lancaster.

It would seem strange that Haweis publicly denounced the reception of Omai, which Banks himself orchestrated, given the intimacy of their correspondence.[29] Haweis wrote: 'The foolish Omai was an expense more than would have maintained a mission to the island. Not so much as an attempt was made to give him any knowledge tending to the saving of his soul: He was led about to stare, and be stared at, at our public places, and be abandoned as those that frequent them.'[30] But this comment serves to substantiate the reading of the correspondence. Haweis was aware that 'the interest in humanity' was a bridge between him and Banks; he knew that his belief in the sufficiency of faith and grace stood at odds with Banks. He criticised Banks's reception of Omai on this very point: Banks had neglected to introduce Omai to faith, instead spending his time gratifying the islander by acquainting him with the civilised world of metropolitan culture.

Two kinds of spiritual improvement were therefore important for evangelicals: the conversion of the soul and its growing sanctification. Improving moral conduct served as a symptom of conversion and was demonstrated in good works. It was an outward manifestation of inward change, which was visualised in the language of natural history. But for Banks there was only one kind of improvement: the improvement of the

---

[28] Sir Joseph Banks to Revd Thomas Haweis, 11 September 1798, SLC, BAI: JSB941102/ 011.03798. For more on what Banks would have thought of Haweis, see the satirical pamphlet widely read in Banks's circle which ridiculed Haweis. *A letter from Omai to the Right Honourable Earl.. of late ... Lord .. the ... translated from the Ulaiatean tongue. In which amongst other things is fairly and regularly stated the nature of original sin; together with a proposal for planting Christianity in the islands of the Pacific Ocean*, Boston Public Library, Massachusetts. The comment that faith and grace were antithetical to Banks is also made by Gascoigne, *Joseph Banks and the English Enlightenment*, 43.

[29] Much has been written of the reception of Omai by Banks and his circle. See E. H. McCormick, *Omai, Pacific Envoy* (Auckland, 1977).

[30] *Evangelical Magazine*, 3, 1795, 263. For another evangelical criticism of the reception of Omai, see George Bennet and Daniel Tyerman, *Journal of Voyages and Travels Deputed from the London Missionary Society to Visit the Various Stations in the South Sea Islands, China, India &C in the Years 1821 and 1829 Compiled from Original Documents by James Montgomery*, 2 vols. (London, 1831), vol. II, 144.

material well-being of the islanders and the natural world. For him this was unrelated to faith, and was sufficient for salvation.

It was Banks's desire to bring about this improvement that was demonstrated in his treatment of the Pacific islanders brought to London. On Cook's first voyage, he acquired an islander called Tupai'a, who later died on the voyage. 'I do not know why I may not keep him as a curiosity', Banks wrote, 'as well as my neighbours do lions and tygers.'[31] This natural historical mode of perception was also evident on the later voyage when Cook took on board Omai. Forster wrote that he was tall with remarkably thin hands and that his features conveyed no idea of the beauty which characterised his fellow islanders. He was said to be of 'the darkest hue of the common class of people'.[32] Cook himself wrote of Omai that he was 'dark, ugly and downright blackguard'.[33] Several decades later, when Fitzroy took Feugian islanders aboard, he wrote that their features would improve when they reached the metropolis.[34] Just as the plants that Banks arranged to be brought to Britain were improved in his hands, the Pacific islanders were also improved and presented as noble savages when in the metropolis.

Evangelicals did not equate islanders to natural historical specimens; they described islanders using a visual language of nature. But this was sufficient for Haweis to co-operate with Banks in the project of improving mankind. Meanwhile Banks saw the missionary society as performing a worthy cause by lifting mankind from barbarity. For him this was a role that would keep evangelicals away from doctrinal meddling.

Sent to harvest

Jesus instructed his disciples about the results of their ministry by using the parable of the sower. Of the good soil, in this parable, he said it 'did yield fruit that sprang up and increased; and brought forth, some thirty, and some sixty, and some an hundred'.[35] When the Society was formed, it had these teachings firmly in mind.

Sanctification was a crucial test of faith for these evangelicals. Revd Charles Simeon, a member of the Clapham Sect and a close friend of

[31] Joseph Banks, *The Endeavour Journal of Joseph Banks 1768–1771*, 2 vols. (London, 1896), vol. I, 305–13, 16.
[32] Georg Foster, *A Voyage Round the World*, 2 vols. (London, 1777), vol. I, 388–9.
[33] James Cook, *A Voyage toward the South Pole and Round the World Performed in His Majesty's Ships the 'Resolution' and 'Adventure'*, 2 vols. (London, 1777), vol. I, pl. lvii.
[34] Cited in Gillian Beer, 'Travelling the Other Way', in *The Cultures of Natural History*, ed. Nicholas Jardine, James Secord and Emma Spary (Cambridge, 1995), 332–3.
[35] Mark 4: 7.

Joseph Hardcastle, treasurer of the Society,[36] preached on *The True Test of Religion in the Soul or Practical Christianity Delineated* to the University of Cambridge in 1817. The true Christian, he claimed, has the duty of 'abiding' in Jesus 'as branches of the living Vine, of receiving from his fulness continual supplies of grace and strength, and of "growing up into all things as our living head" '.[37] He continued:

For what is holiness, but a conformity to the Divine image, as sin to the image of the devil? It was by transgression that man lost that resemblance to the Deity which was stamped upon him at his first creation: and it is by the new-creating influence of the Spirit quickening him to a course of holy obedience, that this resemblance is gradually restored.[38]

Simeon therefore argued that though a true Christian should have faith, he or she should show that faith by deeds.

Among his compilation of five hundred skeletal sermons, Simeon wrote of how 'fruitful' professors were distinct from 'barren professors'. He said: 'an empty vine marks the depraved nature of those, who, notwithstanding all the labour with which they have been cultivated, remain "barren and unfruitful in the knowledge of the Lord"'.[39] Meanwhile, sanctification saw the believer become more like Jesus, who was portrayed in the book of Revelation as a tree of life. Simeon wrote of this tree: 'So *abundant* are its fruits, that all in heaven, and all on earth may eat of them.'[40] Simeon hoped that believers would identify their own spiritual standing on this natural historical typology, where the ultimate aim was to become like Jesus Christ.

Evangelicals had strict codes on the use of figures of speech such as this one. Simeon wrote, 'The similes of scripture, if strained and perverted, are made disgusting; but if soberly and judiciously illustrated, they are replete with useful instruction.'[41] Bogue taught out-bound missionaries how to use illustrations. Figures of speech are important, he emphasised, because of the 'poverty of language' and because of the 'influence that imagination has on language'.[42] He advised his students: 'Words and phrases are

---

[36] Orchard, 'The Origins of the Missionary Society', 451; also see Martin, *Evangelicals United*, 207.
[37] Charles Simeon, *The True Test of Religion in the Soul or Practical Christianity Delineated* (Cambridge, 1817), 9. Jesus compared himself to the true vine in John 15.
[38] Simeon, *The True Test of Religion*, 10–11.
[39] Charles Simeon, *Helps to Composition or Five Hundred Skeletons of Sermons, Several Being the Substance of Sermons Preached before the University*, 2 vols. (Cambridge, 1802), vol. II, 105–6. For 'the empty vine' see Hosea 10: 1.
[40] Simeon, *Helps to Composition*, vol. I, 58. For the 'tree of life' see Revelation 22.
[41] Simeon, *Helps to Composition*, vol. II, 105.
[42] 'Third Lecture on Rhetoric.' Lectures on Rhetoric, transcribed by J. Lowndes, L 14/1, DWL, 23.

multiplied for expressing all sorts of ideas for describing even the most minute differences, the nicest shades and colours of thought which no language could possibly express by proper words alone without the assistance of tropes.'[43]

Bogue instructed his students to identify the occasion when 'inanimate objects are introduced acting like those that have life'[44] as personification, while comparison, he continued, 'beautifully sets off and illustrates one thing by resembling it with another to which it bears manifest resemblance and relation'.[45] Metaphor was said to be 'like a transparent veil which exposes what it covers',[46] while allegory was 'a continued metaphor'.[47] Bogue emphasised to his students that illustrations should never be used 'but when they are stronger and larger than the things themselves which they are designed to represent'.[48] Nature conformed to this rule precisely: illustrating individual spiritual growth by a natural historical theme demonstrated how personal experiences fitted into a larger pattern common to the entire realm of nature.

Bogue continued that metaphors 'should be suited to the nature of the subject'. 'There should be a dignity in them.' 'Such allusions should not be used, as they raise in the mind disagreeable mean and dirty ideas.' 'The resemblance should be clear and conspicuous not far fetched.' 'Metaphorical and plain language should not be jumbled together' and metaphors 'should not be pursued too far'.[49] In relation to personification, he advised: 'it is not to be attempted unless you are prompted by passion'. 'It is not to be continued after the passion.' 'Such objects only as have dignity in them should be personified.' Further, 'there must be suitable preparation made for the introduction of it'. 'In prose this figure must be employed with great reserve, delicacy and modesty.'[50]

Evangelicals practised these rules in describing spiritual growth in the Society's sermons. Individuals who were saved were said to be 'first like a tender plant which makes an uncompromising appearance, and is in danger of being nipped by every chilling frost. Yet watered by the rich dews of heaven, and warmed by the benign influences of the Sun of righteousness, it by degrees gathers strength, strikes deep its roots, and becomes capable of enduring the severest weather.'[51] As time passed and the converted individual reached greater maturity of faith, it was important that he or she was clothed: 'A Solomon in all his glory was not so elegantly arrayed as the lilies of the field, and yet what is the beauty of the fairest

---

[43] Ibid., 26.   [44] Ibid., 36.   [45] Ibid., 39.   [46] Ibid., 27.   [47] Ibid., 30.   [48] Ibid., 27.
[49] All from ibid., 29.   [50] All from ibid. 36.
[51] Quotes in this paragraph from *Sermons and Report to the Missionary Society for 1807*, 58, 60, 60, 63.

flower to that of a saint adorned with the robe of the Redeemer's righteousness, and decked out with the fair flowers of implanted grace?'
Referring to conversion, the speaker asserted that 'it changes the unkindly
soil of the human heart, and restores, in some degree, the moral beauty of
our nature ... Thus the grace of God communicates a comeliness to the
souls, and stamps a dignity on the characters of men which no other means
could possibly effect.' This metaphor was intimately linked with a view of
salvation as a process. The tree was said to continue developing even when
advanced in years. Quoting scripture, the speaker said, 'those that are
planted in the house of the Lord shall flourish in the courts of our God,
they shall still bring forth fruit in old age, they shall be fat, and flourishing,
to shew that the Lord is upright'.[52]

These typologies of growth, development and husbandry therefore created a natural history of the spiritual process of the Christian life and the
conversion of the world. I now consider how this figurative use of natural
history manifested itself in the presentation and treatment of Pacific
islanders by missionaries.

Framing an islander

Every issue of the *Evangelical Magazine* had a biographical article and an
accompanying portrait as its leading story. These portraits took the shape
of medallions, reminding us of pictures that contemporaries would have
worn around their necks.[53] Leading evangelical biographies were presented in the hope that they would stimulate spiritual growth by pointing
readers to lives that were worthy of imitation. The issue for January 1800,
however, did not present a portrait of a British evangelical. It depicted
Temoteitei, a Polynesian islander, brought to England in June 1799 and
put under the protection of the Society[54] (figure 3.1).

Evangelicals were accustomed to viewing portraits of Pacific islanders,
in order to come to an idea of the individuals for whom they prayed. Revd
William Henry, a South Pacific missionary, for example, criticised some
portraits of Pomare II, the king of Tahiti, on account of the appearance of
his eyes, cheeks and lips:

I am sorry that the Portraits of Pomare that have been published do him such great
injustice, representing him as mopish & stupid with his eyes half closed; and

---

[52] Psalm 92: 13.   [53] I am indebted to Patricia Fara for pointing this out to me.
[54] For a similar study, see Michael Newton, 'Bodies without Souls: The Case of Peter the
Wild Boy', in *At the Borders of the Human: Beasts, Bodies and Natural Philosophy in the
Early Modern Period*, ed. Erica Fudge, Ruth Gilbert and Susan Wiseman (Basingstoke,
1999).

Figure 3.1: This portrait appeared as the frontispiece of the January 1800 issue of the *Evangelical Magazine* above the title 'Temoteitei of the Marquesas.' Temoteitei does not establish eye contact with the reader and the mark on his forehead appears prominently.

destitute of all nobleness or dignity of aspect, which was not the case … He was no longer visaged than either of the portraits represented him and his whiskers went down in a streak of about a quarter of an inch broad toward the chin, & then turned round the lower part of the cheek, then up until nearly opposite the upper lip, & then turned forward to it & joined the whisker on it.[55]

A similar mode of vision is demonstrated in the presentation of Temoteitei in the *Evangelical Magazine*.

[55] Cited in Gunson, *Messengers of Grace*, 189.

Though Temoteitei was seen to possess a soul, because he was unconverted he was thought not to possess the Holy Spirit. The first sentence of
the article carried the word 'heathen' which was repeated several times.[56]
Temoteitei's dark skin colour was revealed in the portrait, because he wore
no clothes. This was in contrast to the clothed bodies of the Society's
founders whose likenesses had adorned earlier issues. They wore wigs
and academic gowns, which made them appear distinctive. The desire to
parade Temoteitei's dark skin is significant as the route to salvation,
damnation and the new creation was linked to light and darkness.
Readers were told, at the start of the account, that it would 'promote our
gratitude to Him who has called *us* from darkness to light, and our
exertions to impart the blessings of the Gospel, to them who are still
under the power of Satan, and the shadow of eternal death'. They were
urged to do everything possible to 'dissipate the thick darkness in which
the heathen are involved'. There was thus an explicit pronouncement of the
damnation of Temoteitei's soul, which called for its urgent salvation.

Subtle strategies of visual rhetoric presented this argument in the portrait too. At the end of the eighteenth century, portraiture depended on a
dualistic conception of the body and the soul: the artist attempted, by
depicting the physical likeness of the sitter, to provide an insight into his
inner self, or soul.[57] Temoteitei's lack of clothes and ornament therefore
indicated that his soul was doomed. More striking, however, was the
subject's gaze. The eye was the window of the soul, so that Temoteitei's
lack of eye contact showed that spiritual communion had not been
established.

The significance of Temoteitei's clothing and the appearance of his eyes
becomes clear if we compare his portrait to that of three converted Khoi
Khoi[58] or 'Hottentots' who appeared in the *Evangelical Magazine* with
their missionary Mr Kircherer (figure 3.2). The *Monthly Repository*, in
describing the *Evangelical Magazine*, made special mention of this engraving. It observed that the periodical 'boasts a monthly portrait (somewhat
roughly executed) of some "Evangelical" minister'. In a footnote it carried
on: 'Now and then a layman and even a lady attains the honour of being
represented in "Evangelical" effigy. One or more converted Hottentots are
amongst the "handsome likenesses" '.[59] The Khoi Khoi were described as
handsome, because they had converted, unlike Temoteitei. Their conversion

---

[56] For Temoteitei's article see *Evangelical Magazine*, 1800, 3–14.
[57] See Joanna Woodall, 'Introduction', in *Portraiture: Facing the Subject*, ed. Joanna
Woodall (Manchester, 1997), 5.
[58] For the use of Khoi Khoi for Hottentot, see Pratt, *Imperial Eyes*, 40.
[59] *Monthly Repository*, 1820, 541. I thank Jonathan Topham for this reference.

The Rev.? M.?Kircherer;   Mary.   John.   Martha?

Pub. by T.Williams, Stationers Court, Jan.? 1804

Figure 3.2: The 'Hottentots' or Khoi Khoi with their missionary
Mr Kircherer from the frontispiece of the *Evangelical Magazine*, 1804.
These three converts have been renamed Mary, John and Martha, and are
clothed in white apparel.

experiences had affected their appearance. This was why the Khoi Khoi
wore the same type of clothes as Kircherer.[60] Temoteitei, on the other
hand, was unclothed, bringing to mind biblical verses that spoke of clothing the sinful nature. Another difference lies in the prominence of instruction in the group portrait.[61] The Khoi Khoi are shown listening attentively
to Mr Kircherer, who is instructing them from a book. Temoteitei, on the
other hand, does not even look the reader of the *Evangelical Magazine*
directly in the eye.

Bernard Smith has said that portraits of Pacific islanders in this period
were essentially natural historical.[62] Natural historical conventions of
naming are important here.[63] Whilst the Khoi Khoi were named Mary,
John and Martha, emphasising their Christian identity as converted

---

[60] It has been pointed out to me by Revd Brian Macdonald-Milne, former missionary to the
South Pacific, that Polynesian islanders usually did not wear clothes above the waist. I do
not think that this changes the argument. His lack of clothes was greatly dissimilar to how
the subjects who usually appeared on these pages were presented.

[61] For the setting-up of missionary schools in the South Pacific, see Gunson, *Messengers of
Grace*.

[62] Smith, *Imagining the Pacific*. For the claim that colonised people were seen as botanical
specimens, see also Anne Maxwell, *Colonial Photography and Exhibitions: Representations
of the 'Native' and the Making of European Identities* (Leicester, 1999), 2.

[63] For the argument that naming is central to all collecting, see Pearce, *On Collecting*, 181.

believers, Temoteitei – being unconverted – was made to retain his own name.[64] In the accompanying article he was given the name of the ship on which he had arrived, John Butterworth. One mission enthusiast named John Vine Hall wrote to the directors: 'I seem to have something of a notion in my mind that in some of the Missionary Stations native youths when baptized have had an English name given them – the name of some Christian friend who has contributed the expenses of their education &c. I should like a youth in Tahiti and also in Rarotonga baptized John Vine Hall.'[65]

The writer of the article that appeared alongside Temoteitei's portrait adopted a mode of direct access and measured observation: 'Temo has a continued line from his left temple to his right jaw, and a few irregular marks on his arms and legs.' He said that he had 'drawn' information from Temoteitei which would 'fill several volumes'.[66] Just as plants were labelled with their place of discovery, and who discovered them, we are told: 'Temoteitei was born in Tahouatta, an island about 800 English miles north east from Otaheite. Mendana, a Spaniard, who discovered this, and three other islands adjacent, gave to the whole the name of Les Maquesas de Mendoza: and to the island of Temo's nativity, that of Santa Christina.' A connection was made between Temoteitei and his habitat: 'The natives lie under a burning yet healthful climate; and are generally tall, well made and active. Their complexion is chiefly of a yellowish brown, like Temo, little darker than some English people who have been much exposed to the weather.'[67] Temoteitei was presented using the dual means of a portrait and an article reminding us of how natural historical types were usually depicted.

The distance between the viewer and the subject in Temoteitei's portrait also recalls natural historical conventions of imaging.[68] Temoteitei's portrait shows him alone, unlike the image of the Khoi Khoi. This distance is extended, in the course of the article, as Temoteitei is made to appear inhuman, as he is said to have 'crawled upon the ground and into the water, till he learned to swim and walk'.[69] 'By playing with the carcasses of human victims in a manner that precludes description, he became inured to inhumanity.'[70] The 'improvement' that was necessary to bring Temoteitei out of this state of 'inhumanity' involved another process of 'inuring'. Banks wrote in the *Transactions*: 'RESPECTABLE and useful as

---

[64] This is closely related to the naming of slaves in Britain: they also often lost their names.
[65] Letter dated 29 April 1844 from John Vine Hall to the directors, Home Correspondence, Box 8, CWM, SOAS.
[66] *Evangelical Magazine*, 1800, 4.   [67] Ibid.
[68] See Woodall, 'Introduction.' She has argued that the pleasure in viewing a portrait comes from the substitution of the portrait for *something* distant or absent.
[69] *Evangelical Magazine*, 1800, 7.   [70] Ibid.

every branch of the horticultural art certainly is, no one is more interesting to the public, or more likely to prove advantageous to those who may be so fortunate as to succeed in it than that of inuring plants.'[71]

The natural historical mode of vision further emerges in the denial of social relations between Temoteitei and his interviewer. Portraits are never distinct from the process of production: they are not just end products, but rather the indicators of a social encounter.[72] The author of the article did not allow Temoteitei's words to enter the narrative. He wrote: 'His countrymen have no idea of chronological statements; and it would be vain to enquire from *him* how he has passed the few years of his life.'[73] The social relations of the encounter were like the portrait itself. They saw Temoteitei stripped of his words just as he had been stripped of his attire.[74]

The soul when found is fed

Temoteitei was not the only Pacific islander brought to Britain by missionary enthusiasts. On a conservative estimate there were at least sixteen who were mentioned in the reports of the Society or who were announced in the *Evangelical Magazine* either when they arrived, or when, as most of them did, they died, being unable to stand the climate or European disease, rather like live natural historical specimens.[75] It was hoped that each of

---

[71] *Transactions of the Horticultural Society* 2, 1812, 21.

[72] A. Rosenthal, 'She's Got the Look! Eighteenth Century Female Portrait Painters and the Psychology of a Potentially Dangerous Employment', in *Portraiture: Facing the Subject*, 147.

[73] *Evangelical Magazine*, 1800, 3.

[74] For undressing and the denial of agency, see Maxwell, *Colonial Photography and Exhibitions*, 142.

[75] I have been able to trace the records for sixteen islanders who were placed in the Society's care in the period from its commencement to 1850. David Bogue wrote concerning one of them to Joseph Hardcastle in a letter dated 11 January 1799, Home Correspondence, Box 1, CWM, SOAS. This could have been one of the lads mentioned in Wilson, *A Missionary Voyage to the Southern Pacific Ocean*, 114. Temoteitei was the third, and his records are in *Evangelical Magazine*, 1799, 261–2, *Evangelical* Magazine, 1800, 1–4 and *Evangelical Magazine*, 1800, 522. The fourth was brought to the country by Mr Hodges from Port Jackson and was ten years old. His records appears in *Evangelical Magazine*, 1800, 338. The report for the next year mentions two boys and two men brought under the Society's protection that year. Presuming that one of them was the aforementioned, this provides us with three more. See *Sermons and Report to the Missionary Society for 1801*, 5. Two youths are said to have been brought under the instruction of the Moravians in a school in Mirfield, Yorkshire. See *Sermons and Report to the Missionary Society for 1801*, 10, and *Sermons and Report to the Missionary Society for 1804*, 5 for the record of these two youths. We may already have accounted for one of them. They were both dead by the end of 1804. Two more youths were brought under the Society's protection in 1807. See *Sermons and Report to the Missionary Society for 1807*, 16. One of them was Tapeoe, whose treatment was criticised at length in the press and by a certain individual who wrote to the directors under

these islanders would come to an awareness of their souls, be edified with spiritual food, be converted, grow in holiness and eventually return to their islands as missionaries. Interestingly, Banks's project of improving plants also involved exchange. Revd John Love, one of the founders of the Society, wrote a series of sermons to be used by the Society's missionaries. Addressing the people of Tahiti he said:

Your souls are within your bodies: and when we look at you we perceive that your souls are there within your bodies; they are, as it were, looking at us through your eyes, yet we see not your souls. Our souls are here in our bodies, they loved you when we were far off in our own country, and we brought our bodies nearer and nearer to you; you see that we love you, and this makes us sometimes weep over you, yet you do not see our souls with your eyes, you see them with your minds.[76]

The discovery of the soul involved the opening of a new sense of vision. Revd John Williams wrote explicitly about the form of the soul and how it could be converted. He wrote that the 'soul of man is formed for the reception of knowledge'.[77] The ultimate destination of the soul in this view was heaven; it had to be continually fed with more and more knowledge till it was 'relieved from all its entanglements of the flesh'.[78]

the pseudonym Amicus. For this exchange, see letter dated 1 October 1807 from Amicus to the editor of the *Evangelical Magazine* in Home Correspondence, Box 2, CWM, SOAS. Also a letter dated 26 September 1807 from Revd T. Haweis to the directorate, in ibid. Tapeoe was dead by 1814: see *Evangelical Magazine*, 1814, 569. Three other islanders, Tomma, Terea and Tenavow, and Tapeoe were also mentioned in a lengthy account of the treatment of these islanders written in protest to the directors of the London Missionary Society. See Joseph Fox, *An Appeal to the Members of the London Missionary Society against a Resolution of the Directors of That Society Dated 26 March 1810 with Remarks on Certain Proceedings Relative to the Otaheitan and Jewish Missions* (London, 1810). Revd John Williams mentions one islander whom he brought back to England to aid him with the scriptures, and then also notes that a Captain Green brought back two islanders, one a Rarotongan, and the other 'an interesting lad the principal chief of Nikikiva, one of the Marquesan islanders': see Revd John Williams to the directorate, 21 May 1835; Revd John Williams to the directorate, 5 August 1837; and Revd John Williams to Revd J. Arundel, 23 August 1835, Home Correspondence, Box 6, CWM, SOAS. Two islanders were taken on a relentless tour of missionary societies in 1843, leading to the death of one of them who was the chief, Leora: see Revd J. Alexander to Revd J. Arundel, 30 October 1843, and Revd J. Alexander to Revd J. Arundel, 4 November 1843, Home Correspondence, Box 8, CWM, SOAS. A similar tale was told in relation to Kiro, a Rarotongan, who was put on display at missionary meetings. See Revd A. Leith to the directorate, 31 December 1847 and Revd A. Leith to the directorate, 30 July 1847, Home Correspondence Box 9, CWM, SOAS.

[76] John Love, *Address to the People of Otaheite with a Short Address to the Members of the London Missionary Society* (London, 1796), 14.
[77] John Williams, 'The Missionary Pleading for the Perishing Heathen: A Sermon Preached at Surrey Chapel on Sunday Evening October 8th 1837', in *The Pastoral Echo: Nineteen Sermons by Eminent Dissenting Ministers and Others* (London, 1837), 309.
[78] Ibid., 311.

There was some slippage between Williams' use of the concepts of mind and soul. He said that both were receptacles of knowledge.[79] This knowledge comprised a knowledge of God, an acknowledgement of the sinfulness of humans and an awareness that salvation was possible through the blood of Jesus. In his view, heavenly knowledge was distinct from that pursued by men of science.

We might refer again to the sciences, to astronomy, botany, mechanics, and many other things, of which it may be said that it is not good for the soul to be without. But it not our business to speak of human knowledge tonight, and I think I should be desecrating the important place I occupy should I speak of anything but heavenly knowledge.[80]

Doctrinal instruction, as we have seen, was integral, but such doctrine was expected to reform behaviour too. Exterior appearances were expected to serve as symptoms of the interior state of the heart.[81] Thus the cessation of cannibalism, alcoholism and dancing was vital. As the article in the *Evangelical Magazine* noted, Temoteitei was submitted to a course of education. Similarly, Oli and Mydo, who were probably the first Pacific islanders to be brought under the care of the Missionary Society in 1799, were placed by 'their kind patrons' in 'a school, recently established by the Moravian Brethren, at Mirfield'.[82] As the same account continued, 'Owing however to unpreparedness of mind in early youth, as well as natural indolence, and delicate health in a moist and cold climate, their progress in learning was slow, but they could read and write tolerably well.'[83] Oli was of 'higher birth (probably the son of some chief)' and this distinction manifested itself, according to the evangelical writer, in a range of subtleties including a 'larger intellectual capacity'.[84] Mydo was the first to be converted despite the instruction and the head start that Oli had in his education. We are told that he woke one morning, and addressed the person who waited on him at the school thus:

You told me that my soul could not die, and I have been thinking about it, how it is. Last night my body lay upon that bed, but I knew nothing of it, for my soul was very far off. I was in Tahiti. I am sure that I saw my mother and my companions there. I saw the trees, and the houses and the hills, just as I left them. I spoke to the people and the people spoke to me; and yet all the while my body was lying quite still in this room. In the morning I was come back again into my body, and was at

[79] Ibid., 310.   [80] Ibid., 315–16.
[81] These islanders were put to a Lancasterian mode of education. See Gunson, *Messengers of Grace*, 238.
[82] Bennet and Tyerman, *Journal of Voyages and Travels Deputed from the London Missionary Society*, vol. II, 123.
[83] Ibid., 124.   [84] Ibid.

Mirfield again, and Tahiti was a great many miles off, over the sea. Now I understand what you say about my body being put into the earth and my soul being
somewhere else; and I wish to know where it will live then, when it can no more
return to my body as it did last night.[85]

Mydo had thus, with instruction, discovered his soul. This was an acceptable passage of events to count as credible conversion for the evangelicals.
In the Pacific, however, at times, the symptoms of conversion could be
expressed more creatively by islanders. The most striking example of this is
the Mamaia or Visionary Heresy which Niel Gunson has discussed at
length.[86] This indigenous movement mixed tenets of evangelical
Christianity with pre-Christian culture and questioned the authority of
the Society's missionaries. Central to its teachings was the notion that
personal revelation was possible; many of its leaders and adherents
reported strange dreams, in which they had travelled to heaven and been
in the company of Jesus and other biblical characters. The Mamaia prophets also held that strict adherence to the laws instigated by the missionaries was unnecessary. Revd John Orsmond described the beliefs of
this sect:

They professed (1) that their leader was at the time of inspiration really God (2) that
the missionaries are all liars in as much as they state that the soul never dies (3) that
hell is figurative not real (4) that men ought to eat and drink abundantly and take
any wife they long for that the land may be full of people.[87]

The Mamaia sect in all likelihood was wiped out when it resisted vaccin-
ation against smallpox towards the middle of the century, but it serves as
an example of how Pacific islanders reacted to evangelical conversion.

Souls on display

Missionaries were – especially in the context of lapses such as these – never
certain that they had improved a Pacific islander so that he or she came to a
converted state; or, in other words, that they had collected a soul. Since
they adhered to a dualism between the seen and the unseen, they were
unable to conclude from observed symptoms that their wards had truly
passed the irreversible divide and that they were being sanctified – the two
components of Simeon's test for true religion. There was thus some hesitation in the strategies of display that they adopted in presenting their

---

[85] Ibid., 125.
[86] Gunson, 'An Account of the Mamaia or Visionary Heresy of Tahiti, 1826–1841.'
[87] Cited in ibid., 223.

collections of souls redeemed for the next creation. This uncertainty was alleviated by their theologies of the future life and the future of the world.

It was important that the converted died well: for death and judgement were coincidental, as the deceased individual only came to life again on judgement day.[88] The death-bed functioned to confirm conversion. As their wards died, evangelicals recorded the words that they uttered and the mind-set with which they died and circulated these accounts. Mydo's death scene is a case in point:

> On the 22nd September he was brought upon his bed into the chapel, by his own particular desire, and in the presence of a great congregation, who were all deeply affected by the solemnity of the scene, he was baptized ... in the name of the Holy Trinity, and into the death of Jesus. He received the appropriate name of Christian, being the first of his people to whom it could be given. He was baptized for the dead. Being carried back to his sick chamber, his bodily pains seemed to forsake him; he remained in a comfortable mind, and in the course of the following day expired, leaving a firm conviction on the ears of all who witnessed his last end, that he died the death of the righteous.[89]

This was the evangelical equivalent of putting someone on display: the baptism of Mydo functioned as a public announcement of his conversion. This was authentic because many observed it and also because Mydo was near the point of death. Mydo could now have a new name to denote his status in the new creation. Temoteitei's death scene, on the other hand, was one of pain, as evangelicals attempted to figure out whether his soul had been saved: 'Being exhorted to pray he said, "I do pray, father." – Who do you pray to? – "To Jesus Christ" – What do you pray for – "That he would forgive my sins." – Then you do not pray to the God of Tahoutta? "No, No." '[90]

When Chief Leora died after falling ill following a relentless tour of missionary meetings in England, even though he was thought to be a convert, an evangelical minister wrote: 'I fear that Mr. Heath and the teacher were absent when he died, that there was no one acquainted with his language and the state of mind was unknown.'[91]

---

[88] There were many competing theories of the afterlife and the intermediary state. See G. Rowell, *Hell and the Victorians: A Study of Nineteenth Century Theological Controversies Concerning Eternal Punishment and the Future Life* (Oxford, 1974); Michael Wheeler, *Heaven, Hell and the Victorians* (Cambridge, 1994).

[89] Bennet and Tyerman, *Journal of Voyages and Travels Deputed from the London Missionary Society*, 126–7.

[90] *Evangelical Magazine*, 1800, 522.

[91] Revd J. Alexander to Revd J. Arundel, 30 October 1843, Home Correspondence, Box 8, CWM, SOAS.

Discussing Pacific islanders' deaths was just one form of display, which fitted alongside many others. Topographical accounts of missionary successes around the world and statistical accounts of population and conversion were two others.[92] These were especially vital for a group of missionaries who held so fervently to a faith in post-millenarianism and who hoped to aid the second coming of their redeemer by spreading the news of the gospel to every land and converting the inhabitants. The desire to bring about the second coming of Christ was connected to a desire to bring the collection of souls to completion, and so evangelicals calculated the 'saved and the damned', and coloured missionary maps according to the progress they had made in evangelism.

The display of individuals whose conversion was uncertain was avoided in all of these mechanisms of display. In the case of the baptism of Mydo, the individual was displayed only at the point of death. Uncertainty was minimised as the heart's unseen aspects were thought to manifest themselves at death. Similarly, uncertainty was avoided with statistical surveys. Here it was possible to avoid focusing on the individual and make the whole collection the subject of display. But at other times and in other contexts, live people were displayed. Such exhibitions always showed more hesitance. Evangelicals hoped to show that they were attempting to collect the souls of the unconverted. When these criteria for display were violated, the criticisms of evangelicals fell directly on those in their number who were in the wrong.

The painful tale of Tapeoe exemplifies this well. Tapeoe arrived in Britain in September 1806 on the *Warley East Indiaman* and was introduced to the directors. He was said to show an enthusiasm for learning. Since he had lost his letter of recommendation from the South Pacific missionaries, the directors had no means of ascertaining his character and background, and were unable to determine what state of civilisation he had come to; therefore they refused to take him under their care. Whilst they were in this quandary, Tapeoe was taken into the service of Captain W. Wilson of Fenchurch Street until it was possible for a return passage for him to be obtained. He was abducted by Mr Kelso, an ex-missionary. Mr Kelso was tried and found guilty of mistreating Tapeoe, according to the *Morning Chronicle* of 19 July 1808. The statement of guilt established that:

---

[92] For examples of missionary maps see James Nisbet, 'The Children's Missionary Map of the World' (London, 1844), James Nisbet, 'The Pictorial Missionary Map of the World' (London, 1861). Also for an interesting and lengthy account of how missionary societies hoped to use maps, see Anon., *American Board of Commissioners for Foreign Missions on the Use of Missionary Maps, at the Monthly Concert* (Boston, 1842). For statistical surveys, see Robert C. Schmitt, 'The Missionary "Censuses" Tahiti', *Journal of Polynesian Society* 76 (1967): 27–34.

Kelso had seduced this Otaheitian from Captain Wilson's protection under the profession of teaching him to read, but instead of that had turned the possession of him to the same purpose as Pidcock does his wild animals, making money by the show of beasts (royal lions, Bengal tigers, or kangaroos alive) and keeping the poor man in wretched ignorance and ruling him with a rod of iron that at last Tapeoe finding the situation in which he was placed too oppressive to bear fled for protection to Mr Gillham, Surgeon Blackfriars Road ... Mr G. went with him to Kelso, to obtain his clothing. Instead of this, Kelso forbade Tapeoe leaving him, refused his clothes and on his attempting to take them, seized him and beat him with a chair.[93]

Kelso thus attempted to display Tapeoe before his conversion, and in a fashion that was remarkably similar to that of the exhibition of beasts. A committee of evangelicals came to Tapeoe's rescue. Tapeoe was acquainted with the Lancasterian plan of education and Mr Braidwood of Hackney instructed him 'in the articulation of the different sounds of our language'.[94] After this course of training the missionary enthusiasts could write of 'every opening of his mind to the reception of truth and divine knowledge'.[95] Tapeoe's last days in London were spent walking around the city 'like a little chief'[96] with another three islanders, who had by this time arrived in Britain from the South Pacific, in his charge.

Tapeoe had become like his keepers and achieved the status of civilisation and humanity that they possessed. It was impossible to treat him like an animal in a cage in this context, and special arrangements had to be made, through Banks, for whom a special display was organised, for Tapeoe to be elevated from steerage class to be 'on terms of equality' with 'six persons going out as settlers to his native island' on his passage home.[97]

---

[93] *Morning Chronicle* 19 July 1808. It was acceptable to put Tapeoe in a cage because he had not converted. Converted Pacific islanders, on the other hand, were taken on a relentless tour of missionary meetings by the third decade of the nineteenth century. This led, at least on one occasion, to death by illness. For the death of the chief Leora, see Revd J. Alexander to Revd J. Arundel, 4 November 1843, Home Correspondence, Box 8, CWM, SOAS. 'When Mr Heath was here, he complained much of the conduct of the Directors – and what he said, both publicly and privately left upon many minds the impression that he and the natives were worked beyond their strength and against the remonstrance which they had made.' Also see Revd A. Leith to the directorate, 30 July 1847; Home Correspondence Box 9, CWM, SOAS, for an account of the public display of Kiro: 'I have found that he is invariably worse after a journey, also after the excitement of a meeting & although I have taken utmost care of him he is constantly taking colds.'

[94] Fox, *An Appeal to the Members of the London Missionary Society*, 27.

[95] Ibid., 42.   [96] Ibid., 66.

[97] Ibid., 39. See also letters from Sir Joseph Banks to Revd George Burder, 13 January 1810 and 15 January 1810, Joseph Banks Archives, NHM, BAI: HLC951030/008.03810 and HLC951030/009.03810. And a letter from Sir Joseph Banks to Sir John Beckett, 21 August 1810, relating how he has 'induced' the London Missionary Society to pay for Tapeoe's maintenance till his departure. Joseph Banks Archives, NHM, BAI: HLC951009/021.03810.

Conclusion

Missionaries viewed unconverted Pacific islanders to be like live natural historical specimens. Selection, naming and classification saw the starting point of this linguistic practice; cultivation and improvement followed, and display marked the desired end. These natural historical typologies provided a visual language that helped articulate notions of spiritual development and sanctification. This argument should not come as a surprise because collecting is always about representation: elements of the collection are collectible not merely for what they are but also for what they have been and what they will be. The metaphor of seeing converts as trees came from the Bible: the islanders were now damned, because if they died they would go to Hell, but if improved and converted, their souls would belong to God. And if they persisted in doing good works then their faith would be proven.

The use of natural history as a metaphor for conversion and spiritual sanctification fitted perfectly with early nineteenth-century 'agrarian patriotism',[98] as demonstrated by the collaboration between Banks and Haweis. Missionaries' attempts to save souls and natural historical collectors' attempts to cultivate crops shared much in common. For both groups, collecting and improvement was a process that, as Paula Findlen has pointed out for the case of natural historical collecting, brought together a range of people. At the heart of the collaboration between the Society and Banks was the parallelism between spiritual development and natural history as continuous processes of improvement.

The entanglement between the natural historical language of evangelicalism and the imperial project of natural improvement explains why it is difficult to trace the boundaries of the figurative use of natural history. When did the description of Pacific islanders as trees stop acting as a figure of speech and start dictating their treatment? In answer to this question, we may point to the strict body of rules that evangelicals adopted in using illustrations; and yet Temoteitei's depiction in the *Evangelical Magazine*, Tapeoe's imprisonment in a cage, and missionaries' attention to statistics, maps and death-beds provide evidence for the ease with which individuals became natural historical projects. It has been said that natural history is important because it can provide models for the operation of society, and indeed this was precisely why the missionaries used it so fervently for educative purposes.[99] But in this chapter I have raised a supplementary

---

[98] See Bayly, *Imperial Meridian*.
[99] Nicholas Jardine and Emma Spary, 'The Natures of Cultural History', in *The Cultures of Natural History*, ed. Nicholas Jardine, Emma Spary and James Secord (Cambridge, 1995), 8.

question. In what circumstances does natural history cease to provide models for the self and become the identity of what is described?

In addition to providing an arena for representing its elements, the natural historical collection provides a mirror to the collector. 'Our collections', Susan Pearce writes, 'will with all their potential for selection and dismissal, offer us the romantic chance to complete ourselves, to create significance and meaning out of nothing, by the power of need and imagination, and so to sustain a sense of dignity and purpose. They are both autobiography and monument.'[100] Evangelicals hoped to bring Pacific islanders to their God, but they often established their own identity through their evangelism, reassuring themselves that their missionary endeavours were succeeding and that they were multiplying their flock. There was a continual desire for self-replication in dress, speech and action, just as was discussed in the previous chapter. The missionaries also worked on the principle that when islanders converted they would become evangelists and then return to their islands and mature in holiness.

Since these evangelists worked so hard at converting and nurturing holiness, we can safely come to the idea of how spiritual improvement was at the centre of who they were. Missionaries structured their lives around accounts of conversion and good works, and rebelled against the effects of sin in the hope of the eternal state of heaven. This in turn raises questions about the importance of religiosity in understanding all forms of collection. The desire, adoration and adulation that we have traced in evangelical conversions may be extrapolated to the relationship between other collectors and collections in this period, when evangelicalism was at its height.

Extrapolating further still, I have suggested how a theology of nature may be written into the study of the self in this period. This forms an important link with the following chapter, which is also concerned with the connection between natural history and self-identity in the context of mission. In the next chapter the argument that the cycle of life mirrored the processes of nature will be analysed again. At focus is an equally significant theological moment, namely the demise of the earthly body.

[100] Pearce, *On Collecting*, 254.

4   The body that will bloom: death and its theology of nature

The Revd David Bogue described his ideal missionary as a man with the 'celestial heat of zeal' which would burn 'like unextinguished fire' upon the 'altar' of the breast regardless of 'all the difficulties and discouragements which from time to time set themselves in array against him'.[1] Bogue had yet to become an exacting trainer of missionaries, but his description points to the fortitude and perseverance which he impressed on students after he had founded the Missionary Seminary. This grandiose description was shared by others. At the second annual general meeting, Revd Thomas Pentycross told out-bound missionaries 'that after living for so glorious a purpose, to conclude it will not be your lot to die the common death of all men ... The soil of the South-sea Islands may require your ashes to impregnate it with the most abundant salt of salvation.'[2]

Having considered the relationship between nature and conversion, my attention will now move to the natural historical dimensions of dying, and the manner in which demise was combined with meditations on the oceans and seed. By attending to how nature was linked with death, it is possible to extend the argument of the previous chapter: the entire course of the believer's spiritual journey was conceived in terms of the cyclical processes of nature. In paying such close attention to death, my starting point is the evangelical obsession with demise in the early nineteenth century.[3] Within

---

[1] *Sermons and Report to the Missionary Society for 1795*, 140.

[2] Cited in Gunson, *Messengers of Grace*, 48.

[3] Pat Jalland, *Death in the Victorian Family* (Oxford, 1996), 21. Jalland's is the best discussion of evangelical deaths, but see also Rosman, *Evangelicals and Culture*. There is now a thriving literature on the history of death at home: see Regina Barreca, *Sex and Death in Victorian Literature* (Basingstoke, 1990), Peter C. Jupp and Clare Gittings, eds., *The Changing Face of Death: Historical Accounts of Death and Disposal* (Basingstoke, 1997), Peter C. Jupp and Clare Gittings, eds., *Death in England: An Illustrated History* (Manchester, 1999), Nigel Llewellyn, *The Art of Death: Visual Culture in the English Death Ritual, c.1500–c.1800* (London, 1991), John McManners, *Death and the Enlightenment: Changing Attitudes to Death among Christians and Unbelievers in Eighteenth-Century France* (Oxford, 1981), Garrett Stewart, *Death Sentences: Styles of Dying in British Fiction* (Cambridge, Mass., 1984). For the colonial dimensions of death, see David Arnold, *Colonizing the Body: State Medicine and Epidemic Disease in*

evangelicalism, the battle between the flesh and the soul in this life, the emergence of the new and transformed body and the flight of the soul were all linked with nature. For the religious, nature could act as an 'aid to reflection'.[4] This evangelical concern was part of a wider popular theology that combined elements of animism, fatalism, and a belief in the dynamic interrelationship of the individual and nature.[5] Before the rise of the ordered cemetery and memorial, romantic and organic visions of change and fertility were crucial to the immortalisation of self.[6]

In 1839, Revd John Williams followed Pentycross's advice very literally in impregnating the Pacific with his blood: he was murdered by Eromangans who then apparently ate his body. His story may exemplify how the connection between self and nature could have both private and public elements. The mythical manner in which his death was exalted in the public imagination is evident in contemporary claims that Williams knew in advance that he would die. Representations of the event suggested that he had internalised a natural historical language of development; he had understood how his body would change into a transformed vessel at the resurrection. The landscape of Eromanga was enrolled to explain his death and to reassure evangelicals that the missionary had ascended to heaven. Williams' story is thus in concord with Felix Driver's observation that 'for the death of the explorer to be represented as a martyrdom ... the mundane experience of travel had to be ennobled: exploration was rendered less as a journey across territory than as a quest for truth, the explorer transfigured into the bearer of larger values of religion, science or culture'.[7]

To understand how Williams was cast as a martyr, it is useful to contrast his death with that of Captain James Cook. In his death, Williams became a better Cook for a religiously awakened public. Reports that suggested that Cook had been deified at the moment of his death had angered evangelicals in the late eighteenth century. It was as if the respected navigator had lost control of his passions and given in to a grave

---

Nineteenth-Century India (Berkeley, Calif., 1993), Greg Dening, *The Death of William Gooch: A History's Anthropology* (Honolulu, 1995), Driver, *Geography Militant*, Max Jones, *The Last Great Quest: Captain Scott's Antartic Sacrifice* (Oxford, 2003). For accounts of Christian martyrdom in other periods, see J. R. Knott, 'Characterising Protestant Martyrs', *Sixteenth Century Journal* 27 (1996): 721–34, and B. D. Shaw, 'Body/Power/Identity and Christian Perceptions of the Passions of the Martyrs', *Journal of Early Christian Studies* 14 (1996): 269–312.
[4] Wheeler, *Heaven, Hell and the Victorians*. See also Michael Wheeler, *Death and the Future Life in Victorian Literature and Theology* (Cambridge, 1990). An earlier work on this topic is Rowell, *Hell and the Victorians*.
[5] Ruth Richardson, *Death, Dissection and the Destitute* (London, 1998), 7.
[6] For the beginnings of public commemoration, see Alison Yarrington, *The Commemoration of the Hero 1800–1864: Monuments to the British Victors of the Napoleonic Wars* (New York and London, 1998).
[7] Driver, *Geography Militant*, 91.

temptation. The missionaries who were sent to the Pacific in Cook's wake were advised in strong terms to guard against evil. In Williams, evangelicals found a mariner who had lived a life like Cook's; but instead of adding to the stock of curious knowledge, Williams had spread the gospel and died while in full control of his emotions. His death had brought glory to the Creator God. In addition to this he had become a missionary of evangelical science.[8]

Just as Cook's *Voyages* was important in creating the navigator's name, Williams also published what became a best-seller, under the title, *A Narrative of Missionary Enterprises* (1837). In its pages Williams made a case for being an explorer on a par with Cook. He wrote of Rarotonga:

This splendid island escaped the untiring researches of Captain Cook, and was discovered by myself, in 1823. It is a mass of mountains, which are high, and present a remarkably romantic appearance. It is situated in lat. 21° 20' S., 160° W. long. It has several good boat harbours, is about thirty miles in circumference, and is surrounded by a reef. The population is about 6,000 or 7,000.[9]

As Williams translated islands into number, he authenticated his own claim to be a discoverer and added to Cook's map. The created order was designed to have humans at its head. To live in unison with nature – like the islanders had done – was to oppose that divine plan. The heroic coloniser was the pious individual who rose against the land and put it in its place, firmly in the bounds of human control. In that process he never came under its sway, like Cook had done, in confusing the Creator and the created.

Williams' early biographer tells us of his book that 'once and again he repeated his conviction that if he could induce men of rank and science, with the merchants and shipowners of Britain to ponder over its pages, they would no longer occupy neutral ground in the great contest with heathenism'.[10] He presented fifty free copies of his book to a number of notables, the Royal Geographical Society, the Geological Society and 'other scientific and literary societies'. He also delivered 'two or three lectures at the principal towns in the country, on the geography, formation, natural history, traditions, usages, government, language and social state of the islands ... At Bristol, Bath, Sheffield and elsewhere these lectures were listened to with great interest and liberal sums were obtained from those who heard them.'[11] One evangelical noted that 'Williams'

---

[8] In attributing the title missionary of science to John Williams, I follow recent work on David Livingstone: see ibid. Livingstone was compared with Williams in the nineteenth century. See, for example, Arthur Montefiore, *Heroes Who Have Won Their Crown: David Livingstone and John Williams* (London, 1909).

[9] Williams, *A Narrative of Missionary Enterprises*, 18.

[10] Prout, *Memoirs of the Rev. John Williams*, 454.   [11] Ibid., 448.

Missionary Enterprises alone is of more real value than all the writings of a Clarke, a Butler, a Paley, a Chalmers, a Leland and a Landner united'.[12] Williams was, by such supporters, elevated to a pedestal higher than that occupied by natural theologians.

The discussion of the complicated means by which Williams was made a hero has a direct bearing on the debate between Marshall Sahlins and Gananath Obeyesekere over the deification of Captain Cook.[13] The complexity of how evangelicals responded to Cook's death has been lost by Obeyesekere. One of the evangelical sources he cites reads: 'He allowed the worshipping like Herod did. He did not put a stop to it. Perhaps one can assume that because of the error on the part of Lono – Cook – and because he caused venereal disease to spread there, God struck him dead.'[14] Obeyesekere goes on to argue that, though Hawaiians have been portrayed as 'thinking mythically, their mythic thought is considerably more flexible than the inflexible discourse of the missions which can tolerate almost no internal debate'.[15] This assertion is misguided. Evangelical criticism of Captain Cook went hand in hand with the aim of emulation: the typological representations of evangelicals were flexible. The Sahlins–Obeyesekere exchange may be read as a debate over how the body is interpreted in contact. Obeyesekere contends that Hawaiians must have demonstrated pragmatic rationality; they should have realised that a malnourished European body could not be a manifestation of their god Lono. Sahlins retorts that Hawaiian conceptions of Captain Cook did not follow Western forms of rationality. In his view, Hawaiians subscribed to a spirit-filled world whilst the British did not. Both Sahlins and Obeyesekere subscribe, then, to a dichotomy between 'our' rationality and 'their' rationality. This dichotomy fails for evangelicals: they subscribed to a spirit-filled world too, and nature could provide a set of images that were useful for interpreting the moment of death.

Religious narrations

When the king and queen of Hawaii died in England in July 1824, after being taken ill with pulmonary inflammation thought to be caused by their introduction to a cooler climate, their bodies were taken back to the Pacific

---

[12] John Campbell, *The Martyr of Erromanga or the Philosophy of Missions Illustrated from the Labours, Death, and Character of the Late Rev. John Williams* (London, 1842), Preface, 11.

[13] See Gananath Obeyesekere, *The Apotheosis of Captain Cook* (Princeton, N. J., 1992) and Marshall Sahlins, *How 'Natives' Think About Captain Cook for Example* (Chicago, 1995).

[14] Obeyesekere, *The Apotheosis of Captain Cook*, 161.   [15] Ibid., 168.

in the *Blonde*.[16] According to the missionaries, the ceremony that accompanied the return of these remains was put on at least in part because of the islanders' claim that an act of terrible revenge had been inflicted on their monarchs. The American missionary Revd George Young wrote: 'The death of their King and Queen in London, was regarded by many of them as a judgement of God, inflicted on the islands for the murder of the great Captain.'[17] Captain Byron's voyage aboard the *Blonde* therefore had the specific aim of recasting the memory of the Cook tragedy in the islands. The bodies of the monarchs were deposited in lead coffins, enclosed in wood, covered with crimson velvet, and richly ornamented, with inscriptions in Hawaiian and English.[18]

At this time Cook's reputation amongst the evangelicals had many threads to it. I have already described Revd Thomas Haweis' avid reading of Cook's *Voyages*.[19] In fact Cook's discovery of the islands was said to have set the stage for a divinely ordained plan of mission work. In an address written to encourage exertions towards missionary work, Revd George Burder wrote: 'Captain Cook and others have traversed the globe, almost from pole to pole, and have presented us, as it were, a new world ... May we not reasonably hope that a well-planned and well-conducted mission ... will be attended with the blessing of God and issue in the conversion of many souls?'[20] But at the same time as Cook's travels were thought to have provided the first step in God's master plan for unfolding the Pacific islands, evangelicals derided Cook for losing control of himself and acting irreligiously at his death. The missionary Revd Hiram Bingham wrote that Cook's death was a divine judgement for the sin of allowing the Hawaiians to adore him: 'we can hardly avoid the conclusion, that for the direct encouragement of idolatry, and especially for his audacity in allowing himself like the proud and magisterial Herod to be idolized, he was left to infatuation and died by the visitation of God'.[21] Bingham went on to suggest that Cook had violated the proper relationship between humans and the Deity. The missionary noted that it was vain and rebellious for 'a worm to presume to receive religious homage

---

[16] George Byron, *Voyage of the H.M.S. Blonde to the Sandwich Islands 1824–1825* (London, 1826). According to the American missionary Sheldon Dibble, the monarch decided to visit London from a state of restlessness. See Sheldon Dibble, *History and General View of the Sandwich Islands' Mission* (New York, 1839), 87.

[17] George Young, *The Life and Voyages of Captain Cook* (London, 1836), 462.

[18] James Jackson Jarves, *History of the Hawaiian Sandwich Islands, Embracing their Antiquities, Mythology, Legends, Discovery by Europeans in the Sixteenth-Century, Rediscovery by Cook* (London, 1843), 233.

[19] Above, p. 2.   [20] Lovett, *The History of the London Missionary Society*, vol. I, 20.

[21] Hiram Bingham, *A Residence of Twenty-One Years in the Sandwich Islands or the Civil, Religious and Political History of the Islands* (London, 1969), 35.

and sacrifices'.[22] Revd George Young added: 'in this instance, our illustrious countryman suffered his curiosity to overcome his sense of duty'.[23] This was thought to be unusual for the celebrated voyager, who had condemned the human sacrifice of Tahiti, and whose journal contained many references to Providence.[24] Cook seemed to have fallen prey to a momentary but consequential temptation.

Religious biographers were insistent that Cook's folly could not be dismissed; the navigator was said to have consented to being adored with the full knowledge of what was happening. James Jackson Jarves, who first arrived in Hawaii in 1837 as a sympathiser of missions, and who edited the weekly paper *The Polynesian*, wrote that Cook had observed how the inhabitants of the island worshipped him and allowed this to continue. Poking fun at local traditions, Jarves noted: 'the punctilious deference paid Cook when he first landed was both painful and ludicrous ... as soon as he walked passed, all unveiled themselves, rose and followed him'. In all there were said to be 'ten thousand half-clad men, women and children' chasing or following Cook 'on all-fours'.[25] These actions could not be misinterpreted and so Jarves wrote: 'The natives say that Cook performed his part in this heathen farce, without the slightest opposition.'[26] In the meantime, Young criticised those who argued that Cook's curiosity was sufficient excuse for his folly, by pointing to the fact that he allowed himself to be worshipped twice.[27] Cook's intention to be worshipped, and the implication that full blame for his actions should rest on his own shoulders, were shared features of religious narrations of his demise.

These criticisms need to be contextualised in a wider account of evangelical views of British contact in the Pacific. Navigators and travellers were often accused of neglecting to introduce local people to the benefits of religion, while encouraging alcoholism and spreading venereal disease.[28] The American missionary Revd Sheldon Dibble observed: 'Captain Cook might have directed the rude and ignorant natives to the great Jehovah, instead of receiving divine homage himself. If he had done so, it would have been less painful to contemplate his death.'[29] The self-presentation of missionaries as benevolent and selfless was forged in opposition to the image of godless mariners who sought their own gain. Where missionaries

---

[22] Ibid.   [23] Young, *The Life and Voyages of Captain Cook*, 421.
[24] Ibid., 421–3.   [25] Jarves, *History of the Hawaiian Sandwich Islands*, 102.
[26] Ibid., 103.   [27] Young, *The Life and Voyages of Captain Cook*, 421.
[28] For more on the representation of mariners in this period, see Jane Samson, *Imperial Benevolence: Making British Authority in the Pacific Islands* (Honolulu, 1998).
[29] Dibble, *History and General View of the Sandwich Islands' Mission*, 28.

brought the benefits of British rule through pain and suffering, worldly mariners were said to destroy everything in their path.

This rhetoric explains why religious commentators on Cook's last days were quick to combine the navigator's irreligiosity with his supposed selfishness. Ephraim Eveleth, an American evangelical, wrote, for instance, of how Cook had insisted on a *heiau*, or sacred enclosure, being desecrated to supply the needs of his crew, just prior to his death. As payment for a piece of wood from this site, where the bones of kings and chiefs were deposited, Cook offered two iron hatchets.[30] Exasperated at the Hawaiians' denial of this request, Cook ordered his men to break down the fence of the *heiau* and to convey it to the boats. Cook's lack of benevolence was amply proved for Eveleth by the unequal nature of this exchange. Jarves also wrote of the selfishness of Cook's crew:

[the] most cogent reason operating to create a revulsion of feeling, was the enormous taxes with which the whole island was burthened to maintain them. Their offerings to senseless gods were comparatively few; but hourly and daily were they required for Cook and his followers ... The magnitude of the gifts from the savage, and the meanness of those from the white men, must excite the surprise of anyone who peruses the narrative of this voyage.[31]

In these and other ways, Cook and his contingent were demoted to the lowly rank of other travellers, characterised by greed and worldliness.

While accusing Cook of acting irreligiously and selfishly and wanting to distance themselves from his mistakes, evangelicals wished to follow in the navigator's path. One solution to this paradox was to set about redeeming and remoulding the memory of the death. The rearrangement of the landscape, including the setting-up of a missionary station, was just one aspect of this.[32] There was also a desire to track down those who were associated with the events surrounding Cook's demise, to suggest that their behaviour had been altered under the redeeming influences of evangelicalism. Ellis wrote that there were a number of persons at Kaavaroa, and other places in the island, 'who either were present themselves at the unhappy dispute ... or who, from their connexion with those who were on the spot, are well acquainted with the particulars'.[33] Dibble noted that, 'the heart, liver, &c. of Captain Cook were stolen and eaten by some hungry children, who mistook them in the night for the inwards of a dog'. Emphasising the contact that these men had since had with missionaries, he added

---

[30] Ephraim Eveleth, *History of the Sandwich Islands, with an Account of the American Mission Established There in 1820* (Philadelphia, 1831), 13.
[31] Jarves, *History of the Hawaiian Sandwich Islands*, 108–9.   [32] See above, p. 1.
[33] Ellis, *Polynesian Researches During a Residence of Nearly Six Years in the South Sea Islands*, vol. IV, 131.

that they were now 'aged ... and reside within a few miles of the station of Lahaina'.[34]

Attempts to change the geography of Hawaii and to assert the superiority of Christianity are evident outside the missionary corpus. After depositing the remains of the king and queen, Captain Byron steered for Karakakoa Bay. He noted, upon meeting the chiefs of the district: 'Theft is punished, murder almost unknown, and infants enjoy all the benefits of parental love.'[35] Yet even in the context of all these changes there was still more converting that had to be done. Byron visited the spot where it was believed that Cook's body had been burnt and took away many pieces of the dark lava that lay at the spot. According to Ellis, few visitors left Hawaii without making a pilgrimage to the spot where Cook died. Such tours customarily included the collection of lava, the commentary of a Hawaiian guide and the study of two coconut trees that were perforated by balls shot from the boats on the occasion of Cook's death.[36] Yet Byron was not content with these gestures of commemoration. He went to the royal *marae*, where the son of the high priest of Cook's time was still in charge of relics. He described it as 'filled with rude wooden images of all shapes and dimensions, whose grotesque forms and horrible countenances present a most extraordinary spectacle'.[37] Viewing the artefacts of this district where Cook had been deified, Byron hastily collected some to display in Britain.

The regret of the high priest's son at the desecration of a holy place is noted and yet paraded as a sign of powerlessness. The structures of a culture that allowed a navigator to perish were dismantled and transplanted with Christianity. By the collection of artefacts, Byron asserted the passage of time, and put Cook's folly firmly into history. At the spot where the body was burnt, he erected a cross of oak to the memory of the man: 'Sacred to the memory of Capt. James Cook, R. N. who discovered these Islands in the year of our Lord, 1778. This humble monument is erected, by his countrymen, in the year of our Lord, 1825.'[38] A new artefact and a new memory: the signification of a landscape and a people changed and Christianised.

The memory of Cook's death therefore stimulated a range of positions amongst evangelicals and religious travellers. His last actions were said to violate the proper ordering of creation: he had allowed himself to be worshipped and had acted in a way that was unfitting for a British navigator. He had also displayed a selfishness that was common to all worldly explorers

---

[34] Dibble, *History and General View of the Sandwich Islands' Mission*, 31.

[35] Byron, *Voyage of the H.M.S. Blonde*, 198.

[36] Ellis, *Polynesian Researches During a Residence of Nearly Six Years in the South Sea Islands*, vol. IV, 137–8, 44.

[37] Byron, *Voyage of the H.M.S. Blonde*, 200.   [38] Ibid., 202.

who sought their own gain before the conversion of the Pacific islanders. Yet evangelicals were forced to portray themselves as following in Cook's path, since the missionary enterprise rose out of the seeds of Cook's voyages. This ambiguity was resolved by the civilisation of the people associated with the events of the navigator's last days. As places and people were redeemed, it became possible to atone for the past and to move beyond Cook's folly.

Being selfless

Even as evangelicals attempted to redeem Cook's memory by reshaping the physical appearance of Hawaii and converting the inhabitants of the bay where the navigator had been slain, they urged others to emulate the great man by living a life like his and then dying for the cross instead of worldly passion. The Society's directors decided to warn the missionaries about the power of temptation: 'there may be suspecting kings, super-stitious priests, a blind and perhaps a ferocious people; [you] may be in perils often, and perhaps in deaths; [you] may expect all that hell and earth can devise or execute ... [you] should chiefly dread [your] own heart'.[39] To follow in Cook's wake was to ensure that the self was mastered and that temptations from within as well as without were resisted. In order to exemplify how the navigator's life could be re-embodied in the lives of those that followed him, I will focus on the death of Revd John Williams. The manner in which this missionary was equated to Cook can also be the lens through which we understand how the definition of the self was related to natural history in this period.

In November 1839, on landing on the island of Eromanga, Williams was killed and allegedly eaten. Revd John Campbell wrote of the missionary's death: 'for popular effect, for the reputation of Mr Williams, and for the purposes of history, he died in a proper manner, at the proper place, and the proper time'.[40] In Campbell's thinking, Cook's death also came at the climax of his career.[41] This is why he could write:

What Cook was in his own department, that Williams was in his; the career of the seaman shone resplendent with maritime, the career of the missionary with moral, glory ... the one represented England's power and science, the other her piety and humanity; both had earned the confidence of their countrymen, and the admiration of mankind; – both were killed with the club of the savage.[42]

This analogy between Cook's death and Williams' demise had come into such currency that a children's Sunday School book on Williams,

---

[39] 'Considerations Recommended to the Missionaries', in *Evangelical Magazine* 1796, 334.
[40] Campbell, *The Martyr of Erromanga*, 228.   [41] Ibid., 226.   [42] Ibid., 227.

published much later in the early twentieth century, could begin with an image of Cook's landing at Eromanga and end with one of Williams' death at the same location. Despite seeming to compare the two navigators, these images draw attention to Williams' selfless character. In the first image Cook is shown standing over the Eromangans, with weapon in hand (figure 4.1). Williams' landing, however, emphasises his willing death; he does not even resist the attack. Here it is the assailant who stands above him, swinging a club (figure 4.2). While Cook has not left the boat, Williams' companions are shown far in the background. The missionary's death is therefore emphatically determined and detached, unlike that of Cook. That this work started with Cook's arrival and ended with Williams' death had a powerful rhetorical thrust: Williams completed what Cook began and he did it far more sacrificially.

Accounts of Williams' death suggested not only that he died willingly, but that his demise was pre-ordained. Captain Morgan, who was with Williams, wrote that the missionary was determined to land at Eromanga despite his own hesitation.[43] Mr Cunningham, the Vice-Consul of Sydney, who was with him at the moment of attack, wrote:

I instantly perceived that it was run or die. I shouted to Mr. Williams to run ... Mr. Williams did not run at the instant I called out to him, till we heard a shell blow; it was an instant, but too much to lose. I again called to Mr. W. to run, and sprang forward for the boat. . . . Mr. Williams instead of making for the boat, ran directly down the beach into the water, and a savage after him.[44]

These actions were irrational, both for a thinking man and for the normal frame of mind that Williams possessed. This type of evidence was essential in the evangelical claim that the missionary had been led to his death in a pre-determined way. The spirit that resided within him had destined that he would die and guided him to that very death. The last incomplete entry from Williams' diary was also used to celebrate this thesis of premonition. Two days before his death Williams wrote: 'This is a memorable day, a day which will be transmitted to posterity, and the record of the events which have this day transpired, will exist after those who have taken an active part in them have retired into the shades of oblivion, and the results of this day will be ... '[45] Commenting on this unfinished entry, Campbell said: 'Did not our departed friend, like the prophets of old, write words which he saw not the full import?'[46] The fact that Williams did not sleep on the night before they reached Eromanga also attracted attention.[47] Williams

---

[43] Prout, *Memoirs of the Rev. John Williams*, 578.   [44] Ibid., 580.   [45] Ibid., 569.
[46] Campbell, *The Martyr of Erromanga*, 229.
[47] Basil Mathews, *Yarns of the South Sea Pioneers for Use of Workers among Boys and Girls* (London, 1914), 32.

Figure 4.1: Captain Cook's landing at Erromanga from Basil Matthews, *John Williams, The Ship Builder* (Oxford, 1915). Cook raises a rifle and exerts his relation of power.

Figure 4.2: 'John Williams' landing at Erromanga' from Basil Matthews, *John Williams, The Ship Builder* (Oxford, 1915). Williams falls to his knees, in a pathetic gesture of submission, which contrasts sharply with the presentation of Cook's arrival.

was said, therefore, not only to have known that he was about to die; his excitement demonstrated his close communion with the Deity, and stood in contrast to how Cook lost his religiosity at the moment of his demise.

In coming to all of these conclusions evangelicals paid particular attention to the manner in which Williams mastered his body at death. It was presumed that he would have prayed like Jesus did: 'Father forgive them, for they know not what they are doing.'[48] The saintliness of Williams became so well accepted that the image of him dying while pointing to heaven became an accepted trope of evangelical thinking. Images from Sunday School books of the early twentieth century may be used to show the longevity of this tradition.[49] Here Williams is focused on the world to come, pointing upwards and looking beyond to the heavens. This is quite unlike the manner of Cook's death. Williams' death therefore highlights the character of the evangelical martyr: an individual in control of his body to the extent that he could give it up, like Christ had on the cross. Though Campbell equated Cook and Williams, it is clear that he believed that Williams was infinitely superior to Cook. He wrote: 'John Williams will be venerated as one of the most illustrious Fathers of the New Era, – as one of the royal line of Stephen and Antipas, and other martyrs of our God'.[50] And this was why progress was at the core of evangelical re-inscriptions of Cook. Williams did what Cook had done, only much better.

In these accounts, Williams was presented as powerless; his persona was diametrically opposed to that of the islanders. In a sermon delivered in London immediately after the news arrived, it was said:

The circumstances of his death furnish a mournful illustration of the need of the gospel among the natives of the islands. Their savageism, their cherishing of the settled purpose of revenge, furnish only one phase of the darkness and corruption of the human heart, and nothing but the illumination of the Gospel, can scatter the mental darkness in which they are sitting.[51]

The contrast between the peace, holiness and love of Williams' willing death and the sinfulness of his attackers was vital to retellings of the demise. A description accompanying a popular print of the event claimed

---

[48] See *Evangelical Magazine*, 1840, 298 and *Evangelical Magazine*, 1843, 117.
[49] See Sujit Sivasundaram, 'Redeeming Memory: The Martyrdoms of Captain James Cook and Reverend John Williams', in *Captain James Cook: Explorations and Reassessments*, ed. Glyndwr Williams (London, 2004).
[50] Campbell, *The Martyr of Erromanga*, 273.
[51] Archibald Jack, *Believing Consecration and Service, in Connexion with Missions to Heathen, a Sermon Occasioned by the Lamented Death of the Rev. John Williams, Missionary to the Islands of the South Seas, Delivered in St. Andrew's Chapel, Northshields, on the Lord's Day* (London, 1840), 26.

that the natives 'more like demons than fellow creatures, hurried towards him, and beat him with clubs, speared, stoned, and mutilated his body in the most frightful manner'.[52] Statements such as these related outward signs of brutality to inward states. Whereas the Pacific islanders had been taken captive to rage, Williams had died a preordained death.

For the metropolitan populace the Eromangans could then become icons of cruelty. When the news reached England, one preacher said: 'I have just been making reference to them in my discourses tomorrow. My heart bleeds when I think of the inestimable missionary – and thousands bleed with it.'[53] In the meanwhile, evangelicals were keen to learn the lurid details of how Williams' body was eaten. One minister communicated the information supplied by a nephew of one of his congregation, who was with Williams, to the directors:

Mr. W ran and a powerful native with a wooden sabre was close behind him. Mr. W was in the act of falling when the savage struck off his head at one blow – this head fell into the sea and the body was instantly dragged upon the shore. A fire was kindled and the natives were distinctly seen to roast and afterwards eat the remains. He also states that he has heard Mr. W speak as if he had a presentiment that he should one day be devoured by cannibals.[54]

A twentieth-century missionary wrote that when the Eromangans heard the anguished cry of Captain Morgan and his crew on seeing Williams slain, they reacted in surprise, but 'soon however their savage instincts and love of human flesh revived, and the bodies were then carried into the interior and cooked and devoured. Marks are still to be seen on a slab of rock where Williams's body was measured before being cut up'.[55] Another writer noted:

The body of Williams which they said was short and stout, they carried up the south bank of the river, now Williams's River, laid it down on the top of a large, high rock while they rested, and while doing so 'amused' themselves by measuring the body as it lay there, and cutting holes in the rock to indicate its length.[56]

This commentator continued by giving the account of Williams' death from the Eromangan perspective. He explained that, shortly before the missionary's arrival, a group of foreigners who had landed on the island had stolen a chief's daughter and committed other offences; Williams'

[52] 'The Last Two Days of Rev. John Williams and Mr. Harris', from a description accompanying the print at the School of Oriental and African Studies, University of London, 4.
[53] Letter dated 11 April 1840, From Ralph Wardlaw to Revd J. Arundel, Home Correspondence, Box 7, CWM, SOAS.
[54] Letter dated 24 August 1840 from J. Day to J. Arundel in ibid.
[55] A. K. Langbridge, *Won by Blood: The Story of Erromanga, the Martyr Isle* (London, 1922), 31.
[56] H. A. Robertson, *Erromanga: The Martyr Isle* (London, 1902), 56–9.

death was then an act of revenge.[57] But the exact provenance of this earlier atrocity is unclear. Some accounts suggest that Williams' death was caused by a sandalwooder who had arrived before him. But Revd Charles Spurgeon claimed that it resulted from the 'evil doings of a trader who had gone bad on the island, and who was also the son of a missionary'.[58] Niel Gunson, the historian of the South Pacific mission, notes that Captain Henry, the son of a missionary, engaged in the rum trade while openly assisting the London Missionary Society, and that some regarded the killing of Williams as a direct consequence of the slaughter by Henry's crew in earlier years.[59]

Nature, death and progress

The news of Williams' demise was obviously a great shock to British evangelicals, who had recently been captivated by his tour of England. To understand how they came to terms with this exotic death, it is well to attend to wider views of demise, and their relation to a theology of nature. Because post-millenarian evangelicals equated the changing faces of nature to the stages of their own lives, the manner in which the animal and vegetable kingdoms responded to death was said to be illustrative of the human experience of decease. This belief arose from scripture, where St Paul's answer to the person who inquired about the resurrected body was said to be: 'inconsiderate man, not to have observed the analogy existing on this point in the manner in which the divine power operates in animating seed sown in the earth'.[60]

Before death, humans were thought to possess a soul which resided within a body of flesh. Life for the believer was characterised by a continual conflict between the body and the soul. The believer's body was attracted to worldly concerns whilst his or her soul was directed to heaven. This conflict was described as natural in cause and form:

The whole movement of that which is called a spiritual mind is contrary to fallen nature. It is an up-hill motion and requires great effort ... A man who would live easy, and go where nature leads him, will never attain a spiritual mind. He must enter in earnest in a conflict with nature, and wage war, if not of extermination, at least of absolute conquest.[61]

---

[57] Ibid., 56.
[58] Charles Spurgeon, *Manasseh, a Sermon Delivered on Sabbath Morning, November 30, 1856 at the Music Hall, Royal Surrey Gardens* (London, 1856).
[59] Gunson, *Messengers of Grace*, 171.
[60] Joseph George Tolley, *A Paraphrase of Saint Paul's First Epistle to the Corinthians with Explanatory Notes* (London, 1825), 117. See also 1 Corinthians 15: 14.
[61] *Evangelical Magazine*, 1831, 182.

In this battle, it was paramount that the eyes, arms and legs were constantly watched. Only if these components were guarded would a spiritual mind-set be forged. The implication was that the war on temptation was against nature, because the body was a natural artefact, while the whole of nature was characterised as sinful. This was the war that Williams had won so victoriously, and which Cook had lost. The writer in the *Evangelical Magazine* equated a spiritual mind which could resist natural temptations to a bird at complete rest: 'Turn not thine eye away: let it be constantly fixed on that moving within thee. Have the arm of thy resolution near thee to seize it the moment it attempt to fly. If you were to keep a bird, unfastened, upon the palm of your hand, you would know what it meant to keep a heart with all diligence.'[62]

One writer described the state of the individual at the moment of death as a 'spirit released from the clay ... A world of sin, dying friends, an afflicted body – all left behind.'[63] There was peace and joy because the temptations of the old body were laid aside and the war between the flesh and the spirit was at an end. Those who had conquered nature and who had won the spiritual battle were said to be immediately recognised by 'the robe of righteousness in which [they] are arrayed'.[64] The metaphor of clothing is important because it indicates that rescued individuals were not perceived to be free-floating spirits.[65] While death signified the shedding of the old body, the soul was now seen to reside in a transformed body, fitted for its new condition.[66] One writer noted: 'Such an identity is implied in the very name resurrection – a word which signifies restoration of life to what once before possessed it – not the creation of new matter to be quickened, or the giving of life to formerly existing matter.'[67] The relationship between clothing and the old body was elucidated by another commentator: 'As I have put off my clothes and laid myself upon my bed for repose of the night, so will the day of life quickly come to its period, so must the body itself be put off and laid to its rest in a bed of dust.'[68] This metaphor showed that though death saw the shedding of the outer

---

[62] Ibid., 184.
[63] *Evangelical Magazine*, 1832, 567. For God as a potter, see Romans 9: 21.
[64] *Evangelical Magazine*, 1832, 567. For the 'robe of righteousness' see Isaiah 61: 10.
[65] This metaphor arose from scripture: see, for instance, Revelation 3: 5, for a promise to the believer: 'He that overcometh, the same shall be clothed in white raiment; and I will not blot out his name out of the book of life, but I will confess his name before my Father, and before his angels.'
[66] *Evangelical Magazine*, 1832, 567.
[67] John Brown, *The Resurrection of Life: An Exposition of First Corinthians Xv* (London, 1852), 185–6.
[68] *Evangelical Magazine*, 1845, 574.

garment, there were still vital connections between the present and future states.

This doctrine of continuity was supported by the contemplation of nature. 'It is so common a thing to see the seed which is sown in the earth, spring up in quite different form ... why should it be more surprising for fleshy bodies to spring again from corruption than for vegetable bodies also?'[69] The transformed body was said to come into existence at conversion, but to be realised in its totality at resurrection. From the moment of conversion it had to be nurtured with care and there was 'a growing into this image here on earth'.[70] Continual improvement and growth therefore characterised the life of the believer, resembling the growth of trees. Nature reassured evangelicals that they would experience this improvement:

what an immense difference there is between the trifling little seed which we lay in the earth to rot, and the beautiful flower, or magnificent forest tree which will after a time spring from it. And cannot we, by the help of this comparison, draw some conclusion as to the enormous disproportion which there will be between the body as it is laid in the earth in a state of most dishonourable weakness and corruption, and its splendid condition when we shall be raised in incorruptible power and glory.[71]

Therefore natural metaphors characterised evangelical conceptions of the present body, the future body, the relationship between them and the dichotomy of body and soul.

These doctrines came into their most potent pictorial form in the apocalyptic paintings of John Martin. In *The Plains of Heaven* (1853) the earthly connection between the cycle of nature and the passage of death is reversed. According to William Feaver, 'every line from the horizontal spread of the cedars on Mount Zion to the clusters of angelic figures barely hovering above the lawns, floats in harmony; the face of nature has been rendered timeless, and so, inevitably the roses flourishing so brightly in the foreground, look waxen'.[72] The depiction of nature is ironic in Martin's paintings, portraying life in its fullest form. In heaven it is suggested that nature no longer changes, as it has been created anew. In 1861, a woman who observed one of his paintings wrote:

[69] G. Boddington, *St. Paul's First Epistle to the Corinthians Explained in Simple and Familiar Language* (London, 1839), 197.
[70] Ibid., 199.   [71] Ibid., 198.
[72] William Feaver, *The Art of John Martin* (Oxford, 1975), 199. For more on Martin's paintings, see M. Pendered, *John Martin, Painter, his Life and Times* (London, 1923), J. Dustin Wess, *Darkness Invisible: The Prints of John Martin* (Williamstown, Mass., 1986).

Oh! you should have seen it! There was a river, you know, and boats, beautiful gondolas they looked, taking the redeemed to the shores of heaven. They were shadowy figures in white robes, myriads and myriads of them, for they reached all up in the air to the holy city; it seemed to be in the clouds, coming down from God. The flowers grew on the banks of the river, pink and blue and violet; all colours, but so bright and beautiful; brighter than our flowers here.[73]

These evangelical meditations on the relationship between death and nature shared much in common with other late eighteenth- and early nineteenth-century conceptions of demise. According to Julie Rugg, Rousseau's burial, in an island tomb surrounded by poplars in 1778, encapsulates the link between funerary practices and romantic visions of nature.[74] Echoes of this connection are also discernible in discussions concerned with the arrangement of nature in cemeteries. J. C. Loudon, in his highly utilitarian *The Laying out, Planting and Managing of Cemeteries* (1847), wrote how a cemetery, if 'properly designed, laid out and ornamented with tombs, planted with trees, shrubs, and herbaceous plants might become a school of instruction in architecture, sculpture, landscape-gardening, arboriculture, botany, neatness, order and high-keeping'.[75] The *Quarterly Review*, in the meantime, chose to emphasise the contemplative dimensions of nature: 'When death is in our thoughts, nothing can make amends for the want of the soothing influences of nature, and for the absence of those types of renovation and decay, which the fields and woods offer to the notice of the serious and contemplative mind.' The writer derided the crowded cemeteries of the metropolis and longed for 'the still seclusion of a Turkish cemetery, in some remote place, and yet further sanctified by the grove of cypress in which it is embossed'.[76] Bishop Joseph Butler's classic *Analogy of Religion: Natural and Revealed to the Constitution and Course of Nature* (1736), which was reprinted many times in this period, also consolidated the link between death, the future state and nature. Butler wrote of a 'general law of nature': 'the change of worms into flies, and the vast enlargement of their locomotive powers by such change: and birds and insects bursting the shell of their habitation, and by this means entering into a new world, furnished with new accommodations for them, and finding a new sphere of action assigned them'.[77] Butler asserted that human beings would experience a similar transformation after they died

[73] Cited in Feaver, *The Art of John Martin*, 200.
[74] Julie Rugg, 'From Reason to Regulation, 1760–1850', in *Death in England: An Illustrated History*, ed. Peter Jupp and Clare Gittings (Manchester, 1999).
[75] Cited in John Morley, *Death, Heaven and the Victorians* (London, 1971), 48.
[76] Cited in ibid., 49.
[77] Joseph Butler, *Analogy of Religion: Natural and Revealed to the Constitution and Course of Nature*, ed. W. E. Gladstone (London, 1907; first printed 1736), 21.

and before they were raised again. Butler continued: 'death may immediately in the natural course of things, put us into a higher and more enlarged state of life, as our birth does, a state in which our capacities, and sphere of perception and action may be much greater than at present'.[78] Thus death was seen to be a progressive step in the development of self, which was intimately tied in with debates concerned with nature and improvement.

Williams and nature

In 1841, an engraving made from wood blocks entitled 'The Massacre of the Lamented Missionary Rev. John Williams' appeared in London and was widely circulated (figure 4.3). The print depicts Williams falling into the water with his left arm held up to shield his head. He is depicted looking 'with eyes turned up to heaven for that support which he well knew and felt would not fail him even in that dreadful moment'.[79] Over him 'ready to repeat the blow, stand two of the natives with their clubs upraised, while another by their side, is ready to pierce the heart of the unhappy missionary with his spear'. In all, about a hundred Eromangan men are shown rushing towards the ocean in 'wild commotion, every countenance expressive of the most diabolical malice and rage, armed with spears and massive and murderous clubs, made of the hard wood of the island, slings, and bows and arrows, they all seem intent on the work of death'.[80] It is possible to use this image to illustrate how evangelicals came to terms with Williams' death by using a theology of nature.

The engraving was produced by George Baxter, who had by this time established a reputation and won a patent for colour printing.[81] Baxter used steel plates in conjunction with wood blocks to produce his pictures, and oil instead of watercolour or ink.[82] Subscribers were informed of Baxter's expertise on the bottom left-hand margin of the plate depicting Williams' death. The print originally appeared in a folio volume, together with another which showed Williams' favourable reception at Tana, close to Eromanga, shortly before his death. The death scene was modelled on a watercolour drawn by J. Leary, who had been on the boat, to which

[78] Ibid., 41.
[79] 'The Last Two Days of Rev. John Williams and Mr. Harris', 7. To help in interpreting the claim that Williams looked heavenly, see Elaine Scarry, *The Body in Pain: The Making and Unmaking of the World* (Oxford, 1987).
[80] 'The Last Two Days of Rev. John Williams and Mr. Harris', 7.
[81] For George Baxter, see Asa Briggs, *Victorian Things* (London, 1988), 173–8.
[82] See A. Ball and M. Martin, *The Price Guide to Baxter Prints* (Woodbridge, Suffolk, 1974), 2. Also, for the patent, James Cordingley, *Early Colour Printing and George Baxter* (London, 1950), 7.

Figure 4.3: George Baxter, 'The Massacre of the Lamented Rev. John Williams' (London, 1841). The original image presents the Erromangans in lurid colour with blue eyes and blue grass skirts. From Special Collections, CWM, SOAS.

Williams attempted to return before he died (figure 4.4). Leary's description of the tragedy and an account of the islands by Captain Cook and Captain Dillon formed the remainder of the book. It was sold to subscribers for £2 2s; to non-subscribers for £2 12s 6d; or in gold frames with description around the plates for £4 2s.[83] The distributor and printer was John Snow, the Society's publisher.

In his engravings George Baxter apparently 'drew from nature'.[84] His first colour print was of butterflies. Robert Mudie's books, *The Feathered Tribes of the British Islands* (London, 1834) and *Man: His Physical Structure and Adaptations* (London, 1838), were illustrated by him.[85] His illustration of clouds in J. M. Moffat's *The Book of Science* (London, 1835) was praised by the author: 'The artist, Mr. Baxter, has thus been enabled to furnish representations of the forms and appearances of the clouds which for accuracy and effect may compete with drawings in water colours.'[86] This attention to natural detail is also evident in Baxter's portrayal of the death of Williams. The original watercolour drawn by Leary survives and has been annotated by Baxter with such phrases as 'hilly', 'deep valley', 'the mountain not so steep', 'bushes and men running through', 'these men should be in deeper water', 'natives – *dark* complexion', and, most revealingly, 'Williams should be more heavenly.'

These changes were necessary to make the image consonant with evangelical views of nature and death. Bernard Smith, in discussing this image, has focused exclusively on Williams' pose and its relationship to prints of Captain Cook's death, while neglecting evangelical attitudes to nature.[87] Because evangelicals interpreted the mountains, the seas and the rocks anthropomorphically, the appearance of these objects at the moment of death could add meaning to the image. For example, Leary's watercolour had four well-defined peaks quite close to the shore, but Baxter's print had just one mountain which faded into the background. In describing the values of Jesus' kingdom, scripture held that 'every valley shall be exalted, and every mountain and hill shall be made low: and the crooked shall be made straight, and the rough places plain: and the glory of the LORD shall be revealed, and all flesh shall see it together: for the mouth of the LORD hath spoken it'.[88] For Baxter, the fading of the peak on the shore of Eromanga could symbolise the passing of earthly splendour. Here

---

[83] For prices and a description of these prints, see C. T. Courtney Lewis, *George Baxter, his Life and Work* (London, 1972), 100ff.
[84] C. T. Courtney, *George Baxter, the Picture Painter* (London, 1924).
[85] For more on this see Courtney Lewis, *George Baxter, his Life and Work*. For the *Evangelical Magazine*'s review of Mudie's *The Sea*, see *Evangelical Magazine*, 1836, 21.
[86] Courtney, *George Baxter, the Picture Painter*, 61.
[87] See Smith, *European Vision and the South Pacific*, 321.   [88] Isaiah 40: 4–5.

Figure 4.4: J. Leary, 'Massacre of the Rev. John Williams' (London, 1841). From the Nan Kivell Collection, National Library of Australia, Canberra. Three blue mountains in the distance serve as a backdrop to a crowd of brown Erromangans who rush to strike Williams. One Erromangan stands boldly on the rock in the foreground with his hand raised to the air, typifying the noble savage.

DILLON'S BAY, ERROMANGA.

Figure 4.5: Dillon's Bay, Erromanga, from *Evangelical Magazine*, 1843,
413. This image draws attention to the aridity of Erromanga. As three men
watch, a ship enters the harbour. The barren plain on the opposite shore
and the empty tract of land behind them emphasise their sense of isolation.

Williams would be killed, while in heaven he would be crowned a martyr.
In an article on mountains in the *Evangelical Magazine*, a writer noted that
'Time is every hour committing gradual but constant depredations on
those surprising monuments of almighty power ... how should it teach
us to set our affections on the things above.'[89]

Two years after Baxter's print appeared, the *Evangelical Magazine*
carried a plate depicting Dillon's Bay, Eromanga, where Williams had
been slain (figure 4.5). The page following the engraving carried a description of the landscape, which presented the argument that nature was to
blame for Williams' demise. It was 'possible, indeed that the wild barrenness of its rocks and hills have helped, with other more potent causes to
nurture in their bosom those habits which seem to defy at present, the
approach of the Gospel's genial influence'. The spot where Williams was
slain was said to have 'a bold and very rugged coast' whilst the bay was said
to show 'stern uncultivatedness'.[90] Leary's watercolour, with its four
majestic peaks, did not present a sufficiently fallen view of the environment
surrounding Williams' demise. Baxter's changes to the original image

[89] *Evangelical Magazine*, 1806, 457. For more on the connection between mountains and the
sacred, see M. H. Nicholson, *Mountain Gloom and Mt. Glory* (New York, 1959).
[90] *Evangelical Magazine*, 1843, 414.

might thus be related to evangelical theologies of the mountains. The *Missionary Magazine* for 1842 noted: 'those mountain peaks are the obelisks on which, in the blood of their martyrdom, are inscribed the memorials of devoted zeal, and the glory of the gospel'.[91]

But this connection between the environment and Williams' demise could also be turned on its head, by the suggestion that the Eromangans had revolted against nature in killing Williams, without conforming to its ruggedness. In an early twentieth-century missionary history of Eromanga, it was observed: 'the contrast between the beauty of the island of Erromanga and the degradation of its inhabitants is as light and dark'.[92] In the description accompanying Baxter's print, the scene that he had depicted was described in these words:

On the mountain, which is romantic, a waterfall descends its closely sinuous and sparkling course to the savannah, which, glowing in the depth of its dark green, spreads over the plain, watered at its foot by a gleaming brook, that seems to hurry along its lively course from the waterfall to the sea, coming from amidst the tangled foliage of the savannah, like a child in its joy and gladness, and hastening to the boundless ocean which forms the best and most sublime emblem of eternity.[93]

While this description of the Eromangan shore is distinct from that which appeared in the *Evangelical Magazine*, it combines a romantic survey of the environment with a measure of the unknown. The savannah is dark green and deep, the brook is gleaming, and the foliage is tangled and appealing. There may indeed be hints of the Garden of Eden here.

Just as Baxter changed the appearance of the mountains from Leary's original, he also made the water appear deeper and more turbulent. This modification might also be related to evangelical theologies of nature. The fury of the ocean could, for example, be linked to the spiritual condition of the Eromangans. A poet wrote of the natural features of the island where Williams had fallen:

> But long the powers of darkness had held dominion there;
>   And rites of horrid cruelty polluted all the air;
>   And the cliffs that frown above them, and the waves that round them roll,
>   Spoke of wrath, and not of mercy, to the terror stricken soul.[94]

References to the relationship between the sea and death were widespread in the early nineteenth century. Symbolism usually represented the dying as passing over a great sea to the eternal shore beyond. The popular

---

[91] *Missionary Magazine and Chronicle*, June 1841, 89–90.
[92] Langbridge, *Won by Blood*, 21.
[93] 'The Last Two Days of the Rev. John Williams and Mr. Harris', 7.
[94] *Evangelical Magazine*, 1844, 405. For the connection between the sea and the sacred, see Cynthia Behrman, *Victorian Myths of the Sea* (Athens, Ohio, 1977).

nineteenth-century funeral hymn, 'Abide with Me' captures the sense of
life as a passage through 'cloud and sunshine', until 'heaven's morning
breaks'.[95] In an early book titled *Contemplations of the Ocean, the Harvest,
Sickness and the Last Judgement* (London, 1802), Richard Pearsall wrote
that 'The wicked are like yon troubled sea, vexations to themselves and one
another; they many times blaspheme God ... Peace is a stranger to their
breasts, for the way of Peace they have not known.'[96] Therefore the
connection between Baxter's furious sea and the Eromangan temperament
was a real one in the minds of observers.

   A link could also be made between the trial of the saints and the
tempestuousness of the ocean. For example, in its review of *The Landing
of the Heaven Bound Voyager* (1833), the *Evangelical Magazine* noted:

The good man is like a vessel on the sea of life, wafted onward by the genial
influence of Christian hope; and if occasionally the uniform quietude of his course
should be disturbed by conflicting gales, yet as the confident mariner, he is not
dismayed, knowing that were the ocean ever in calm he could never reach his
wished for haven.[97]

A similar connection between the seas and the passage of life is evident in a
tract titled *Navigation Spiritualized*, which was written by John Flavell and
reissued in 1822. He wrote: 'The saints are now fluctuating upon a troublesome and tempestuous sea ... Many a hard storm they ride out, and
many straits and troubles they here encounter with, but at last they arrive
at their desired and long expected haven.'[98]

   The sea for the evangelical was also an important reminder of the
attributes of God. The infinity of the oceans was said to be indicative of
the infinity of God's love.[99] The description that accompanied Baxter's
print noted that the brook appeared to be journeying 'like a child in its joy
and gladness, and hastening to the boundless ocean which forms the best
and most sublime emblem of eternity'.[100] The *Evangelical Magazine* carried a sermon preached by the late Williams. This included the anecdote of
a South Sea islander who remarked that 'the love of Christ is like the

---

[95] H. F. Lyte, 'Abide with Me' (1793–1847). For a good analysis of this hymn, see
    J. R. Watson, *The Victorian Hymn* (Durham, UK, 1981).
[96] Pearsall, *Contemplations on the Ocean*, 58. This is a reference to Isaiah 57: 20: 'But the
    wicked are like the troubled sea, when it cannot rest, whose waters cast up mire and dirt.'
[97] *Evangelical Magazine*, 1833, 62.
[98] John Flavell, *Navigation Spiritualized: Or, a New Compass for Seamen, Consisting of
    Xxxii. Points of Pleasant Observations, Profitable Applications, and Serious
    Reflections: ... Whereunto Is Now Added, 1. A Sober Consideration of the Sin of
    Drunkenness. 2. The Harlot's-Face in the Scripture-Glass, Etc.*, ed. Revd C. Bradley
    (London, 1822; first printed 1682), 228.
[99] Ibid., 18.   [100] 'The Last Two Days of Rev. John Williams and Mr. Harris', 7.

ocean. In all ages men have been taking from its waters, yet the ocean remains as full as ever, in like manner, men in all ages have been drinking of the stream of Christ's love yet there remains a fulness that can never be diminished.'[101] Williams continued:

One thing we know, we must die; and if we would be saved, we must come to Christ and believe his love. Think not that I have exaggerated in speaking it; look at the glow worm, and then at the tropical sun shining in its splendour, and you will see the infinite disproportion between man's highest conceptions and the love of Christ. We cannot discover the shores of the ocean, no more the bounds of the love of Christ, we cannot tell the length of eternity; nor the joys of the heavenly world, neither can we the love of Christ.[102]

Baxter's style was central to the communication of these points. Reviews of his work in the *Evangelical Magazine* praised his ability: 'We regard it an honour to our country to have given birth to an artist capable of producing such a print in colours as the one before us.'[103] Another review held that 'while their qualities as pictures will awaken admiration – to the friends of liberty, justice and religion – the moral associations which surround them will impart an additional charm'.[104] The connections between the sea, the mountains and death were moral, no doubt: for they spoke of the brevity of life, the urgency of evangelism and the reversal of earthly hierarchies. Baxter's new technique of colour printing allowed these connections to appear more forceful.

The image of Williams' death, for example, was said to be life-like. A reviewer held that it 'is almost too realizing to admit of calm and placid examination'.[105] Baxter contributed large portions of his profits to the Society.[106] In the case of the print of Williams' death, the public were told that Baxter had already gifted fifty guineas before the print was sold and that all further profits would be forwarded to Mrs Williams.[107] In subscribing to the print, readers did not merely arrive at moral reflections, they also contributed to those whom Williams had left behind; they translated their meditations into actions. Baxter had judged his evangelical audience accurately. His fame is attested by the unpleasant dispute between Baxter and Snow, the Society's publisher. While the cause of this dispute is not completely clear, it has been suggested that Baxter's prominence in the public eye may lie at its heart.[108]

[101] *Evangelical Magazine*, 1843, 168.   [102] Ibid., 170.
[103] This is from the review of Baxter's print of the coronation, *Evangelical Magazine*, 1842, 699.
[104] This is from the review of the portraits of Queen Pomare and George Pritchard, *Evangelical Magazine*, 1845, 389.
[105] *Evangelical Magazine*, 1841, 192.   [106] See *Evangelical Magazine*, 1845, 533.
[107] See *The Patriot*, 19 April 1841 and 17 May 1841.
[108] See Courtney, *George Baxter, the Picture Painter*, 79.

Trade in tragedy

Just as much as Williams emulated Cook and recast the navigator's death in an evangelical mould, there were many who followed in Williams' wake who wished to replicate the missionary's life story. Dozens of books came off the evangelical press that served to commemorate the martyr-traveller. These ranged from philosophical treatises to boys' adventure books. John Campbell's *Maritime Discovery and Christian Missions, Considered in their Mutual Relations* appeared in 1840 and celebrated Williams' life and his achievements in navigation and ship-building. Campbell published again under the title: *The Martyr of Erromanga or the Philosophy of Missions Illustrated from the Labours, Death, and Character of the Late Rev. John Williams*. This appeared in 1842 and went through two further editions. He also reissued the farewell proceedings for John Williams, together with an account of his death, and six thousand copies of this were published. Within the decade pamphlets celebrating Williams' life also appeared.

For the period up to 1954 I have been able to trace no fewer than ten books published on Williams.[109] Many of these were children's books and carried statements such as: 'Children like to imitate and they like to experiment. Here is an opportunity for both.'[110] Another claimed: 'Its aim is to reach boys of the Scout type, at the age when the new emotions of space-hunger, hero-worship and sex instinct are bringing them into a new world, and the age at which the majority of those who take any decisive line at all come to their decision.'[111] For the evangelical and the Christian, mechanical ingenuity was a manly trait. Male children were expected to be interested in building ships and were provided with the necessary cut-outs. They were also asked to contribute to the cost of a line of ships that were designed to send missionaries to the South Pacific: these

[109] Anon., *John Williams, the Missionary* (London, 1849), Robert Collens and Beryl Collens, *John Williams, a Sunday School Celebration* (London, 1949), Norman Davidson, *John Williams of the South Seas* (London, 1925), J. J. Ellis, *John Williams, the Martyr Missionary of Polynesia*, 3rd edn (London, 1890), Ernest Hayes, *Wiliamu, Mariner Missionary* (London, 1922), Albert Lee, *John Williams, the New Missionary Series* (London, 1921), Basil Mathews, *John Williams, the Ship-Builder* (London, 1915), Phyllis Matthewman, *John Williams, a Biography for Children* (London, 1954), Montefiore, *Heroes Who Have Won Their Crown*, Cecil Northcott, *John Williams Sails On* (London, 1948). On the John Williams ships, see Anon., *The Missionary Ship 'John Williams'* (London, 1844), Anon., *The Return to England of the Missionary Ship 'John Williams' Containing an Account of Her Voyages During Three Years as Related by Capt. Morgan, and Messrs. Barff, Buzacott and Mills* (London, 1847), Anon., *Our John Williams 1844–1944* (London, 1944), Mary Entwistle, ed., *Islands Everywhere: Stories for 7–9 Year Olds* (London, 1939), Basil Mathews, *The Ships of Peace* (London, 1919), Cecil Northcott, *South Sea Sailor, the Story of John Williams and his Ships* (London, 1965), J. Reason, ed., *The Ship Book 1844–1944, Stories, Games, Models Etc.* (London, 1944).
[110] Winifred Warr, *Practical Books No. 6. South Seas, a Handbook for Leaders* (London, 1947), 37.
[111] Mathews, *Yarns of the South Sea Pioneers for Use of Workers among Boys and Girls*, 2.

were named the John Williams ships. By the launch of *John Williams VI*, the money was said to come from children all over the Empire.[112]

The desire to raise a generation of missionaries of the calibre of John Williams was not restricted to Britain. The island of Eromanga and others of the region also came to serve as lasting monuments to Williams' memory. Churches were built on several islands in memory of Williams. Monuments were erected very soon after the event in Rarotonga. It was crucial that the very people that caused Williams' martyrdom were converted. Particular attention was paid by later missionaries to the family of Williams' murderer. When the Gordons arrived in Eromanga in 1857 they wrote: 'Kowiowi – the murderer of Williams – was killed fighting three months before our arrival. We visited his widow, a dear little woman, living in their war cave. Kowiowi had two sons; the younger son joined our Mission, the other son used to come sulkily about, but remained a heathen in our day.'[113] This 'other son' also embraced the gospel and took part in the laying of the stone for the centennial memorial of the death of Williams. The family of the murderer was therefore redeemed, and this brings to mind the quest to redeem the Hawaiians after Cook's demise. The Missionary Society did not have to wait long to see their desire of emulation fulfilled. The Gordons, who arrived as missionaries to Eromanga in 1857, were martyred, as was their successor, George Gordon's brother.[114]

Conclusions

Evangelicals used a theological language of nature in coming to terms with death. The oceans, the mountains and the bareness of the shores of Eromanga could have a myriad meanings for those who contemplated the popular print of Williams' demise. This form of analogy was a scriptural one, but its use in the exotic landscape of the Pacific was particularly arresting and successful. The religious public already thought of the islands in Edenic terms, and so an event as momentous as the death of a missionary hero produced questions about the status of the landscape and the sinfulness of the islanders. Brutal acts such as the murder of a messenger of the gospel would have no place in heaven where nature would be perfect. The attention to the failings of the site of Williams' demise called for further evangelisation of the islands.

The theology of nature surrounding Williams' death could offer comfort and hope. It encouraged believers to use their contemplation of seeds and

---

[112] See article entitled 'The Story of the Six "John Williams": A Pioneer's Work Has Continued in the Six Ships Named After Him', uncertain provenance, South Seas Odds, Box 11, CWM, SOAS.
[113] Langbridge, *Won by Blood*, 17.   [114] See ibid., 87ff.

worms to move from past and present to future. It therefore involved leaps of belief and imagination. The images supplied by this form of meditation were personal, and effective in forging self-identity. At the same time, however, the confirmation of Williams' heroism, in the environment of Eromanga, was a public act. Private conceptions of self could therefore meet public definitions of heroism in the natural realm. Visions of the environment could move with ease between these seemingly opposite significations.

The manner in which Williams was compared with Cook involved the question of how the created should relate to the Creator. Although Cook was said to have contradicted the proper relation between humans and the Deity and to have acted selfishly at his death, missionaries had to draw on his life in order to place themselves within the tradition of Pacific exploration. To deal with their ambiguous relationship with Cook, evangelicals modified their memory of the navigator's death by reshaping the geography and religion of the bay where Cook was killed. They called on missionaries to follow in Cook's path, and to die for the cross instead of passion. When Williams was slain by Eromangans, his death could therefore better the manner of the navigator's demise. Williams' control of the environment was such that he could also appear a more worthy naturalist than Cook; he had extended the reaches of known knowledge for the sake of the gospel.

In showing the relation between private meditations of nature and public proclamations of the mastery of nature, this chapter serves as the turning point of the book. If the discussion thus far has studied how the self was related to nature in the Pacific, the remainder of the book will show how nature served as a slate for religious and public improvement. Evangelicals could make use of displays of nature to depict distinctions between savagery and civilisation, damnation and salvation. The next chapter considers how the buildings and plantations of mission settlements mediated in such a public narrative.

It is important to make this transition from studying how evangelicals defined themselves to a discussion of how evangelicals portrayed themselves to others and others to themselves. As Greg Dening has shown in relation to the death of William Gooch, and Chris Healey in writing about the memory of Captain Cook in Australia, the way we write history is a product of the public field of memory, which encompasses the circumstantial process of telling a story and chronicling an event.[115] To remember how evangelicals defined themselves in relation to nature and to forget that nature was a public site would be inappropriate.

---

[115] Dening, *The Death of William Gooch*, and Chris ealey, *From the Ruins of Colonialism: History as Social Memory* (Cambridge, 1997).

5   The plants of the land: building settlements of civilisation

Whenever Revd John Williams watched an island emerge from the waters of the Pacific, if the 'forms and features of moral loveliness and spiritual life' blended together with the 'natural landscape', then 'the picture instantly imprinted its own image upon his memory and his heart'. While he appreciated the sight of 'isles rich with fruits and redolent with flowers, and beautiful as earth's primeval bowers' he did not have 'the eye of a sentimentalist or a poet'. His 'taste like his general character was practical'. Williams sought 'for something more than the mountain and the dell, the forest and the stream, the crested wave and the coral strand'. Nature's beauty arose for him when the divine injunction to master and order the environment was obeyed. A tall chapel, an ordered settlement and an industrious people; these were the 'bright lights' that brought a landscape to completion. If these 'stood in the foreground' it was as if 'nature seemed instinct with new and nobler life and clothed in her most attractive attire'. The scene became a composite whole as every part sang the Creator's praise, from the mountain to the chapel.[1]

The organisation of missionary settlements held a peculiar interest for the evangelists in the Pacific. The way stations appeared from the sea served as the first evidence of missionary presence to arriving visitors, who were curious to take account of the effect of evangelism. By paving paths and building chapels, missionaries hoped to reassure subscribers that their efforts counted as success, just as they urged islanders to take on board a new lifestyle which involved agriculture, settlement and order. This agenda was sustained through the material form of the settlement, and by the use of visual and linguistic practices of description, which are evident in the sermons and correspondence of missionaries. In paying attention to the crafting of nature, I follow W. J. T. Mitchell, who observes that landscape is 'not a natural scene, and not just a representation of a natural scene, but a *natural* representation of a natural scene, a trace or icon of nature *in*

---

[1] All of the quotations for this paragraph appear in Prout, *Memoirs of the Rev. John Williams*, 347–8.

nature itself, as if nature were imprinting and encoding its essential structures on our perceptual apparatus'.[2] Distinguishing the allegedly real form
of the buildings and gardens of the mission settlement from the manner in
which they were represented is therefore a dangerous project. On the
contrary, we need to move behind the mission settlement and see how it
was made to sustain an ideology, while appearing neutral.

The agricultural improvement of mission stations might also be explained
by how metropolitan agronomy had a colonial agenda. The promoters of
agronomy, Sir Joseph Banks, Sir John Sinclair, Arthur Young and their
ardent supporter and correspondent, Revd Samuel Marsden, the Society's
representative in Sydney, were connected by a web of correspondence. On
Marsden's advice, the Society's missionaries built settlements with chapels
at their centre, which radiated light out to sea. Agronomy is now said to be
crucial to the formation of ideologies of colonialism. It is therefore unsurprising that it should have this place in missionary enterprise.[3]

But even as evangelical ideology might be traced back to Britain, it was
reinvented in practice in the Pacific. Islanders responded to the instruction to
be industrious by exercising their own agency. They deployed existent traditions of material culture and ideas of plantation in coming to terms with new
knowledge. Meanwhile, secular critics reported how missionary plantations
and chapels lay in ruin. Justin Willis and John Mackenzie have already
drawn attention to how the architecture and layout of missionary settlements
might be interpreted.[4] Yet the confidence of missionary rhetoric should not
be taken at face value: the manner in which the evangelists' practice was
reshaped and questioned will become clear from the discussion here.

---

[2] W. J. T. Mitchell, 'Imperial Landscape', in *Landscape and Power*, ed. W. J. T. Mitchell
(Chicago, 1994), 15.

[3] For how agronomy was wedded to empire, see Bayly, *Imperial Meridian*, Drayton, *Nature's
Government*, and Schaffer, 'Field Trials, the State of Nature and the British Colonial
Predicament'. There is also of course a wider literature within colonial history which is
concerned with the environment. See David Arnold, *The Problem of Nature: Environment,
Culture and European Expansion* (Oxford, 1996) and Grove, *Green Imperialism*. Also for the
debate surrounding Alfred Crosby's book, *Ecological Imperialism: The Biological Expansion of
Europe 900–1900* (Cambridge, 1986), see B. R. Tomlison, 'Empire of the Dandelion: Ecological
Imperialism and Economic Expansion, 1860–1914', *Journal of Imperial and Commonwealth
History* 26 (1988): 84–99. For the history of agriculture, see B. A. Holderness and Michael
Turner, eds., *Land, Labour and Agriculture, 1700–1920: Essays for Gordon Mingay* (London,
1991), G. E. Mingay, *Land and Society in England 1750–1980* (London, 1994), G. E. Mingay,
Rural Life in Victorian England (London, 1998), Joan Thirsk, ed., *Agricultural Change: Policy
and Practice 1500–1750* (Cambridge, 1990), Joan Thirsk, ed., *Chapters from the Agrarian
History of England and Wales 1500–1750* (Cambridge, 1990), Joan Thirsk, *Alternative
Agriculture: A History from the Black Death to the Present Day* (Oxford, 2000).

[4] Justin Willis, 'The Nature of a Mission Community: The Universities' Mission to Central
Africa in Bonde', *Past and Present* 140 (1993): 127–54, and John M. MacKenzie, 'Missionaries,
Science and the Environment in Nineteenth-Century Africa' (unpublished manuscript).

To be an agronomist

On 28 August 1809, an unusual cargo left Portsmouth on board the *Ann*. There were boxes of books containing publications on agriculture, commerce, history, religion and geography; 193 male prisoners; and five merino ewes with young. But the most important personage on board was Revd Samuel Marsden, chaplain in Parramatta, who was returning to the penal colony of New South Wales after a hectic sojourn in Britain. The merino ewes were no less than a personal present to Marsden from George III, in order to express his commendation of the chaplain's efforts in breeding sheep and experimenting in the cultivation of the new continent.[5]

Marsden first left Britain in 1793 as the son of a butcher and the grandson of a labourer, trained to be a minister by the Elland Society, an evangelical organisation of the Church of England, connected with Revd William Wilberforce and Revd Charles Simeon and other members of the Clapham Sect. His ascent of the ladder of respectability could not have been more marked. In 1793 he left as a redeemed working-class youth, just married and facing an uncertain future; in 1809 he was a renowned religious hero, who had succeeded in combining the notoriously difficult tasks of civilisation and conversion. The *Eclectic Review* described Marsden as 'a character that seems expressly formed by Providence' to 'Christianize and civilize the barbarians' and 're-civilize the hordes of wretched culprits that are vomited by our prison-ships upon its shores'.[6]

Marsden's new-found fame had much to do with his combination of agriculture and evangelism. In describing his sense of vocation, he avoided making a distinction between manual work and the exegesis of the revealed Word:

I am a Gardener, a Farmer a Magistrate & Minister so that when one duty does not call me another always does. In this infant colony there is plenty of manual labour for everybody. I conceive it a duty for all to take an active part ... Yesterday I was in the field assisting in getting my wheat. To-day I have been sitting in the civil court hearing the complaints of my People. To-morrow if well must ascend the pulpit and preach to my people.[7]

Banks was impressed with Marsden's fortitude and so was Arthur Young, the Secretary of the Board of Agriculture. Marsden had been in contact

---

[5] The details for this paragraph were extracted from 'Account of the Rev. Samuel Marsden's exertions for the benefit of the British settlement in New South Wales', in *Evangelical Magazine*, 1809, 498–503 and 537–9. (Article copied verbatim from the *Eclectic* Review.)

[6] Ibid., 499.

[7] Cited in A. T. Yarwood, *Samuel Marsden: The Great Survivor* (Melbourne, 1977), 51–2, Marsden to Mrs Stokes, 26 October 1795.

with Banks as early as April 1803 on the importance of improving colonial sheep and of the good prospects for wool in the colony.[8] Young wrote to Banks in March 1805 that 'Mr. Marsden's wools & management are very interesting: and the specimen of linen equally so.'[9] Banks himself became President of the Merino Society, a position that he held until his death. In Britain farmers had been hesitant to breed the merino, fearing that the sheep's wool would degenerate. Consequently, George III decided to establish his own flock so as to exhibit without doubt the superiority of the beast. It was natural for Banks to shepherd the royal flock, despite the fact that George III had never officially appointed him to this role.[10] As President of the Royal Society Banks had turned increasingly to the science of agriculture. It was Banks who arranged for both Arthur Young and Revd Samuel Marsden to receive gift merinos.[11]

Young and Marsden were not only similar in their receipt of merino sheep as royal benefactions: one fact scarcely noted in relation to Young's life is that he converted to evangelicalism in 1799. Central to the early steps of his spiritual development was Revd William Wilberforce, the very figure that had exerted a formative influence on Marsden. The event that triggered Young's conversion was the death of his favourite daughter Bobbin. When Bobbin died, the first act that Young performed was to hoe her garden. Almost every entry in his diary for the days immediately following her death contain references to this garden. '20th – Again looked at her garden, and a new one she had marked out and planted under a weeping willow. No day arrives but some new object is presented to move all the springs of affection and regret; and what day can pass in which these melancholy feelings will not predominate?'[12] Another entry reads: 'Examined the willows she planted on the island. Oh! that they were thriving oaks that promised longer duration, but they may last as long as anybody that will care for the planter.'[13] While occupying himself in this husbandry, Young devoured several books, including Butler's *Analogy* and later Wilberforce's *Practical View*. He asserted that this latter work was decisive in his conversion. In April 1799 he wrote: 'I have no pleasure, and wish for none, saving the comfort which religion gives me; and the sooner

---

[8] See ibid., 90.
[9] Cited in ibid, 104. Arthur Young to Joseph Banks, 21 March 1805.
[10] Joseph Banks, 'A project for improving the breed of fine-wooled Spanish sheep, now in the possession of his Majesty into all parts of Great Britain, where the growth of fine clothing wools is found to be profitable', *Annals of Agriculture*, 1800, 285–93.
[11] See Harold Carter, *His Majesty's Flock: Sir Joseph Banks and the Merinos of George III of England* (Sydney, 1964), 119. See also Arthur Young, 'Don. A Merino Ram &c', *Annals of Agriculture*, 1792, 529–33.
[12] Arthur Young, *Autobiography*, ed. M. Betham Edwards (London, 1898), 282.
[13] Ibid., 284.

I make it my own pleasure the wiser I shall be. I go to no amusements, and read some Scripture every day.'[14]

Both Bobbin's garden and Young's laboratory were located at his farm at Bradfield. Sites for the practice of the science of agriculture were therefore closely related to sites for the private and public meditation of nature. Marsden's residences in Parramatta displayed a similar overlap in function. The French naturalist M. Péron, who visited New South Wales and eventually published a travel journal in 1807, noted that the clergyman's farm was made up of 151 acres of land, of which 103 were devoted to different kinds of cultivation. Marsden had made provision for 800 sheep, ten horses or mares, twenty-six horned cattle, thirty pigs and ten goats to graze. Two decades later Marsden was farming over 5,000 acres of land. Marsden's need to impress his congregation through manual work as much as preaching serves as one explanation for his interest in agriculture.[15] But a comparison with Young is instructive here. Young's agriculture was consonant with his evangelical enthusiasm because it apparently brought him into closer communion with the Deity, while allowing him to follow the divine injunction to control and master nature. Young noted that reading Cowper's religious letters had made him 'more attentive to every beauty ... there is something very amiable in the manner in which he converts every flower, tree and twig to enjoyment.'[16] While a country gentleman could come to ideas of his providential role in employing his labourers fairly by walking in his gardens, the new science of agriculture also performed a didactic function. Young wrote in the *Annals of Agriculture*:

It is the happy distinction of this science to be equally applicable to every age of life, it is adapted to the warmth and animation of youth, to the keen spirit of enquiry that characterises the middle age, and the maturer years find in it that compatible mixture of quiet and activity, of tranquility and business, varying to the state of the mind, that is congenial to the feelings and consistent with the powers of declining age.[17]

Agriculture, like gardening, allowed Young to reflect on his spiritual standing, to consider the cycle of life and his relation to the Deity. Cowper's religious meditations on nature and the pious science of agriculture were linked in instructing believers in matters of religion and morality.

Early in his life and before his conversion, Young outlined a grand scheme for the colonisation of the Pacific islands.[18] He instructed colonists

---

[14] Ibid., 320.   [15] This is A. T. Yarwood's argument.   [16] Young, *Autobiography*, 416.
[17] Arthur Young, 'On the pleasures of Agriculture', *Annals of Agriculture* 1785, 468.
[18] Arthur Young, *Political Essays Concerning the Present State of the British Empire* (London, 1772), 456.

to choose a convenient spot, build a fortress there, and then position a canon. 'The next business would be (if the season be proper) that of cultivation. All the implements, cattle, stock &c of an English farm should be landed by ships; and unless the island was very populous hogs and sheep, &c, turned wild to breed ... Seed of all kinds should be left for trials.' It might seem surprising that Young noted next that the 'the chaplain of the fort should be an honest well-meaning clergyman'. The minister's main occupation, according to Young, was not the task of preaching but civilising the inhabitants 'and extending their wants'.[19] Young would well have described Marsden's role in these terms. Marsden was appointed a resident adviser and supervisor of the Society's South Pacific operations in 1804, and eventually a foreign director of the Society. In this role he arranged for provisions to be sent out to missionaries in the Pacific islands, for sick evangelists to recuperate under his care, and for missionaries who were fleeing the wrath of islanders to minister to congregations in the penal colony while a decision was made as to where to station them next.

When a delegation from the Society visited in August 1824, they were particularly impressed with their agent in Australia. Tyerman and Bennet, who constituted the delegation, described the town of Parramatta as 'situated on a level plain, cleared of trees'; its streets were said to be 'regularly laid out, crossing at right angles'. With a population of three thousand, the town could boast a garden with British vegetables for each house. 'The houses of the colonists who follow agriculture, each in his little domain, are generally neat and comfortable abodes: some may even pretend to elegance.' Thirty-two miles outside Parramatta, the delegation turned off the main road to visit the farms belonging to Mr Marsden where they 'observed a fine flock of Merino Sheep, and a large herd of cattle grazing in rich pastures'. They noted: 'Mr Marsden's residence occupies an eminence, commanding an ample view of town and country, and possessing every other desirable local advantage.'[20]

Through the early nineteenth century Marsden had a decisive impact on the operations of the Society in the Pacific.[21] His views on agriculture in the meanwhile were well known and controversial amongst evangelicals at home who valued the gospel before all else. Marsden's enthusiasm for tending the land must be located in the context of a metropolitan interest in

[19] Ibid., 461.
[20] Bennet and Tyerman, *Journal of Voyages and Travels Deputed from the London Missionary Society*, vol. II, 145–9.
[21] For more on Marsden's views of mission and civilisation, see Brian Stanley, 'Christianity and Civilization in English Evangelical Mission Thought, 1792–1857', in *Christian Missions and the Enlightenment*, ed. Brian Stanley (Richmond, Surrey, 2001), 183ff.

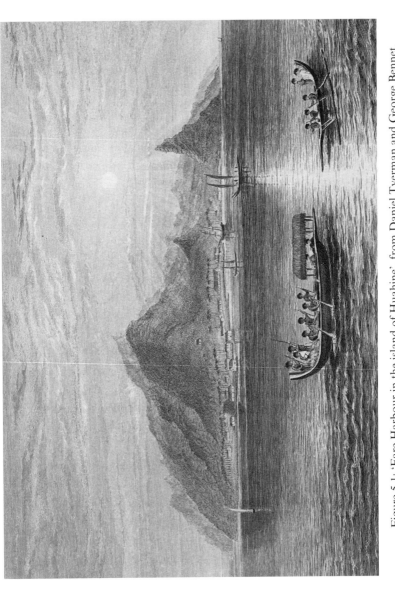

Figure 5.1: 'Fare Harbour in the island of Huahine', from Daniel Tyerman and George Bennet, *Journal*, vol. II, plate ii. As the sun gleams across the ocean, the mission settlement at Fare Harbour is presented in full view. The tract of ocean before it reminds the viewer of the labours of exploration that are required to journey to Huahine.

agronomy, and in the light of his correspondence with figures such as Banks. The making of model farms with plots for the improvement of nature, and ordered houses for the management of the poor, were enthusiastically advocated by Young; and this notion of the ideal settlement may well be related to the setting-up of South Pacific mission sites.[22] In the meanwhile, Tyerman and Bennet, the Society's delegation that called on Marsden, might usefully be seen as a pair of inspectors bent on regulating the civilising mission of the Society by travelling between as many of its far-flung stations as possible.

Huahine

Revd Daniel Tyerman, formerly a Congregational minister in Southampton and Cornwall, and George Bennet, a Sheffield philanthropist, sailed around Cape Horn and then proceeded to Tahiti, the Leeward group of the Society Islands, the Sandwich Islands, and then New South Wales, the Torres Straits, Singapore, Canton, Calcutta, Benares, Mauritius and Madagascar, where Daniel Tyerman met his death. Throughout their journal, Tyerman and Bennet provided their readers with a visual account of the mission stations, to compensate evangelical subscribers for their lack of first-hand experience of missionaries at work. According to Alison Twells, the central narrative of Tyerman and Bennet's journal is the 'moral miracle' of how Tahiti and the islands of the South Pacific had been transformed at conversion.[23] Descriptions of the Pacific islands usually comprised a plate depicting the mission station from the sea, an account of its appearance, the habits of the inhabitants and the produce of the island concerned.

Huahine was a typical case: it claimed two plates in Tyerman and Bennet's narrative. One image depicted the island as it appeared from the sea, and readers were directed to the chapel at the centre of the image, the mission house on the right of the chapel, and the house of chief Mahine near the sea on the left (figure 5.1).[24] With reference to Huahine, Tyerman and Bennet opined: 'At first the appearance was conical, blue and dimly discernible; but, as we approached, the outline broke

[22] For more on this see my doctoral dissertation, Sujit Sivasundaram, 'Nature Speaks Theology: Colonialism, Cultivation and Conversion in the Pacific, 1795–1850' (Ph.D. dissertation, University of Cambridge, 2001), 156ff.
[23] Alison Twells, 'A Christian and Civilised Land: The British Middle Class and the Civilising Mission, 1820–42', in *Gender, Civic Culture and Consumerism: Middle-Class Identity in Britain 1800–1940*, ed. David Nicholls (Manchester, 1999), 55.
[24] Bennet and Tyerman, *Journal of Voyages and Travels Deputed from the London Missionary Society*, vol. II, 184.

Figure 5.2: 'Scenes at the rear of Fare Harbour in the Island of Huahine', from Daniel Tyerman and George Bennet, *Journal*, vol. II, plate x. A missionary stands beneath a breadfruit tree, while another European looks up towards the coconut tree, observing the islander who has climbed to its crown.

into distinct hills, and in the glow of the sunset many sharp peaks were seen crowding through the evening sky.'[25] This plate depicted the result of the civilising mission, by presenting the symmetry and pattern of the station at one glance. The wide expanse of sea might be read as a symbol of the labour of exploration required to reach the station. The importance of such a plate arises because, as Paul Carter writes, coastlines were a 'condition, and perhaps origin of colonialism' inextricably linked to the Enlightenment project that 'seemed to concentrate in the greatest density, and in the most accessible form, that multiplicity of objects without which inductive knowledge was helpless to proceed step by step towards universally applicable generalization'.[26] Tyerman and Bennet's second plate of Huahine did not depict a closer view of the buildings, but provided readers with a view of the island as seen from behind the chapel (figure 5.2). The travellers directed their readers to interpret this engraving thus: 'The tall trees are cocoa-nuts; in the centre is the Breadfruit Tree; and in the foreground on the right, the Panus Odoratissimus or Prickly Pear.'[27] If the image of Huahine, as seen from the sea, denoted the result of the civilising mission, this second image signified the island's call and potential for greater improvement. Evangelicals were urged by this image to improve the interior of Huahine as much as they had changed the beach.

The breadfruit and the coconut tree were described at length in the text, effectively enrolling readers in the project of agricultural exchange and improvement. Tyerman and Bennet described the breadfruit as fertile and luxurious. The 'manifold bounty of Providence' was said to be attested in the gift of the tree to the islanders. The myriad uses to which it could be put were then listed. The breadfruit supplied the islanders with food, clothing and timber, 'each in its kind abundant, and excellent'. 'Their canoes are hollowed out of its trunk, or framed from its planks; the beams, rafters and flooring of their houses are hewn out of its substance; and it also furnishes a good pitch, in the gum which exudes from holes bored into its stems.' The manner in which Pacific islanders made clothing out of the bark of the breadfruit was described. And as the clinching proof of the tree's usefulness, readers were advised that the fruit is the 'principal support of the people'. The islanders were said to 'seldom make a meal without a large portion of it. They call it *miory*.'[28]

---

[25] Ibid.

[26] Paul Carter, 'Dark with Excess of Bright: Mapping the Coastlines of Knowledge', in *Mappings*, ed. Denis Cosgrove (London, 1999), 135.

[27] Bennet and Tyerman, *Journal of Voyages and Travels Deputed from the London Missionary Society*, vol. II, 97.

[28] Ibid., 222–4.

The coconut was also described in a similar vein: attention was paid to the process of its maturation. 'The trunk of this remarkable tree is a bundle of fibres, closely connected by a cementing matter. Within two or three feet of the ground, these fibres spread forth into thousands of small roots, which insinuate themselves through the superficial earth, and spread horizontally twelve or fourteen feet from the hole, in all directions.' Tyerman and Bennet then noted how the husk could be twisted into ropes of various sizes; the shell of the nut could be used as a drinking-cup; and the beverage could serve as a refreshing and cooling drink in the tropics. 'The kernel, when scraped out of the shell, is either eaten raw, or being squeezed through the fibres of the husk, yields a pleasant and nutritious milk, which is sometimes mixed with arrow-root, and a kind of pudding is compounded of both.'[29] The visual depiction of Huahine was therefore combined with the natural historical details of these plants. Both modes of expression called for a scheme of experimentation, transplantation and improvement.

Emma Spary writes: 'the breadfruit was the ultimate desideratum of improving acclimatizers – it was described as the perfect food for mankind, doing away with the need for other vegetable foodstuffs and balancing the constitution'.[30] Spary documents how experiments on the breadfruit continued throughout the Revolution in France. Special containers and baskets were designed by François Lebreton, a correspondent of the Société Royale d'Agriculture de Paris, to assist in acclimatising the mangosteen, the breadfruit and other fruits from the West Indies and the South Sea islands. However, in the British context, after Captain Bligh's failure, the agricultural improvement of the Pacific fell into the hands of evangelical missionaries. Tyerman and Bennet therefore reassured their readership that exchange was already well under way by including a long list of plants and livestock introduced into the island. The first few items on the list are sufficient to provide a flavour of the whole:

We find that the following valuable exotics have been introduced into this island:–
    The pine-apple and the papu; both brought hither by the unfortunate Captain Bligh.
    The superior kinds of cotton, brought by the Missionaries. There is a small indigenous cotton-tree, of little value.
    The coffee plant, lately introduced, of which some very promising specimens are growing in Mr. Ellis' garden.
    Oranges, lemons and limes; also tamarinds, planted by Captain Cook, but principally cultivated with success by the first Missionaries, and now everywhere flourishing abundantly.

---

[29] Ibid., 229–30.
[30] E. C. Spary, *Utopia's Garden: French Natural History from Old Regime to Revolution* (London, 2000), 129–30.

The custard-apple, brought by Mr. Ellis from Rio Janeiro; of which he has three plants, now producing fruit for the first time.

The idea that stagnation and excess were sinful motivated this project of import and export. In this view, evangelicals followed others who considered luxury as a fundamental and generic vice, from which other, subordinate vices would ensue.[31] Evangelicals could then hold that they were virtuous in relation to unconverted Pacific islanders who lived a life of idle and plenty without labouring for their mite. Tyerman and Bennet, in describing Huahine, noted that, prior to conversion, 'the principal part of their time was spent in eating, sleeping and profligacy; but now their hours are generally employed in honest and profitable labour, or useful and pleasant engagements'.[32] With conversion, however, the vagrant habits of the islanders were now in remission; instead of eating 'idle bread wherever they could find it' they now lived the settled life of the agriculturist.[33]

Yet the question of why God had blessed idle Pacific islanders with an environment which was so luxurious was a troublesome one. Evangelical theologies of nature operated on the basis of cause and effect, and therefore Tyerman and Bennet noted:

While contemplating the exuberance of the vegetation here, and recollecting that thus it must have been poured with unceasing prodigality from the lap of the earth and returned thither, season by season, without having answered any proportionate end, as provision for brute or human life – few vestiges of either being anywhere discernible – we were ready to enquire, 'Wherefore all this waste?' But He, without whose will not a sparrow falls to the ground, can have made nothing in vain. And here we may rationally believe that the perpetual renewal and decomposition of vegetable matter, in all its curious and exquisite forms of blade and stalk, of leaf, flower, seed, from the moss on the crag to the cocoa-nut and bread-fruit tree – has been preparing from ages past, a soil in the desert, of which the produce, through ages to come, shall nourish a numerous and happy population, whose industry and wants, as they multiply on the earth, shall lead them alike to cultivate the deep declivities of the mountains and clear the impervious vastnesses of the forests for food and for room to dwell in.[34]

The divine end was then clearly stated by the travellers: God had been preparing the islands for the message of salvation, and with Christianisation the population would grow and spread over all the vast wildernesses of nature, improving, experimenting and making nature even more productive. Nature would no longer produce fruits and food which

---

[31] John Sekora, *Luxury: The Concept in Western Thought from Eden to Smollett* (London, 1977), 48.

[32] Bennet and Tyerman, *Journal of Voyages and Travels Deputed from the London Missionary Society*, vol. II, 218.

[33] Ibid., 202–3.   [34] Ibid., 225.

would be interred in the ground; the environment would support an industrious Christian population. This providential theme emerges throughout Tyerman and Bennet's description of Huahine. It is also evident in discussions concerned with the formation of the islands.

The delegation noted that in the islanders' 'days of ignorance' they had believed that the long coral reef alongside the island was 'a rib of one of their gods'. Struck by the apparent simplicity of this belief, the travellers explained to the islanders as well as they could, how 'these marvellous structures are formed by multitudes on multitudes of the feeblest things that have life, through ages working together, and in succession, one mighty onward purpose of the eternal God'. In explaining the origin of the islands thus, the deputation deployed the newest ideas of geological science. But as they did this they made certain to substitute the 'heathen' theology of nature for an evangelical equivalent: God still had a place in their explanation. Having explained the origin of the islands in these terms, the recent innovations introduced by missionaries could also fit in with this providential plan. 'We showed them how thus the motus [reefs] had been gradually raised above the flood, and become lovely spots of verdure, capable of maintaining both animals and men; producing trees for food and for building; as well as plants to nourish hogs and fowls, or sheep and cattle, such as had been introduced in Eimeo.'[35]

The arrival of the Christian message then brought the act of creation to completion and fulfilment. Missionaries attempted to introduce these ideas of agrarian providentialism to the islanders as well. But, in practice, it appears that islanders reinvented their beliefs in response to the arrival of European material culture. Tyerman and Bennet noted how the local people they encountered believed that the sky was 'a substantial dome, the concave side (like a cocoa-nut cup turned upside down) being spread over the sea, and held in place by the stars, answering the purpose of fasteners, or nails with shining heads'. They went on to note that the islanders had no idea of an object such as a nail or fastener before the arrival of Europeans; so this account of origin must have been formed in response to the arrival of new material culture. The delegation also recorded how local peoples interpreted the arrival of foreign ships using their own traditions: 'When a strange ship arrived from a great distance, they supposed it had come from another inverted cone of the sky, through a hole in the lower part of their own.'[36]

These anecdotes illustrate that the substitution of Christian theologies of nature for indigenous ones was never complete or simple. Pacific

---

[35] Ibid., 207.   [36] Ibid., 288.

islanders, in learning to interpret the skies and the environment, reconstructed earlier versions of their creation stories in response to the knowledge that Europeans brought. Similarly, when confronted with strict orders to plant seeds, grow crops, and observe the processes of nature, so as to come into greater communion with the Deity, and live an industrious and efficient life, Pacific islanders again reconstructed the meaning of plantation. Tyerman and Bennet noted, in reference to an inhabitant of Huahine:

We have been told that the first nail ever seen in this island was taken from a boat at Raiatea. It was a spike-nail, and brought thither by the possessor as something of rare value ... Afterwards another lucky fellow got hold of a nail, and not knowing how such a thing came into existence, he shrewdly conjectured that it must have been formed by a process of vegetation. Wherefore to propagate so valuable an exotic, he planted his nail in the ground, but waited in vain for the blade, the bud, the blossom and the fruit.[37]

The theology of nature advocated by evangelicals in the Pacific involved a visual language of progress and a programme of agricultural exchange. Commentators hoped through their improvement of nature to bring the divine act of creation to completion, whilst making sense of the excessive luxury of the islands. Islanders, however, appropriated these theologies creatively in accordance with existent beliefs, without repudiating one system of natural history in favour of another.

Civilisation or conversion?

Despite the evidence that evangelical theologies of improvement were exchanged at the point of encounter, missionaries hoped to overthrow one system of beliefs and replace it with another. Conversion was said to involve the inward transformation of the heart; but evangelicals hoped that this internal change would lead to a revolution in social organisation.

In a volume titled *Incidents of Missionary Enterprise* (1844) the full extent of the change witnessed in the Pacific was described as 'vain to attempt to deny' for it had been 'astonishing and entire'. Before missionaries arrived islanders were apparently 'content to revel amid the abundance of a munificent soil and climate, which superseded in a great measure the necessity of labour for subsistence. They cared little for anything else save indolence, amusement, dissipation and war.'[38] They had

[37] Ibid., 248–9.
[38] Andrew Bonar, ed., *Incidents of Missionary Enterprise Illustrative of the Progress of Christianity in Heathen Countries and of the Researches, Sufferings and Adventures of Missionaries* (Edinburgh, 1844), 72.

been ignorant of writing and arithmetic; they had been under the absolute subjection of kings and chiefs; and habits of thieving, drunkenness, infanticide and destruction of the sick and elderly were alleged to be widespread. After conversion, however, the people were said to be 'governed with clemency, and according to equitable laws, objects neither of oppression to the powerful nor of plunder to the poor'.[39] Another writer noted that at each station there was now a 'renovated and happy population – all industrious and sober – all educated and pious'. These scenes of change were physically and morally the very epitome of the millennium – 'all nature lying in beauty and man standing up in the likeness of his Maker's image'.[40] Though these accounts of change appeared regularly in missionary sources, they should be treated with caution because of their rhetorical role in convincing subscribers to support evangelism in the Pacific, and because secular writers and travellers often presented a different view.

The novelist Herman Melville, who travelled extensively in the Pacific, noted:

The hypocrisy in matters of religion, so apparent in all Polynesian converts, is most injudiciously nourished in Tahiti, by a zealous and, in many cases, a coercive superintendence over their spiritual well-being ... On Sunday mornings, when the prospect is rather small for a full house in the minor churches, a parcel of fellows are actually sent out with rattans into the highways and byways as whipperin of the congregation.[41]

The *Westminster Review*, drawing on Melville's travels and the accounts of Charles Wilkes, who commanded an American voyage to the Pacific, noted: 'The missionaries have cleared away from the field of their own vision the old sacrifices, garlands, and festivals, and have caused the old idols to be laid down as doorsteps, to be trampled on every hour; but they themselves admit, as we have said, that a sincere Christian is a great rarity.'[42] Much earlier in the century, the *Quarterly Review* presented a similar story in describing the work of the American missionaries on the Sandwich Islands. The reviewer explained how the islanders had given up their traditional customs of livelihood without appropriating European practices of cultivation. 'Thousands of acres of land, that produced the finest crops are now sandy plains. Provisions are extremely scarce ... The poor simple natives are continually threatened with eternal punishment if they neglect "the one thing needful".'[43] The *Westminster Review*, in summarising this state of affairs, presented the diametrically opposed sentiment

---

[39] Ibid., 78.   [40] Ferguson, *Affecting Intelligence from the South Sea Islands*, 2.
[41] Herman Melville, *Omoo, a Narrative of Adventures in the South Seas; Being a Sequel to the 'Residence in the Marquesas Islands'* (London, 1847), 177.
[42] *Westminster Review*, 1856, 28.   [43] *Quarterly Review*, 1827, 440.

to that portrayed in the millennial picture of natural beauty described by the evangelical movement: 'We have driven out Nature with a fork, and she has returned with a vengeance; or Death has come into her place.'[44]

Despite the divergence between evangelical commentators and their critics, both parties shared an expectation of change and progress, which was linked to a debate over the precise relation between civilisation and evangelism. The author of an article in the *Evangelical Magazine* for 1807 argued that a convert would always accept the gospel before character was transformed. He disagreed with those who held that a people had to make reasonable progress in civilisation before the reception of Christianity. According to the writer, this view was unacceptable as it minimised the power of the gospel. The message of the cross would not be hindered either by deficient understanding or by uncivilised habits. 'It is expressly declared that the most roving and untutored tribes shall rejoice in the Messiah's salvation, even while they retain their unpolished characters and manners.'[45] This position was the orthodox evangelical standpoint. By stressing the importance of the gospel, commentators could hold to the primacy of the Bible as the word of God. Those who agreed with this view held that unbelievers had a repressed knowledge of Christianity, and by implication that untutored minds could comprehend complicated theologies. A former missionary to the South Pacific wrote: 'Some may ask with incredulity, how the missionaries have been able to impart to these barbarous tribes ideas so abstruse and truths so profound. To such we reply, that it was unnecessary, to *impart* the ideas represented in the foregoing list of Scripture truths, because the missionaries found those ideas already existing in the native mind.'[46] The *Quarterly Review* poked fun at how South Pacific missionaries believed they had found the doctrine of the Trinity in the islands:

When Wesley finds the Trinity among the savages of North America, and these missionaries in Taheiti, are such discoveries to be considered as affording any support to the doctrine, or as rendering the witnesses suspicious? ... There are few superstitions without some mythological bird; the Greeks and Romans had their harpies, and their Jupiter his eagle; the Mahommedans their Simorg, and their Celestial Cock, whose morning voice of adoration awakens all the Chanticleers of earth; the followers of Zerdusht their Bird of Bahman, who wars upon the spirits of evil; the Japanese their Foo. Thus also the people of Taheiti believe that their *morais* and burial places are frequented by a sacred bird, who feeds on the sacrifices, and in whom the Eatooa descends when the priest invokes him. They believe that the soul as soon as it quits the body is swallowed by the bird, and purified by being digested through him. What more likely than that the missionaries hearing of this Eatooa Bird, and full as it appears they were of Mr. Maurice's

---

[44] *Westminster Review*, 1856, 48.   [45] *Evangelical Magazine*, 1817, 12–15.
[46] *Congregationalist*, 1875, 506.

speculations upon the Trimourtee, should ... have hastily concluded that they had found the Trinity in Taheite?[47]

In practice, however, most missionaries did not adhere to the view that the preaching of the word should always precede conversion. At the Missionary Seminary in Gosport, missionary candidates were advised to combine other employments with preaching. Among 'barbarous people' they were advised to apply themselves to agriculture and common arts such as carpentry. These were said to 'assist' in 'finding support for other missions' while giving missionaries 'favour' among the 'Heathen'. Bogue, the missionary tutor, emphasised that the project of civilisation was important because employments such as agriculture would communicate 'benefits to the heathen, benefits of which all can judge'.[48] Williams, in the meanwhile was criticised for concerning himself too much with the duties of civilisation, leaving no room for biblical instruction.[49] The Nonconformist *Eclectic Review* noted:

Whatever political changes these islands may undergo, no part of the world seems to call more loudly for the introduction of the arts of civilized life, and, in connexion with them, for the great engines of moral improvement, education and the Bible ... This is an important measure; but it will require to be followed up with a partial colonisation, both with teachers and artisans, in order to give permanence to any plans of melioration.[50]

Each of these writers was an evangelical, who believed that conversion was important, and yet the visibility of civilisation was an easy and important sign of success.[51]

Williams, for instance, was ever conscious of how the outside world was watching the progress of the evangelical mission in the Pacific. He compared the station of Aitutaki to 'a city erected on a hill'. 'Many are the eyes looking at you. The church at Raiatea yea and every one of your Brethren in all those islands. Our eyes (Mr. Threkeld and self) and those of all the Missionaries. The eyes of the great Society in London and

[47] *Quarterly Review*, 1809, 38–9.
[48] Nineteenth Lecture on 'Encouragement to Missionaries'. Lectures on missionary Work, transcribed by J. Lowndes, L 14/9, DWL, 243.
[49] Letter dated 20 September 1823 from J. Williams, Incoming Letters from the South Seas, Box 4, CWM, SOAS.
[50] *Eclectic Review*, 1823, 33.
[51] The argument that in practice civilisation often went alongside conversion, rather than after it as orthodox evangelicals hoped, is also made by Stanley, 'Christianity and Civilization in English Evangelical Mission Thought, 1792–1857'. See also Ian Douglas Maxwell, 'Civilization or Christianity? The Scottish Debate on Mission Methods, 1750–1835', in *Christian Missions and the Enlightenment*, ed. Brian Stanley (Richmond, Surrey, 2001).

of all the believers in England. Above all the eyes of Jesus our Lord are directed at you.' He went on to tell his converts that those who watched them were waiting to find some fault in their behaviour. 'They will watch you with Rats Eyes to find little cracked places in your conduct.'[52] With so much publicity for the mission, and with such avid interest in its progress, both missionaries and converts were urged to have something to show. The outward appearance of a civilised settlement seemed the perfect choice in convincing subscribers of the progress the mission had made. This reasoning was central to the Society's Western Committee's suggestion that missionaries should reside together in groups and form settlements without scattering themselves amongst the islands.[53]

Yet there were those who dissented from this practice, returning to the theological standpoint advocated in the *Evangelical Magazine* that unseen conversion should always precede civilisation, without being pursued alongside or after improvement. Revd William Pascoe Crook, the Society's South Pacific missionary, criticised Revd Samuel Marsden on this very point. Crook arrived in New South Wales, after fleeing from murderous islanders, and was put to the task of educating fifty to seventy day pupils with the assistance of two male prisoners at Marsden's church, while awaiting a decision about whether to return to the islands. Marsden's biographer notes that his difficulties with Crook 'arose from the conjunction of two naturally hostile personalities, the one insistent on respect for his authority, the other supremely egotistical and by his own admission believing himself the only effective evangelist and teacher in the Southwest Pacific'.[54] In 1813, Crook wrote a letter concerning Marsden's character to his friend, Revd S. Tracy, which eventually made its way to the Society's directorate. He expressed his surprise at how unsuccessful Marsden had been in his ministry, telling Tracy that he only knew of one person who had been converted in ten years of Marsden's ministry. 'Judge then', he wrote, 'how incorrect must that be of Mr. M's exertions in the Eclectic Review & Evangelical Magazine.'[55] Crook's point of censure concerned Marsden's overemphasis on civilisation. On visiting him in Parramatta to borrow some books, Crook noted how he had found him among his Spanish sheep. 'Mr. M. kept on with his business and when after some time we interrupted him and asked permission to take the books it was granted and we had little conversation about missions.'[56]

---

[52] Letter dated 6 July 1823 from J. Williams, Incoming Letters from the South Seas, Box 4, CWM, SOAS. The phrase 'city on a hill' is from Augustine, and fits in with eighteenth-century Christian philosophies of settlement; see C. L. Becker, *The Heavenly City of Eighteenth-Century Philosophers* (New Haven, Conn., 1932).

[53] Report of the Western Committee regarding the formation of larger settlements in the South Sea islands. From Incoming Letters from the South Seas, Box 3, CWM, SOAS.

[54] Yarwood, *Samuel Marsden: The Great Survivor*, 107.   [55] Ibid., 147.   [56] Ibid., 146.

But, in actual fact, Crook was the exception in holding these views. Most other missionaries followed Marsden's example and busied themselves in the civilising arts, even as they hoped to convert the islanders.

Planting the land

Each of the missionaries differed in the scheme that he advocated for the agricultural improvement of the islands. For instance, Revd James Hayward, who returned to London, told the directors that the culture of cotton was best adapted to the circumstances of the islands. Following the cultivation of cotton, he recommended coffee, coconut oil and the vine.[57] Revd John Williams subscribed to a separate progression of crops.

> The tobacco I think will be most lucrative at first but I think will turn to very good account with a *proper* person to manage it, the coffee we also have in the islands, each of which will find a ready market in New South Wales. If the Tea seeds would be procured or any other spice seeds they would thrive well.[58]

Despite the divergence of opinion amongst the missionaries, all held that a series of agrarian industries could elevate islanders from helplessness. As one crop followed another, local people could be weaned off their idleness and the luxury of the islands would be transformed to efficient management.

With this programme in mind, several missionaries were appointed to the Pacific with the specific title of 'agriculturalist'. John Gyles was appointed as an agricultural missionary to Tahiti, and arrived there in 1818 to grow sugar. Before taking up his post in the Pacific he had worked as a plantation manager in the West Indies, where he had gained experience of the slave trade.[59] Gyles' appointment to the Pacific is said to have been the first 'systematic attempt at "civilisation"' for the Pacific mission.[60] His contract stipulated that it was his duty to communicate the art of cultivating sugar cane, coffee and cotton gratuitously to all persons on the island and 'generally to teach according to the best of his skill, whatever may tend to the promotion of agriculture or other useful application of the Soil or natural products of the Country'.[61] His assignment ended in failure; his colleagues viewed him with suspicion and the king of Tahiti was said to have offered little support.[62] Gyles was back in England by 1820.

---

[57] Observations on the stations of the South Sea islands by J. Hayward, 1819, Incoming letters from the South Seas, Box 3, CWM, SOAS.
[58] Letter dated 24 November 1821 from J. Williams, in ibid.
[59] Gunson, *Messengers of Grace.*   [60] Ibid., 271.   [61] Ibid.
[62] For the king's hostility see, for instance, letter dated 9 August 1819 from W. Henry, South Seas Incoming Letters, Box 3.

Following this false start, Elijah Armitage and Thomas Blossom departed together in 1821. Armitage's official appointment was as a cotton spinner to Tahiti while Blossom went as a carpenter and as Armitage's assistant. Armitage is said to have provided a 'typical example of the social aspirations of the mechanic class'.[63] His father, Elkanah Armitage, had risen considerably in the cotton manufacturing business, while one of his brothers became mayor of Manchester in 1848. Upon reaching Tahiti, Armitage set to the task of establishing a cotton manufactory in Roby's Place, Tahiti. The local people, reportedly, did not assist with this endeavour. At Williams' invitation, Armitage then moved to Rarotonga to introduce the cotton plant there. He eventually returned to England in 1836, having met with failure. By investigating the plans of these three agricultural missionaries, it is possible to understand the notion of civilisation within the nineteenth-century mission and why visibility was often used as its rationale.[64]

As soon as Gyles arrived in Tahiti in 1818, he is said to have fixed on a 'spot a mile in from Mr. Crook's dwelling for the sugar plantation'. On surveying the location he noted: 'I found it very convenient for a settlement having a fine River navigable for boats to the spot that I have chosen for the Work.'[65] A settlement was crucial to the sugar works, as those who were associated with it could then come to an idea of their separate existence, as attested by the segregation of space. Hayward could tell the directors in 1819 that one of Gyles' primary obstacles was that 'there was no wood in the islands adapted for fences – that hitherto used for gardens decays in the course of 10 to 12 months'. Without fences it seemed that the respectability of a sugar factory could not be impressed on observers.[66] Rivalries arose between Gyles and the more traditional missionaries who spent their time preaching in the chapels, teaching in the schools and translating the scriptures. There were at least two reasons for dissent. Hayward told the directors that Gyles had not been selective in his choice of helpers. 'He would have employed for the purpose two ungodly men one of them a runaway convict from Port Jackson and the other a runaway seamen.'[67] Therefore Gyles did not respect the connection between civilisation and conversion. Neither, apparently, did he see the dangers of

---

[63] Gunson, *Messengers of Grace*, 40–1.
[64] For criticisms of the cotton and sugar-cane plantations not discussed here, see *Westminster Review*, 1856, 33.
[65] Letter dated 21 November 1818 from G. Gyles, Incoming letters from the South Seas, Box 2, CWM, SOAS.
[66] Observations on the stations of the South Sea Islands by J. Hayward, 1819, Incoming Letters from the South Seas, Box 3, ibid.
[67] Ibid.

talking about the production of rum from his sugar. 'Mr. G. has said the Natives may as well have spirits to drink as to the lusting in their minds after it.' And again, Mr Gyles 'observed that rum might easily be made for [the missionaries'] use and upon their objecting that it would be disapproved of by their Directors, he replied that it did not depend on them'.[68]

When Armitage and Blossom arrived in Tahiti to cultivate cotton, a similar set of events unfolded. Armitage immediately set about the task of demonstrating the advantages of civilisation by producing 'a new suit for young Pomare to be ground entirely of the produce of the island from first to last'.[69] By 1824, they had built a factory. Blossom explained why they had little support: 'The people here must see everything before they believe anything. It is just the case with their houses. Since we have got our houses made neat and comfortable (though not yet finished). They have almost all begun to build them new houses.'[70] Blossom told the directors that he had put up water wheels without any help from the islanders. When the machines started working, they helped visualise improvement in material form and Armitage apparently noticed a change in the islanders' interest. 'Several principal Females came & observing with what ease she [Mrs Armitage] could draw the thread & twist it were prevailed on to make the attempt by coming to learn.'[71] Soon the novelty of this sight had worn off. Blossom wrote, 'To our surprise the spinners all struck, not exactly for wages, nor do we know what it is for. But they said they would not spin any more at present.'[72] Shortly afterwards there were reports that the factory had been broken into and several pieces of equipment stolen, and an unpleasant exchange of comments arose between William Henry and Elijah Armitage over Henry's part in the failure of the cotton concern.[73]

The agenda of plantation and civilisation had failed. Interest could be aroused again only by extraordinary gestures, such as dyeing cloth in unusual colours. Armitage wrote in 1827 that this 'had been the greatest excitement of anything that I have attempted'.[74] Eventually Armitage resigned himself to failure, attesting to how the islanders reasoned from their vision:

cloth woven here though much more durable is not so neat in its appearance & on that account they will not be disposed to labour much for it & when they have got a

---

[68] Ibid.   [69] Letter dated 16 May 1822 from Thomas and Sarah Blossom, in ibid.

[70] Letter dated 26 December 1824 from T. Blossom. Incoming Letters from the South Seas, Box 4, ibid.

[71] Letter dated 1 October 1825 from E. Armitage, Incoming Letters from the South Seas, Box 5, ibid.

[72] Letter dated 12 February 1826 from T. Blossom, ibid.

[73] For this exchange see letters dated 1826, ibid.

[74] Letter dated 8 September 1827 from Elijah Armitage, ibid.

few yards they do not think of making more until they are again in want so that I have always had more new spinners than old ones which is the great difficulty to overcome.[75]

In addition to failing in the task of civilisation, these three agriculturalists were perceived as a threat to the mission by their more traditional colleagues, who restricted themselves to teaching and Bible exposition. The *Quarterly Review* echoed this class-based revulsion: 'The shoe-maker who may have left his stall and the tailor who has escaped from the shipboard to commence evangelical preaching would think it degradation to instruct these poor islanders in the use of the awl or the needle. According to this rule, the more time that is spent in preaching, praying and singing the better.'[76] Those dealing with the scriptures in the South Pacific mission thought of themselves as bourgeois members of society, while agriculturalists such as Armitage, Blossom and Gyles were seen to be of a different class.

The sentiment that civilisation was the only way forward, and that those missionaries who preached, prayed and sang should pay more attention to the arts, underpinned the criticism of the *Quarterly Review*. Within the missionary movement, however, the debate was a difficult one. Would Pacific islanders improve in spiritual standing before they improved in behaviour? Melville wrote: 'All the plantations went famously for a while; the natives swarming in the fields, like ants, and making a prodigious stir. What few plantations now remain, are owned and worked by whites.'[77] For the novelist it seemed that the missionaries had failed in the task of civilisation.

Building churches

While plantations were one means of providing islanders with the opportunity to visualise improvement, gleaming white chapels were also expected to play a role in this project of civilisation. In his widely read *Narrative of Missionary Enterprises* (1837) Williams described in vivid terms how the Raiatean people responded to their chapel when it was unveiled to them:

The chiefs and common people, men, women and children, hurried to the spot: and when the covering was removed, a sheet of beautifully white plastering was presented to their astonished view. All pressed forward to examine it; some smelling it,

---

[75] Letter dated 15 May 1832 from Elijah Armitage, Incoming Letters from the South Seas, Box 7, ibid.

[76] *Quarterly Review*, 1827, 439. For the dispute surrounding the accuracy of certain facts represented in this review, see William Orme, *A Defence of the Missions in the South Sea and Sandwich Islands against the Misrepresentations Contained in a Late Number of the Quarterly Review in a Letter to the Editor of That Journal* (London, 1827).

[77] Melville, *Omoo, a Narrative of Adventures in the South Seas*, 190.

some scratching it, whilst others took stones and struck it exclaiming, as they retired, 'Wonderful, wonderful!' The very stones, in the sea and the sand in the shore, become good property, in the hands of those who worship the true God, and regard his word.[78]

These chapels were often built on the very sites of the old temples.[79] Their interiors displayed the relics of the former religions in ways that violated their original function. 'If you went into one of the places of worship in that island', one evangelical wrote, 'you would see two curiously carved images supporting the pulpit rails. They were once the gods of the people. And had you knelt at the communion rail you would find that it was supported by the shafts of spears which the warriors of Tonga had once used in their wars and against each other.'[80] Evangelicals noted that the old temples were dark and gloomy in contrast with the white chapels, and expected islanders to notice this transformation. Tyerman and Bennet wrote of a *marae*, or temple: 'In surveying this wreck of Satan's throne, melancholy retrospection carried our spirits through the dark ages which had passed over these lands while they were full of the habitations of cruelty and wickedness.'[81] Evangelicals also used such words as 'uncouth', 'monstrous', 'rude' and 'massy' in describing the temples.

Though the positioning of artefacts and the whitewashing of the walls was expected to present a message of transformation, islanders did not perceive the chapels to be diametrically opposed to the *maraes*. Williams wrote that local people killed a number of pigs to mark the opening of a chapel, just as they did when they opened a *marae*, while the notion that the king should enter a sacred place first was still obeyed.[82] Curiously, Melville destabilised evangelical narratives of change from darkness to light by writing that within the chapels 'little light is admitted, and every thing being of a dark colour, there is an indefinable Indian aspect of duskiness throughout. A strange woody smell, also – more or less pervading every considerable edifice in Polynesia – is at once perceptible. It suggests the idea of worm-eaten idols packed away in some old lumber-room at

---

[78] Williams, *A Narrative of Missionary Enterprises*.

[79] Bennet and Tyerman, *Journal of Voyages and Travels Deputed from the London Missionary Society*, vol. II, 163.

[80] Lee, *John Williams, the New Missionary Series*, 47. The Pacific case was not atypical. John Mackenzie, in describing how the Anglo-Catholic Universities Mission's cathedral in Zanzibar was built on the site of a slave market notes: 'missionaries saw a new moral geography as overlaying another, former dark deeds expunged by western engineering and architecture'. MacKenzie, 'Missionaries, Science and the Environment in Nineteenth-Century Africa'.

[81] Bennet and Tyerman, *Journal of Voyages and Travels Deputed from the London Missionary Society*, 242.

[82] Prout, *Memoirs of the Rev. John Williams*, 528, 285.

hand.'[83] Melville's account of the chapels brings their fragility and unstable construction to the fore. 'At one time there were no less than thirty-six on the island – mere barns, tied together with thongs, which went to destruction in a very few years.'[84]

The evangelical missionaries, however, perceived the chapels as diametrically opposed to the *maraes*, and described them as stable icons of the success of their mission. The same criteria that were used in judging the chapels were used in observing the *maraes* so as to indicate progress. Precise measurements were provided for the *marae* in Huahine: 'This measured a hundred and forty six feet in length, by eighteen in width.'[85] When Revd John Williams built a chapel on an island, he also recorded its appearance in terms of size and materials, and made a point of noting whether the building was better, larger and more stylish than those he had already seen on that island or elsewhere.[86] This attention to size and construction is related to the missionaries' belief that they brought with them a superior form of material culture. It might also be linked to how visibility was an important proof of conversion. In Raiatea, the need for visibility led evangelicals to build a chapel by the sea.[87] From this location the building could radiate light far out to sea, and reassure the fears of desperation in a dark ocean. In describing the Raiatean chapel, one evangelical noted: 'The greatest wonder of the place however were the great chandeliers made by the missionary, carrying sufficient lamps to illuminate the building by night – an unheard of thing hitherto in the islands.'[88]

When evangelical travellers saw white they were reminded of home; they imagined that the shore ahead was inhabited with converts like themselves. 'At the head of this bay', Tyerman and Bennet noted, 'we were surprised to see several neat-looking white houses, built in the English fashion, as used in the Christianised islands, and on an elevation a staff, with a white flag flying upon it, as a signal that we were descried and invited to land.'[89] The landscape of the South Pacific had to be clothed in specific colours to visualise conversion. If a chapel stood in the foreground of majestic mountains, radiating light to the sea at night, then the message was clear. That island resembled Britain and had embraced the robes of Christianity;

---

[83] Melville, *Omoo, a Narrative of Adventures in the South Seas*, 169.   [84] Ibid., 167.

[85] Bennet and Tyerman, *Journal of Voyages and Travels Deputed from the London Missionary Society*, vol. II, 240.

[86] Prout, *Memoirs of the Rev. John Williams*, 283, 19.

[87] Bennet and Tyerman, *Journal of Voyages and Travels Deputed from the London Missionary Society*, vol. II, 69.

[88] Hayes, *Wiliamu, Mariner Missionary*, 26.

[89] Bennet and Tyerman, *Journal of Voyages and Travels Deputed from the London Missionary Society*, vol. II, 492.

the millennium, which redeemed all of the created realms, had arrived. Even Melville noted how chapels united with nature in praising the Diety:

The islanders love to dwell near the mountain streams; and so, a considerable brook, after descending from the hills and watering the valley, was bridged over in three places, and swept clean through the chapel ... Flowing waters? what an accompaniment to the songs of the sanctuary; mingling with them the praises and thanksgivings of green solitudes inland ... But the chapel of the Polynesian Solomon has long since been deserted. Its thousand rafters of hibiscus have decayed, and fallen to the ground; and now the stream murmurs over them in its bed.[90]

Measuring metamorphosis

In coming to terms with the alleged transformation of the environment brought about by plantations and chapels, evangelicals drew on a set of metaphors that were highly suggestive of change. For instance, languages of darkness and light and fertility and aridity were often used to describe settlements. If the mission station was visualised as white and fertile, it apparently indicated conversion; if it was seen as dark and parched as a desert it was said to lie in sin.

The language of darkness and light appeared in a variety of genres. Early preachers to the Society used it in their sermons. 'I cannot tell how many millions are enveloped in the thickest darkness. Of the thousand millions of human beings who inhabit the globe, perhaps nine hundred millions never heard the Gospel. How prodigious the numbers.'[91] And again: 'There is no time to be lost ... Fly-Oh-Fly on the wings of love, and try to pluck them from the flames. The inhabitants of the whole world have been estimated at about 731 millions, 420 millions of which are in Pagan darkness.'[92] Articles in the *Evangelical Magazine* also carried many references to darkness. One titled 'Spiritual Darkness' claimed that this was the 'most impressive' scriptural metaphor for describing the unconverted state.[93] The use of darkness was said to convey the fear, misery and danger that characterised the unsaved. The soul is 'plunged into a pit of spiritual darkness, where he enjoys not those animating those heart-reviving blessings, which are associated with the light and power of the glorious gospel!'[94] And again, 'unconverted sinners are, doubtless, in a state of darkness; they are servants to Satan; they are exposed to wrath – and this is the fruit of darkness; they are in the road to Hell, – and this is the place of darkness'.[95]

[90] Melville, *Omoo, a Narrative of Adventures in the South Seas*, 167.
[91] *Sermons and Report to the Missionary Society for 1799*, 25.
[92] *Sermons and Report to the Missionary Society for 1811*, 40.
[93] *Evangelical Magazine*, 1810, 460.   [94] Ibid., 461.   [95] Ibid., 462.

Evangelicals, meanwhile, were walking in the light, for they were following their heavenly father.[96] One poet described the millennial morning thus:

> Yes, it shall rise that glorious morn shall rise,
> Even now its first pale glimmerings are begun,
> Even now I see on the far distant skies
> The golden traces of the rising sun.[97]

Buildings and churches also drew on this metaphor. A chapel in Rurutu in the South Pacific, for example, was described as having white seats, black floors, white windows and whitewashed walls.[98] Churches were said to symbolise the body of Christ and were expected to radiate light. Revd John Love wrote to Pacific islanders about the building that Moses had built at the command of God. This, he said, symbolised the coming Messiah. For 'it represented that he would be wonderfully pure and bright like gold. It represented that the glory, love and mercy of Jehovah would be displayed in him. It represented that God's heavenly ministers would look down from the skies wondering at this glorious Man.'[99]

These uses of the language of darkness and light allowed the agony of damnation and the desire for conversion to become real. Metaphorical language such as this suggested how believers should respond to the material changes in the Pacific. Missionaries also referred to mission stations as fields. One speaker explained the significance of the word at an annual general meeting of the Society: 'The field of missionary labours is the world: this lower world with all its continents and islands, with the millions of inhabitants which it contains.'[100] While evangelicals saw the unconverted as a parched desert, the redeemed nation was characterised by its luxuriance. In describing the lands to be evangelised, one speaker at an annual general meeting observed: 'Behold ... a parched desert where no water is, where the thirsty traveller pants and dies, where cattle cannot live, where grass cannot flourish.' But when the gospel was preached, suddenly the appearances were reversed: 'waters springing out of the hills and murmuring along the valleys, the fields standing thick with corn, sheep covering the plains and trees crowning the tops of mountains'.[101]

---

[96] References to light and darkness appear frequently in scripture. Jesus, for instance, compared himself to the 'light of the world', see, John 8: 12.
[97] *Evangelical Magazine*, 1827, 60.   [98] *Evangelical Magazine*, 1829, 510.
[99] Love, *Address to the People of Otaheite*, 33.
[100] *Sermons and Report to the Missionary Society for 1814*, 42.
[101] *Sermons and Report to the Missionary Society for 1796*, 80. Several passages in scripture contain this image. See, for instance, Psalm 107: 35: 'He turned the desert into pools of water and the parched ground into flowing springs.' Also Isaiah 35: 1: 'The desert and the parched land will be glad; the wilderness will rejoice and blossom.'

Spiritual improvement came to be connected, then, not just literally, but metaphorically, to the cultivation of the land. One apologist wrote of the progress of the South Pacific mission in terms that would seem strange given the failure encountered by Gyles, Blossom and Armitage:

> In a short time the outward soil began to lose some portion of its original sterility, the heath, the fern, the sedge, the bulrush gradually disappeared; green spots and ears of grain were seen sprinkled along the surface, the rude domain of nature was progressively narrowed by the daily encroachments of art; stagnant pools drained – streams deepened – torrents confined; so that what was hitherto useless, unsightly, wasteful was converted to the support of life, and became at length the fertile source of a productive husbandry. The natives it will be added, who in the meantime, had watched the efforts of the new settlers with marked incredulity, no sooner observed the extraordinary metamorphosis which their united labours had accomplished, that inflamed with a desire 'to do likewise' they not only listened to the instructions of their agricultural teachers but lent a willing hand to the tools of the field, and became sharers in the abundance of the harvest.[102]

Both these metaphors – light and darkness and barrenness and plenty – demonstrate that a study of missionary settlements cannot be restricted to the physical form of the stations. It is crucial to locate the negotiation of vision, and see how missionary perceptions were conditioned by the plants and buildings that constituted the settlement and the linguistic tropes used to describe the level of success. A study of both these genres of representation will enable historians to destabilise the distinction between the land and its languages of description.

Conclusions

I have taken a different route to that traversed by Mary Louise Pratt in discussing the early nineteenth-century colonial gaze. Pratt writes that the seeing man was the monarch whose imperial eyes passively looked out and possessed.[103] She describes this rhetoric of visualisation as a trope of discovery that 'only seeing, and the writing of seeing, can fully constitute'.[104] In this scheme the European man imposes his presence on the scene, aestheticises the landscape by treating it as a painting, in terms of symmetries, and then describes it with a density of adjectives. Pratt summarises her argument by writing: 'the monarch-of-all-I-survey scene, would seem to involve the particularly explicit interaction between aesthetics and ideology, in what one might call a rhetoric of presence'.[105]

[102] Anon., *Polynesia, or Missionary Toils and Triumphs in the South Seas, a Poem* (London, 1839), v.
[103] Pratt, *Imperial Eyes*, 7.   [104] Ibid., 206.   [105] Ibid., 205.

While Pratt grounds her analysis in the terms of a hegemonic discourse of colonialism, I have focused on the material artefacts that lie at the intersection of diverse fields of knowledge, such as the merino sheep, the breadfruit, the cotton plantation and the chapel. The practices of exchange, meditation and cultivation that are associated with these artefacts cannot be classed as evangelicalism or science. All of these artefacts were enrolled in the missionaries' civilising mission. That vision was produced, circulated and displayed by means of the objects of early nineteenth-century agronomy. While Pratt focuses her argument on the moment of discovery, I have considered a more long-term notion of perception in accordance with lived experience in the islands. As residents in the Pacific, missionaries hoped to change the land, so that it provided didactic lessons to islanders. The traditional notion of hegemony that is often associated with ecological histories is questionable: Pacific islanders reconstructed the visions that were presented to them, seeing chapels as *maraes* and nails as plants.

The public spaces of the evangelical mission station depicted hierarchies between converts and 'heathens' and civilised and depraved, using the languages of fertility, progress, light, building and plantation. Nature did not only aid the self-definition of the believer, it could act as a site for the articulation of identity and the establishment of stratifications for the whole of society. The metropolitan ancestry of this evangelical ideology lies in the land schemes of figures such as Banks and Young. By being industrious in relating to nature, missionaries hoped to exemplify the life of the ideal convert. Some Pacific islanders responded to this order; but most of them continued to use pre-existent traditions about the value of material culture and the nature of organic growth in coming to terms with the instructions of their teachers.

From the point of view of the missionaries, the appearance of the settlement was crucial in promoting the success of the mission. The need to appease supporters at home with impressive images of new chapels and productive plantations drove the organisation of mission stations. In fact, secular visitors often saw beyond this rhetoric of change and reported the failure of missionary aspirations. More fundamentally, the evangelical programme of civilisation fell apart at its core: missionaries hoped to overthrow one set of practices by replacing it with another. What occurred was far more complex: there was exchange and accommodation between evangelists and their charges. At the opening of a chapel, for instance, existent traditions with respect to sacred spaces were employed by islanders.

By paying attention to the shared face of nature, I have confined myself to the outdoors, noting how settlements were seen from the sea, and how views of the inner regions of islands were intended to stimulate further colonisation. This leaves unproblematic a distinction between the natural and the artificial, and the interior and the exterior, in evangelical narratives of conversion. The next chapter tackles this question squarely by showing how what may be called the indoors also displayed nature in order to depict stratifications of believers and non-believers. At focus is the Society's museum in London.

The discussion that follows also includes a study of clothed bodies, showing how this public site also fulfilled the function of stratification. Clothing cannot be categorised as either indoors or outdoors, but is a classic case of a practice that moves between these domains. By discussing landscape, clothing and museology together, this chapter and the next stand together in presenting the argument that nature was a public site of theology. They also draw attention to the possibilities that arise in subscribing to a more extended definition of what could count as a natural site.

6   The idol of weeds: the exchange and display of nature

In an engraving from the London Missionary Society's museum, which appeared in the *Lady's Newspaper* for 1853, a twelve-foot god brought from the island of Rarotonga by Revd John Williams stood alongside a giraffe which was alleged to be 'the finest specimen which has reached this country ... shot in the Griqua country, South Africa, by the missionary party of the late Rev. John Campbell in 1814'[1] (figure 6.1). A couple, a child led by her mother and a lone gentleman taking notes were shown peering at cases filled with shells used for money, the dresses of local chiefs, pottery and spears. In the accompanying text it was noted that the museum afforded both 'pleasure and instruction' to visitors.[2] That so many objects were on display, and that the artefacts covered terrain ranging from the domestic to the natural, demonstrated the extent to which Christian civilisation could replace existing belief systems. If a traditional costume was on show, visitors could assume that in the Pacific, Africa or Asia there was a convert who now wore European dress and professed a new faith. Of the South Pacific collection, the journalist noted: 'The various objects here grouped have at the present day become in most of the South Sea Islands objects of greater curiosity than in this country. The dress of the Tahitian warrior here exhibited, has for some years back been abandoned for European costume.'[3]

From one point of view the Society's museum was a storehouse of the products of people who lived in unity with nature; this was one definition of 'heathenism'. By exhibiting nature and artefacts made from nature evangelicals hoped to show how they had successfully transformed the unconverted. In return for the abandoned gods, supporters of the missionary enterprise exported a myriad tools of civilisation, such as clothes, printing presses and books. It was hoped that converts in the Pacific would learn the appropriate objects to cherish, and the precise relationship between the material and spiritual realms. Missionaries taught islanders

---

[1] *Lady's Newspaper*, 16 April 1853.   [2] Ibid.   [3] Ibid.

Figure 6.1: 'I wish to send these idols to *Britain*, for the Missionary Society, that they may know the likeness of the gods that Tahiti worshipped.' These were the words of King Pomare, whose enthusiasm to transport his gods to Britain apparently led to the formation of the London Missionary Society's Museum, depicted here. Pomare's letter was also on display at the museum. From *Lady's Newspaper* for 1853.

that nature had been created by their God; so it was not to be revered for itself. Instead natural elements were to be deployed for the purposes of public improvement. The wood that constituted abandoned artefacts in the Pacific was thus on occasion used to make rafters, chapels and houses.

In the Pacific the giving-up of artefacts was followed by a new system of exchange. Stealing, greed and barter were said to have been replaced by evangelical notions of charity, according to which islanders were urged to toil on the land and contribute generously to the missionary cause. Islanders were instructed to present the Society's evangelists with gifts of pork and cultivated land as recompense for their efforts. The missionaries were hoping then to create a godly settlement which mirrored patterns of exchange common in Europe. But the islanders' ascent to new practices of trade should not be assumed. By using an islander's explanation for the origin of an artefact sent to London, and by discussing the manner in which local people reacted to the instruction to give up their possessions, I aim to make some space for Pacific responses to European material practices.

The Society's museum can only be understood in the context of this web of exchanges between the Pacific and London. In the islands, and in the metropolis, attitudes to nature could serve as a public benchmark for assessing civilisation and religious sensibility. The attribution of such a comprehensive agenda to the Society's museum is surprising in the context of the current historiography. The argument that early nineteenth-century museums relied on such concepts as wonder and freak rather than classification and analogy is a common one. Accordingly, by the middle of the nineteenth century museums participated in the making of capitalist societies, the nation state and the modern public by their systems of classification. With the rise of classification, disciplinary languages concerned with authenticity and origin replaced non-verbal forms of experiencing objects.[4] Despite the undoubted attraction of this view, it privileges familiar modes of organisation associated with modern science above now forgotten forms of categorisation, which may have arisen in the early nineteenth century when there were fluid classifications and when what counted as nation, civilisation, religion and science was contested.

The arrangement of artefacts in the Society's museum suggests that it might be possible to link the early modern cabinet of the world in which the microcosm was expected to mirror the macrocosm of nature's

---

[4] Thomas, *Entangled Objects*, 131, and Paul Greenhalgh, *Ephemeral Vistas: The Expositions Universelles, Great Exhibitions and World's Fairs, 1851–1939* (Manchester, 1998), 9. Also Carol A. Breckenridge, 'The Aesthetics and Politics of Colonial Collecting: India at World Fairs', *Comparative Studies in History and Society* 31 (1989): 195–216.

arrangement, with the late nineteenth-century disciplinary museum, with its emphasis on boundaries. The importance of considering the place of religion in this shift becomes clear if we pay attention to the term 'fetish'. Used originally to denote a sacred object, worshipped for its magical powers or because it was inhabited by a spirit, this term became a keyword in the twentieth century for those who sought to understand the distinction between capitalist consumerism and sexual significance by discussing how objects could cross from occupying mythic status to become consumable entities. What was and is the difference between fetishistic collecting and natural historical or ethnographic collecting? How do the sacred and the sexual mediate in relations with the material world? If these questions are to be answered for the nineteenth century, it is clear that more attention should be paid to evangelical religion. It was precisely at this time that displays of 'idols' became common in the metropolis; they were arranged to urge viewers to separate these different practices and to come to a particular relation with the natural and the divine. When Britons saw fetishes on display, they refined their own view of the spirit world to correspond to the unseen, the immaterial and the rational.

The article that accompanied the engraving in the *Lady's Newspaper* for 1853 noted that the missionary museum was set up because King Pomare of Tahiti had sent his collection of gods to the directors of the Society, asking the directorate to display them to the English people. I will consider the formation of this museum and suggest that the Pacific context of acquisition and the metropolitan context of display need to be interpreted side by side. Following Richard Altick's claim that the Society's museum is uninteresting, surprisingly little attention has been paid to this collection by historians.[5] This chapter will indicate how the museum's cases represented the historical evolution of colonised people from unconverted to converted and from naturalistic to rational. Though Pomare came to have a particular identity for evangelicals, that historical significance was important because he epitomised the submission of the entire island of Tahiti. After his conversion, his people were said to have followed the monarch's lead. The second half of the chapter will discuss how islanders appropriated the tools of European civilisation. The discussion will focus on the example of European clothing and the system of trade that emerged in the islands.

---

[5] Richard Altick, *Shows of London* (Cambridge, Mass., 1978). For a study of the later history of the London Missionary Society's museum, see Annie Coombes, *Reinventing Africa: Museums, Material Culture and Popular Imagination in Late Victorian and Edwardian England* (New Haven, Conn. and London, 1994).

Scripture's spoils

The frontispiece of Williams' *Narrative of Missionary Enterprises* (1837) shows the missionary, together with his wife and another missionary couple, receiving the gods of the island of Rarotonga. Lying before Williams and his company are nine large staff-gods wrapped in bark-cloth. To the right six people are shown bearing another god standing erect on a litter formed of two poles with crossbars. This representation of the event might be used as a starting point for a discussion of how evangelicals collected artefacts in the Pacific. In the text of his book Williams wrote of this event: 'Some of the idols were torn to pieces before our eyes; others were reserved to decorate the rafters of the chapel we proposed to erect; and one was sent to England, which is now in the Missionary Museum.'[6] This last artefact was the staff-god that appeared so prominently in the *Lady's Newspaper*. In an engraving from the *Illustrated London News* for 1859 it seemed to tower even more dramatically above visitors to the museum (figure 6.2). From Williams' account of the provenance of this artefact, it appears that as well as this staff-god there were several others that were similar in form, which were destroyed to mark the conversion of the island. Even the object that was sent to London was changed: the phallus was cut off before display, attesting to the representational power of evangelicalism.[7] Its place in the missionary collection was predicated on the fact that as a whole the institution spoke not so much of preservation, but of how the objects in its rooms had been abandoned by their owners, who had come to value civilisation.

Tales of the abandoning of gods were common in the evangelical press, and visitors to the museum might well have been reminded of such accounts even as they viewed the artefacts on display from the South Pacific. When the Tahitian converts and teachers, Papeiha and Vahapata, oversaw the conversion of Aitutaki in 1822: 'The whole population then came in procession, district after district, the chief and the priest leading the way, and the people following them, bearing their rejected idols, which they laid at the teachers' feet.'[8] At public ceremonies like this, Williams, who was keen on spectacle, ensured that religious domination was clearly articulated. Customs such as the burning and eating of former gods were common. Williams advised an indigenous missionary to keep the best-preserved artefacts: 'if you obtain idols burn

[6] Williams, *A Narrative of Missionary Enterprises*, 98.
[7] P. H. Buck, 'Arts and Crafts of the Cook Islands', *Bulletin of Bernice P. Bishop Museum* (1971), 319.
[8] Williams, *A Narrative of Missionary Enterprises*, 330.

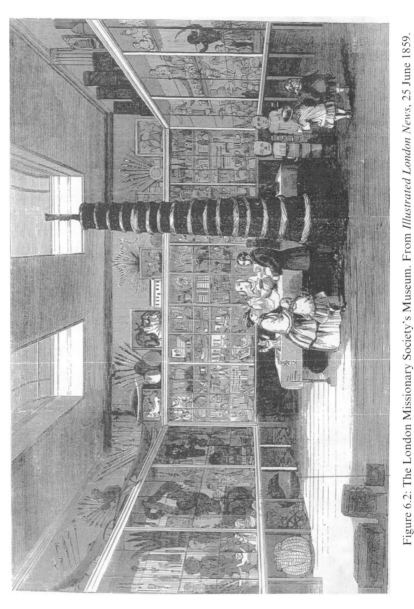

Figure 6.2: The London Missionary Society's Museum. From *Illustrated London News*, 25 June 1859. The Rarotongan staff-god towards the centre of the illustration towers over the visitors to the museum. Two children are shown standing before two other gods brought from the South Pacific.

some (but not the best) before their faces that they may see the consuming of them ... leave the greatest part and send to Raiatea as an encouragement to us and we will send them to England as a rejoicing to them'.[9] An engraving from the *Evangelical Magazine* for 1819 depicted how the gods of Tahiti were destroyed by fire, while the construction of European houses had already begun in the background.[10] The collection of South Pacific artefacts therefore fitted into the theatrical display of conversion. These ceremonies adopted a military style in trumpeting the coming of the new faith.

The use of abandoned gods to build chapels and houses spoke of how 'idols' had been put to material improvement. One South Pacific missionary, Revd Charles Pitman, writing home about a chief's reaction to his former 'idols', demonstrated how the opposition between civilised evangelicalism and depraved 'heathenism' could be presented as a clash between light and darkness.

The chiefs expressed a wish that two of their verua-kinos (literally evil spirits) or idols might be uncovered of their cloth, to wrap around, or ornament the rafters; to which we agreed ... I said to one of the chiefs, who was near me – 'Behold the gods you formerly worshipped.' He replied 'We were Etenes, we were in darkness then. Surely the prince of darkness must have gnashed his teeth at such a sight.'[11]

Before the conversion of the island, the Rarotongan gods had been revolting in the eyes of the missionaries, but the wood that made them could now be put to good use. Light could dissipate darkness, and revulsion could be substituted by functionality. An engraving depicting the 'idols' presented by King Pomare of Tahiti exemplifies how evangelical aesthetics contributed to impressions of the demonism of 'heathenism'. One of the 'idols', Tii, was described as 'ugly'; it was said to represent 'powerful beings dwelling in the *Po*, or night'. To this artefact, viewers were informed, 'sorcerers direct their prayers when they want to injure a person'.[12] Horrified by descriptions such as these, missionaries used abandoned 'gods' for the project of civilisation, to demonstrate how former religious practice had been brushed aside.

Curiously, while missionaries hoped to demonstrate the superiority of their religion and its material culture by the collection of artefacts, they also showed an interest in how islanders had used the objects before giving

---

[9] Letter dated 6 July 1823 from John Williams, Incoming Correspondence from South Seas, Box 4, CWM, SOAS. For the acquisition of local artefacts in dress, see Fara, 'Images of a Man of Science'.

[10] See Thomas, *Entangled Objects*, XX.

[11] Letter from Mr Pitman, from Rarotonga, dated 6 November 1827, addressed to the directors, *Evangelical Magazine*, 1828, 449–50.

[12] *Evangelical Magazine*, 1818, 539.

them up. The South Pacific missionaries Bourne and Williams wrote to Bennet and Tyerman, the travelling deputation of the Society, urging them to collect information about how 'idols' were used before acquiring them, as such information would 'add much to the interest with which you would show them to your different friends in your journey, and at England'.[13] Often ethnographic comments were important because they showed that local religions were similar to Christianity, but significantly different. The similarities demonstrated that there was scope for evangelism, whilst the differences confirmed the superiority of the missionary's system of beliefs. For example, when South Pacific customs of sacrifice were described, Old Testament notions of sacrifice came to mind. The missionary Revd Henry Nott wrote in the *Evangelical Magazine*: 'As to the manner of offering human sacrifices, let it be observed, that they were never offered on an altar, but either buried in the ground, or hung upon a tree for a while, to be buried afterwards.'[14] But evangelicalism's distinction lay in its separation of nature and the divine: South Pacific deities were said to take naturalised forms, unlike the Christian deity. Nott wrote: 'The gods of the South Sea islands were numerous, inhabiting the air, the earth and the sea. The albatross, the heron bird, the dove, and the swallow, the dog, the rat, the lizard, and the centipede, the daring shark and the terror-striking sword fish, with a multitude of smaller fishes deified by the Tahitians.'[15]

Missionaries hoped to replace this naturalism with a scientific conception of nature, so that nature would refer to the unseen Christian God. This agenda is also discernible in missionaries' displays of abandoned gods in the Pacific. When the 'idols' from Aitutaki were brought to Raiatea by sea, 'The Man Varua ino (the Evil Spirits) were seen through the telescope hanging through to the yard-arms of the vessel, as she entered the harbour.'[16] The Raiateans' use of a telescope exemplified how they had embraced a new relationship with nature. They now investigated nature, without revering it. This investigation was possible because of the light diffused by the gospel. The 'idols' from Aitutaki were hung in the 'large chapel' 'especially about the pulpit, desk &c.' The whole building was 'lighted up' and the gods presented a 'brilliant appearance' to the eye of the person trained in the scientific mode of vision, which divided the material from the spiritual.

A charged process of acquisition therefore lay behind the presentation of South Pacific artefacts in London. The communal abandoning of sacred artefacts, the destruction of most of these gods in fire, the use of the wood

---

[13] Letter from Messrs Bourne and Williams, missionaries, dated Raiatea, 11 August 1823, addressed to Revd D. Tyerman and Geo. Bennett, Esq. *Evangelical Magazine*, 1824, 455.
[14] *Evangelical Magazine*, 1837, 40.   [15] Ibid., 38.   [16] *Evangelical Magazine*, 1825, 162.

that constituted a fair few of them for the project of civilisation – all of this would have come to the minds of visitors to the museum. At the point of acquisition these artefacts could be seen, without contradiction, as military trophies and ethnographic treasures; specimens of naturalism and the raw products of civilisation. Upon conversion, islanders were urged to come to new meanings for their 'idols'. Another Raiatean at the exhibition of the gods of Aitutaki is said to have noted in reference to the role of indigenous missionaries in the collection of artefacts: 'They called our ship, a ship of God, and truly it is. It has carried the Gospel to distant lands, and brought back the trophies of its victory.'[17]

Militarism, ethnography and scripturalism

The Raiatean's use of a military language to speak of these artefacts is significant. This form of speech was common amongst evangelicals, and easily adopted by converts. The catalogue of the missionary museum in London, for instance, advertised how it held the 'trophies of Christianity'.[18] In describing the missionary museum, one evangelical wrote that it was 'a monument of the glorious triumph of the cross, achieved by the Christian armies of our country'.[19] A South Pacific missionary noted, in reference to artefacts he had sent to London, that 'the coffin with all their gods we have forwarded'.[20] When evangelicals toured the missionary museum they rejoiced in the victory of their gospel: the emotions of visitors to the metropolitan collection might then be related to those experienced by missionaries who watched local peoples abandon gods. Forms of speech and representation crossed between the Pacific and London. I move now from the context of acquisition to that of display.

The Society's museum, established in 1814, held a diverse collection of objects. The first items received from the public included the 'Skin of a Sloth' and a 'Guana (Serpent)'[21] sent in by Mr Harriot of Demarara and 'two Chinese Ladies Shoes, a piece of Chinese Matting, curious specimen of Sea Weed, and a pair of Buffalo Horns, from India' sent in by Revd D. Clark of Dartford.[22] Shells were displayed alongside the head of a hippopotamus, the tusk of an elephant, a mole rat, drums, baskets of local manufacture, and a pillow from the South Sea islands. The range of

---

[17] All quoted in ibid., 162–3.
[18] Anon., *Catalogue of the Missionary Museum, Austin Friars* (London, 1826), iv.
[19] Letter dated 29 April 1839 from H. S. Cumming, Deans Row, Walworth, Home Correspondence, Box 7, CWM, SOAS.
[20] Letter dated 5 July 1822 from T. Blossom, Incoming Correspondence from South Seas, Box 3, ibid.
[21] *Evangelical Magazine*, 1817, 503.   [22] *Evangelical Magazine*, 1822, 44.

this collection was not random. The museum was designed to depict the web of superstition that engulfed other societies and celebrated the righteousness of Christian victory.

On the one hand, these artefacts brought approbation to the missionaries who had acquired them. While at home, Williams turned to the artefacts that he had brought from the Pacific to publicise his success. 'Very frequently on these occasions, the curiosities he had brought from the islands were drawn from their hiding places, and the various contents of several cases covered the table or the floor.' Williams connected these artefacts with his own person: he 'arrayed his own portly person in the native tiputa and mat, fixed a spear by his side and adorned his head with the towering cap of many colours, worn on high days by chiefs, and as he marched up and down his parlour, he was as happy as any one of the guests whose cheerful mirth he had thus excited'.[23] Williams became, in the eyes of his friends, a military chief in the army of missionaries, one who had conquered the forces of darkness and ushered in the pure reign of Christianity. His acquisition of objects confirmed his victory in the spiritual battle. After his martyrdom, the interest in the museum was enhanced by the fact that his son assisted in reorganising the collections in a 'most careful and intelligent manner'.[24]

The compilers of the catalogue of the missionary museum wrote of how the collection pointed to the success of the Society's evangelists: 'the success with which God has already crowned our labours, should act as a powerful stimulus to our efforts, far more zealous than ever, for the conversion of the heathen'.[25] Though the description of the collection was minimal, the references that did appear linked particular artefacts to the missionaries who obtained them. The catalogue listed 'various shells from the Molucca Islands presented by the Rev. Mr. Kam'; 'the Klip Springer and the Steem Bok from Africa, presented by the Rev. J Campbell'; 'Birds of Paradise and other Birds from Amboyna'.[26] The article in the *Illustrated London News* noted: 'The contents of this museum are not only valuable in consequence of their interest as specimens of particular phases of art and workmanship, but also from their being connected with eminent missionaries.'[27]

The collection depicted the extent to which nature reigned over colonised societies and how the peoples to whom the missionaries had been sent could not distinguish between nature and the divine. Domestic

---

[23] Prout, *Memoirs of the Rev. John Williams*, 479.
[24] *Illustrated London News*, 25 June 1859, 620.
[25] Anon., *Catalogue of the Missionary Museum*, iv.   [26] Ibid., 44.
[27] *Illustrated London News*, 25 June 1859, 620.

utensils and instruments of war in the missionary museum, for instance, were depicted as natural objects. The South Pacific islanders' water bottle was shown to be a coconut, a cloak worn by the inhabitants of the North West Coast of America was labelled as being 'made of the entrails of an animal'.[28] In the text which accompanied the engraving in the *Illustrated London News*, it was noted that Pomare's gods were 'simply logs of wood with scarcely an attempt at form, and the large object in the foreground of the engraving is an idol called Tanquron, and is formed of rags and grasses. There are other matters of worship which are only bunches of feathers, curved stones, and portions of rough shell.'[29] In fact Williams wrote of the staff-god from Rarotonga: 'Near the wood were red feathers, and a string of small pieces of polished pearl shells, which were said to be the *manava* or soul of the god.'[30] The Society hoped to renew all of fallen nature: peoples in union with nature were therefore still in sin. By demonstrating the extent of nature's reign, missionary leaders called for public support in their battle against demonic forces.

Alison Twells, in describing a collection of missionary artefacts of the Sheffield Literary and Philosophical Society, sent home by George Bennet, one of the Society's deputation, suggests that they contributed to the construction of a new relationship between Britain and the 'heathen' world in the first half of the nineteenth century. 'Shaped by evangelical and enlightenment notions of human "likeness", of all peoples as members of one family, this relationship was also based upon an assertion of cultural inequality and difference, expressed in terms of a model of social change whereby all peoples were positioned on a developmental continuum from savagery to civilisation.'[31] This same argument may be made with respect to the metropolitan Society's museum. After commenting on the construction of South Pacific objects, the writer in the *Illustrated London News* observed: 'From these rude examples the visitor may pass to the more finished works of India, China &c.'[32] The developmental scale, which positioned various peoples on a continuum, culminated with the British. And so visitors were expected to compare objects on display with their own productions. For example, a pair of Chinese spectacles was said to be 'exactly like the railway eye-preservers now in use at home'. At the same time as 'savage' inhabitants of the South Pacific were derided for their formless 'idols', it was said: 'Some of the carved work on paddles &c

---

[28] Anon., *Catalogue of the Missionary Museum*, 9.
[29] *Illustrated London News*, 25 June 1859, 620.
[30] Williams, *A Narrative of Missionary Enterprises*, 98.
[31] Twells, 'A Christian and Civilised Land', 60.
[32] *Illustrated London News*, 25 June 1859, 620.

by the savage inhabitants of the South Seas Islands are in some instances, remarkable for both design and execution.'[33] Throughout the collection there was a tension between similarity and difference. All the peoples of the world could be ranged on a hierarchy which emphasised difference; the British were at the head of the scale so as to signify superiority, yet the fact that all peoples could be compared at all denoted similarity.

The displays aimed to help viewers meditate on scripture. The *Evangelical Magazine* in 1817–18 ran a series of articles on the British Museum, demonstrating how a visitor could use the collection to come to a greater understanding of the Bible. One contributor to this series explained his intention of explaining the 'acquaintance of the apostle Paul with THESE VERY ANTIQUITIES *now in our possession* as a nation; and by means of them to explain certain of his allusions imperfectly understood'.[34] He went on to describe sciagraphy, the art of shadow painting, which was widely prac- tised in the time of Paul, and which was evident in certain objects in the collection of the British Museum, including some 'Hamilton Vases'. This led in turn to an exposition of Hebrews 10: 1, which this writer translated as: 'the law having the very Shadow of good things to come, and not the very Image of the things'. Similar scriptural allusions were also noted in the catalogue for the missionary museum. The head of the unicorn or rhino- ceros or reem was annotated: 'This great and formidable animal is supposed to be the Unicorn of Scriptures, Job. xxxxix. 9–12.'[35] The scriptures were central to all evangelical practice: by visiting the missionary museum viewers were promised a greater understanding of the Bible. The artefacts illustrated how the promises of scripture were being fulfilled as the gospel spread abroad in victory, while the objects themselves depicted verses in scripture which related to objects of natural history unseen in Britain.

The keepers of the missionary museum struggled to make their collection present all these messages. In 1839, H. Cumming, who described himself as 'cradled and nurtured amid curiosities', wrote to the directors of the Society complaining about the condition of the museum.[36] He asserted that the collection had been allowed to remain in a state 'not only of utter confusion and chaos, but in a state of ruin and decay'. Cumming continued, 'the moth has committed its ravages wherever nutriment was to be obtained leaving the hairless skins to mark its progress, the Spider has spun its web in every corner and the extraordinary works both of God and Man are alike obscured and disfigured with dust and cobwebs'. Cumming volunteered to

[33] Ibid.   [34] *Evangelical Magazine*, 1818, 13.
[35] Anon., *Catalogue of the Missionary Museum*, 11.
[36] Letter dated 29 April 1839 from H. S. Cumming, CWM, SOAS.

reorganise the collection by identifying the provenance of its objects. This suggestion reveals a tension between the various aims of the museum. A collection organised by origin would have divorced scientific and ethnographic information from a view of the biblical triumph over naturalism. The differences became even more apparent as the century progressed. By the end of the century the keepers attempted to arrange the collection thematically. The natural history cases, for example, were categorised as Polyparia, Insecta, Mollusca, Reptilia, Pisces, Aves, Mammalia, Pachydermata, Rodenta, Edentata, Carnivora, Quadrimana, etc.[37] By 1891 a number of artefacts from the Pacific were transferred to the British Museum; 178 African exhibits, mainly 'weapons and axes', were bought by the Pitt Rivers Museum in Oxford.[38]

Narrating a god

In the early decades of the missionary museum's existence, however, militarism, science and ethnographic comparison could sit at ease. The manner in which one of the gods of the South Seas, variously labelled A'a, Taaroa Upoo Vahu and Tauroa Upao Vahre, was displayed reveals how evangelical representations of material culture interacted with indigenous narrations. This object was said to be the 'Supreme Deity of Polynesia, a wooden figure covered in parts with children'.[39] It is now acclaimed as one of the finest extant pieces of Polynesian sculpture (figure 6.3).[40] It is taken to be a representation of the creator and sea god of the Polynesians in the act of creating gods and men. When it was first acquired the artefact was filled with further small gods and men.[41]

The *Missionary Sketches* for 1824 presented this object in a scientific mode of vision (figure 6.4). The 'idol' was measured and its readings were reported beneath the portrayal: 'Height 3 feet 10 inches; across the head 1 foot 2 inches; width across the chest (including the arms) 1 foot 3 inches.' Since the back face and the front face of the object appeared side by side, the reader was given the opportunity to scrutinise the artefact in detail, whilst being afforded the impression of a neutral gaze. The artist presented the god against a black background, adding an extra dimension to view. The back face of the 'idol' was hollow and revealed a dark crevice. The

---

[37] Anon., *Catalogue of the Missionary Museum Bloomsfield Street, Finsbury* (London, 1900).
[38] See Andrew Porter, 'Religion and Empire: British Expansion in the Long Nineteenth Century, 1780–1914', *Journal of Imperial and Commonwealth History* 20 (1992) 16.
[39] *Illustrated London News*, 25 June 1859, 620.
[40] Alfred Gell, *Art and Agency: An Anthropological Theory* (Oxford, 1998), 137.
[41] W. B. Fagg, *The Tribal Image: Wooden Figure Sculpture of the World* (London, 1970), plate 76.

Figure 6.3: A view of 'A'a' as it appears in the ethnographic collection of the British Museum. This object is intricately carved from hardwood and is now reputed to be one of the most celebrated pieces of Polynesian sculpture.

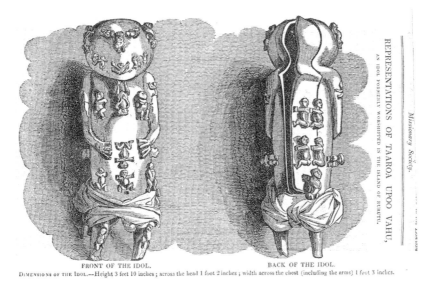

FRONT OF THE IDOL.   BACK OF THE IDOL.
DIMENSIONS OF THE IDOL.—Height 3 feet 10 inches ; across the head 1 foot 2 inches ; width across the chest (including the arms) 1 foot 3 inches.

Figure 6.4: 'Taaroa Upoo Vahu.' From *Missionary Sketches* for 1824.
The god A'a is presented clinically here: the front and rear side appear
together, and its phallus is covered with cloth.

cloth wrapped around the artefact hid from the reader's gaze the phallus
that lay beneath. The manner in which the object was presented therefore
brought objectivity and moral assessment together. A similar style of
representation might be traced in William Ellis's depiction of this artefact
in *Polynesian Researches* (1829). The frontispiece of the second volume of
his work depicted 'a front and profile view of Taaroa'. Again the artefact
was described clinically: 'The image from which these views are taken, is
nearly four feet high, and twelve or fifteen inches broad, carved out of a
solid piece of close, white, durable wood.'[42] A cloth hung loosely from the
waist, hiding the phallus.

This scientific and evangelical mode of vision might be contrasted with
how the artefact fits into indigenous norms of meaning. Alfred Gell writes
of this artefact: 'What is particularly remarkable about A'a is the explicit
way in which this image of "singular" divinity represents divinity as an
assemblage of relations between (literally) homunculi. In so doing, the A'a
obviates the contrast between one and many, and also between inner and
outer.'[43] The surface of the artefact is thus covered with little figures that

[42] Ellis, *Polynesian Researches During a Residence of Nearly Six Years in the South Sea
Islands*, vol. II, 220.
[43] Gell, *Art and Agency*, 139.

repeat, in addition to gods and men having been housed inside A'a. There is thus no boundary to differentiate the god from its creations. In presenting the back and front of the artefact side by side it might be argued that the editors of the periodical were attempting to come to terms with the object's complex personhood.

The display of Taaroa Upoo Vahu therefore saw a Polynesian narrative of religion forcefully set aside for one that was in accord with the sensibilities of the readers of the periodical. The confusion that could arise in the passage from one meaning to another is well demonstrated by contemporary traditions held by the islanders of Rurutu with respect to this object. According to modern Rurutans, there were three gods inside this object when it was first made by a hero called Amaiterai. Amaiterai made the god after visiting London, in accordance with a challenge set for him by the king of Rurutu, to win the hand of the monarch's daughter. In London Amaiterai encountered the God of Wisdom (who was later brought to the islands by the missionaries) and he sought to make an artefact that embodied this deity. A'a was the object that resulted from his efforts.

The gods inside the artefact represent God the Father, God the Son and God the Holy Spirit. 'In other words, the A'a is the Tabernacle in which the Trinity arrived on Rurutu, by the agency of the Rurutan hero, long before the missionaries themselves arrived.'[44] In coming to a new meaning for this object, the Rurutans have therefore creatively appropriated evangelicalism.

Reclothing the native

After giving up their gods, costumes and other productions to the missionaries, the islanders were introduced to European material culture. The manner in which they responded to these artefacts – for instance, new clothes – might be used to raise the question of how effectively islanders appropriated evangelical practices. In effect this allows me to trace the historical ancestry of the Rurutan account of the origin of A'a, by showing how the understanding of material culture possessed by local peoples was Christianised. By using the example of clothing, it is also possible to shed light on the evangelical ideology of separating the material and spiritual realms.

Missionaries often took sets of clothes with them to the Pacific, in order to provide a form of attire for their converts which was consistent with their new identity. Missionaries hoped to set aside forms of clothing that predated conversion, and which used natural materials. One of the laws

---

[44] Ibid., 137.

enforced by the missionaries read: 'Females must not appear in the house of God, adorned with flowers. The transgressor shall pay a fine of 3 Baskets of Cotton.'[45] Females, and other converts, were encouraged to wear white to Sabbath services. As Melville commented, 'For what reason necklaces and garlands of flowers, among the women were forbidden, I never could learn; but it is said that they were associated, in some way, with a forgotten heathen observance.'[46] Many travellers reported that the most striking scene of transformation they witnessed at the mission stations was the sight of Sabbath congregations dressed in European attire. 'It is one of the most gratifying sights the eye can witness on a Sunday in their church ... The women are all dressed in bonnets after the fashion of some years back ... Their attire is as near English as they can copy.'[47] Melville, however, was unenthusiastic about the new attire:

The 'kihee whihenee,' or petticoat, is a mere breadth of white cotton, or calico; loosely enveloping the person, from the waist to the feet. Fastened simply by the tuck, or by twisting the upper corners together, this garment frequently becomes disordered; thus affording an opportunity of being coquettishly adjusted ... But what shall be said of those horrid hats! Fancy a bunch of straw, plaited into the shape of a coal-skuttle, and stuck, bolt upright, on the crown; with a yard or two of red-ribbon, flying about like kite-strings ... Curious to relate these things are esteemed exceedingly becoming.[48]

Natural materials were used in making these European clothes, but the process of manufacture implied that nature had been mastered. On the island of Moorea, for example, the women were said to wear bonnets 'back platted on sword grass or some other plant or grass. The men also have got hats like the common straw hats, made of the same materials, which has a very decent and respectable appearance.'[49] Missionaries attempted to make local people industrious in their relationship to nature. Hats and bonnets served as evidence that they were making progress towards this aim; feathers and beaks did not have this function. Williams forwarded bonnets to the directors, taken from the hands of two Raiatean females, which were 'made by themselves and not made with any idea of being sent'.[50] These artefacts could be used to demonstrate how Raiateans had ascended the scale of civilisation.

---

[45] Literal translation of a French copy of Tahitian laws, Incoming Letters from South Seas, Box 3, CWM, SOAS.
[46] Melville, *Omoo, a Narrative of Adventures in the South Seas*, 181.
[47] Letter from Sam Harvey, the captain of a whaling ship about the 'social condition of the people of Tahiti'. *Evangelical Magazine*, 1839, 620.
[48] Melville, *Omoo, a Narrative of Adventures in the South Seas*, 180.
[49] Quarterly Report on the South Pacific Mission, Incoming Letters from South Seas, Box 3, CWM, SOAS.
[50] Letter dated 14 July 1822 from J. Williams, Raiatea, ibid.

The manner in which missionaries controlled islanders' clothing is similar to how evangelicals at home sought to control the dress of pious women. One writer in the *Evangelical Magazine* complained of 'many persons especially females, adopting an *expensiveness* in their style of dress, extremely unsuitable to their station in life, and their means of support'.[51] 'Just economy enters little into their thoughts', the writer continued, and addressing the women concerned said, 'the cause of the gospel, of benevolence, of the illumination and salvation of mankind calls for your aid'.[52] Another writer addressed evangelical women:

Once more we solicit you to regard this prevailing conformity to the world in expensive and unsuitable apparel, as it robs the treasury of the Most High, and impedes the progress of the gospel. Ah! how often are our solicitations for a trifling increase of the accustomed contribution to a missionary or other religious institution, repulsed by the most decided assurance that the utmost is already subscribed, while a slight glance at the person addressing us, reveals the presence of the unnecessary ribbon, the superfluous lace, and the flower that does not add to nature's charms, and which have cost the wearer much more than the sum she refuses to give for the salvation of the world.[53]

Women were urged to save the money spent on dress, so that they could contribute this sum to the missionary cause. The clothes that women wore to church were seen to be crucial in setting an example to others. Sunday School teachers, for example, were urged: 'think of the young immortal beings, who regard you as their patterns, and beware of encouraging in them a taste which may probably lead them to set at nought your instructions'.[54]

Meanwhile, Pacific islanders' inability to attend service served as a reason for British evangelicals to be modest in clothing. After a hurricane on the island of Rarotonga, many orphans were left destitute without clothes. A writer in the *Evangelical Magazine* noted: 'this fact so painful in itself is rendered still more distressing by one of the effects it has produced, namely the necessary detention of the children from the house of God, involving the loss of that religious instruction which must be regarded as far more necessary to their minds than even clothing to their bodies'.[55] The strict dress code for church attendance spanned the globe from Britain to the Pacific. The overdressed evangelical woman in Britain could deprive the incorrectly dressed islander of attending service by her extravagance.

Islanders were aware of how their new clothes signified an altered relationship with nature. Two Rarotongan orphans wrote to thank British

---

[51] *Evangelical Magazine*, 1815, 315.   [52] Ibid., 316.   [53] *Evangelical Magazine*, 1841, 384.
[54] Ibid., 385.   [55] *Evangelical Magazine*, 1839, 363.

evangelicals for the clothes they had received. 'We have not been able to attend the house of prayer: the want of cloth has been the reason. Our native cloth soon rots – it is only the skin of a tree and will not keep good long; therefore we are greatly rejoiced by this English cloth you have sent us that we may be covered.'[56] Nature's clothing was therefore repudiated, and manufactured clothes embraced. By these means islanders manifested a greater appreciation of the useful arts and a growing awareness of nature's inadequacy. Unconverted Pacific islanders saw the form of clothing adopted by converts as a manifestation of difference. A British traveller watched as two converts went ashore to tell the inhabitants of another island why they had converted to the new religion. He reported: 'Fearless they landed in a canoe which we had brought for this purpose, and were well received by numerous natives who covered the beach. We expected every moment to see their European clothing, torn from their persons; but no injury was attempted, and they began to converse with the people.'[57]

The relationship between the practices of dressing in Britain and those in the Pacific may be extrapolated to other artefacts of exchange. Evangelicals demonstrated a curious ambiguity with regard to objects. On the one hand, certain clothes had to be repudiated, for they signified extravagance; on the other they had to be embraced since they were symptomatic of conversion. Similar practices of control applied to gods. On the one hand, Williams rejoiced as he watched the islanders burn their 'idols'. On the other hand, he desired to take some of them home, to display his successes as a missionary. At home, the sciences were often depicted as worldly pursuits that should give way to the proclamation of the gospel, but in the Pacific the use of scientific instruments denoted conversion. The first missionaries who reached the South Pacific wrote: 'Our clock excites wondrous attention. Every tool we make use of attracts the notice of the spectators, with which we are commonly surrounded. Many of them will mutter out bitter regret and reflections on their own country, because so ignorant of the ingenious arts with which we are acquainted.'[58] Evangelicals practised the art of simultaneously repudiating and collecting objects.

Exchange as religion

Missionaries hoped to teach converts to find this balance between repudiation and use. Brian Durrans notes that the term 'religious' is highly unstable in the context of the display of artefacts. For what counts as

---

[56] *Evangelical Magazine*, 1842, 203.   [57] *Evangelical Magazine*, 1825, 302.
[58] Wilson, *A Missionary Voyage to the Southern Pacific Ocean*, 233.

religious may at the same time conjure associations which may not be classed as religious.[59] This point is directly applicable to evangelical displays of Pacific material culture. The museum's display was intended to depict the web of superstition that engulfed the Pacific, while pointing to how islanders' former religious beliefs did not distinguish the material from the spiritual. Yet, at the same time, islanders were presented with a new type of clothing, which illustrated by the manner of its manufacture how the natural and the divine were separated in their new state as converted Christians. When Pacific islanders learnt which objects to value and which to deride, they learnt what constituted their new religion.

The emergence of a new system of trade in objects is discernible in missionary texts. Williams, in advising a new set of missionaries, made particular note of the system of barter adopted by the islanders, estimating it to be '6 to 10 large blue beads for a large pig'.[60] He advised the outgoing missionaries to take large sky-blue beads with them as 'these are the gold of the country'.[61] Another South Pacific missionary lamented the fact that the rate of barter was constantly increasing in the islands because of the merchant ships that called at mission stations, which 'give the natives in barter for provisions three times the value in articles, the Missionaries can afford to give'.[62] Missionaries were dependent on the local people for their subsistence. The ordinary diet of the missionaries was 'pork, breadfruit, Tarro and sometimes mountain plantains ... a great part of which they purchase from the natives and at times at a dear rate'.[63] Another missionary complained, 'we are obliged to purchase food and if we have not clothing for Barter the natives will not give it'.[64] Missionaries were concerned that customs such as stealing were re-emerging. One missionary wrote: 'the great bane to civilization and industry in Tahiti is the continuance of the arbitrary and unjust measure that no respect is paid to private property, every man's hogs, breadfruit and every species of property he possesses, even to the mat he sleeps on, is liable to be taken from him without the least recompense'.[65]

---

[59] Brian Durrans, '(Not) Religion in Museums', in *Godly Things: Museums, Objects and Religion*, ed. Crispin Paine (London, 2000).

[60] Letter dated 25 August 1835 from J. Williams, Home Correspondence, Box 6, CWM, SOAS.

[61] Ibid.

[62] The Report of the Western Committee Regarding the Formation of Larger Settlements in South Sea Islands, Incoming Letters from South Seas, Box 3, ibid.

[63] Mr. Hayward's answers to queries regarding the subsistence of the Missionaries, ibid.

[64] Letter dated 21 September 1825 from C. Pitman, Incoming Letters from the South Seas, Box 5, ibid.

[65] Letter dated 15 February 1821 from R. Bourne, Incoming letters from the South Seas, Box 3, ibid.

In seeking to transform this state of affairs, missionaries laid down a set of laws relating to property. 'Every hog, strayed, but marked upon shall be considered as the property of the person whose mark it bears. Hogs, without marks strayed, become the property of the Missionaries.'[66] Missionaries also sought to inculcate practices of evangelical charity amongst their converts. To this end, native missionary societies were set up so that islanders could contribute sums to support missionary endeavours elsewhere. The *Evangelical Magazine* for 1830 noted, 'their contributions, which, from the want of a circulating medium, have consisted of the produce of the soil, have been, if their means be considered truly liberal'.[67] Islanders were praised for giving what they could. One missionary wrote:

I am sure, that had you been able, just before the sailing of the *John Williams* to the westward, to peep into the storehouse at Apia, piled with heaps of property, collected to aid in the great work of Missions, accustomed though you are to number the thousands of *Pounds* in Bloomfield-Street, these stores of simple native contributions, would, nevertheless, have called forth a smile of pleasure.[68]

Missionaries urged converts to give them gifts in appreciation of their services. On Moorea, one missionary reported: 'land was given up to the missionaries as their own containing Breadfruit and cocoa-nut trees &c and besides *that* presents of food were and are brought them by the people, such as Breadfruit, Taro, Cocoanuts, plantations, fish &c. The article of Pork we have to buy, but even *that* we have sometimes presents made us.'[69] At the indigenous missionary societies, arrowroot oil was the main article to be subscribed. The Huahine Society, formed in 1828, for example, set out as its main rule that its members were those 'that contribute five bamboos of cocoanut oil annually, or else three balls of arrow root or one pig or four baskets of cotton'.[70] Though islanders duly contributed arrowroot oil, missionaries had to convince the directors in London that this was a worthy article of commerce. It was difficult to transport commodities to London, as vessels called at the mission stations only irregularly. One missionary complained that a 'great quantity of casks and iron hoops'[71] were wanted to transport the oil, whilst another wrote that 'many tons' of the oil had been 'wasted for want of vessels to put it in'.[72] One evangelical at home wrote to the directors suggesting that if they should

---

[66] Literal translation of a French copy of the Tahitian laws, ibid.
[67] *Evangelical Magazine*, 1830, 86.   [68] *Evangelical Magazine*, 1846, 56.
[69] Letter dated April 1821 from W. Henry, Incoming Letters from South Seas, Box 3, CWM, SOAS.
[70] The Huahine Society for Promoting a Knowledge of God, Instituted October 6th 1828, ibid.
[71] Letter dated 4 February 1819 from W. Henry, ibid.
[72] Letter dated 16 May 1822 from T. and J. Blossom, ibid.

'send out an experienced tradesman (say a plodding Scotsman) & let the article be imported in a similar manner under the guarantee of the Society that the article was genuine, it does appear to me that a very great increase to the funds of the Society would be realized'.[73]

For missionaries, the importance of islanders' subscriptions lay in the fact that they nurtured evangelical charity. Islanders were not urged to give solely because of the financial implications; charity was designed to replace earlier practices such as stealing and barter, as conversion progressed. Pacific islanders were quick to ask that their contributions be acknowledged. The Raiatean church, for example, wrote:

We have collected property for the years that have passed by, three. We have completely cleared up, we now send it to you to look at if you please to write our names in the reports of the Society, write them & print them & send us one or two that our hearts may rejoice. May you have health & peace in doing the work of the Lord.[74]

One missionary wrote to the directors urging that they acknowledge the contributions made by islanders, because a converted group of islanders had formed into a sect which claimed that contributions were being used for purposes other than those for which they were collected.[75] Explaining the necessity for acknowledgement, they wrote:

It would be of importance had you heard of the Prophets &c of Tahiti and of the Visionaries of Maupiti but perhaps you are not aware that one half of their disaffection and speech is against the subscription to the Society ... and all they have against us is our being agents to the Society, consequently embezzlers of People's property, and not a few of the simple have been beguiled by them to the injury of the subscriptions.[76]

The desire for acknowledgement on the part of the islanders might be compared to the way that evangelicals at home desired to see their names in print when they contributed sums to the missionary cause.[77] The strategies that were adopted in describing islanders' giving may be compared with descriptions of the worthy poor in Britain. A letter from a poor contributor was published in the *Evangelical Magazine*, serving as an example to others. The contributor wrote:

---

[73] Letter dated 24 August 1843 from G. Gill to the directors, Home Correspondence, Box 8, ibid.

[74] From Church of Christ at Raiatea, dated 1825, Incoming Letters from the South Seas, Box 4, ibid.

[75] For more on this sect, see Gunson, 'An Account of the Mamaia or Visionary Heresy of Tahiti'.

[76] Letter dated 15 November 1830 from G. Platt, Incoming Letters from the South Seas, Box 7, CWM, SOAS.

[77] See above, chapter 1.

I have been a penny a week subscriber for fifteen years or more to the London Missionary Society. I believe God has greatly blessed me for it, but from reading the above-mentioned Magazines, I came to this conclusion, that I would give five pounds to the Missionary Society more than my penny per week. I now send the five pounds to you, with my poor prayers that God would bless all the nations of the earth, and every poor heathen with the Gospel of Jesus Christ.[78]

In a similar vein, one of the speakers at a meeting of the missionary society of Rarotonga said, 'these are the subscriptions from the churches of Rarotonga – it is very little; but we have not money as you have – what we get we are happy to give'.[79]

Pacific islanders who did not follow these examples were criticised for being greedy. One missionary wrote: 'it is the spirit of accumulating property that causes the people to spend more time than formerly on their own lands ... When all assemble together at the missionary station and a few days after the Sabbath many of them go off again to build a house on their land, to get back for making cloth, in coca-nuts to make oil.'[80] Evangelicals at home who hoarded their wealth were also criticised: 'It is a mournful thing when an aged professor is found clinging to the perishable dust of this world, when the glories of immortality are beginning to open on their view. Surely the thought of heaven ought to relax their tenacious grasp of earth, and to prompt obedience to the Master's precept, "Lay not up for yourselves treasures on earth".'[81]

Though Pacific islanders gave up their gods and took on European clothes, they did not submit without resistance to these new notions of property and to their altered relationship with nature. One missionary wrote about the heretical sect:

Some champions for the Visionary Sect have made it their business to endeavour to make our people believe that they are purchasing the salvation of their souls with this oil that they subscribe. This sect of which I speak, under a false pretence of Devotion wish to undermine the Laws of the Land – the preaching of the Gospel – the Teaching in the Schools – and of course the services of the Missionaries.[82]

Rare comments like this in missionary literature provide glimpses of the local response to missionary practice. Pacific islanders were reinventing forms of evangelical charity to resemble the religions that they had denounced, and the gods to which they prayed.

[78] *Evangelical Magazine*, 1839, 569–70.   [79] *Evangelical Magazine*, 1843, 150.
[80] Letter dated 1 January 1830 from W. P. Crook, Incoming Letters from the South Seas, Box 7, CWM, SOAS.
[81] *Evangelical Magazine* 1835, 407.
[82] Letter dated 18 March 1829 from D. Darling, Incoming Letters from the South Seas, Box 7, CWM, SOAS.

Conclusions

Ludmilla Jordanova writes that 'visitors to exhibitions cannot be treated as passive recipients of ideological positions, conveyed through all the physical aspects of the museum'.[83] This is why it is important to remember the Visionary Sect at the close of this chapter and to state that evangelical theologies were not consumed passively. And yet displays of artefacts were implicated in this process of conversion and civilisation by presenting the argument that nature was distinct from the divine and by pointing to what constituted the old religion in London and the new religion in the Pacific. The cases of the Society's museum could, in this context, portray the vanishing and superstitious cultures of unconverted lands. It is of this calibre of display that James Clifford writes: 'The world's cultures appear in the chronotype as shreds of humanity, degraded commodities, or elevated great art, but always functioning as vanishing "loopholes" or "escapes" from a one dimensional fate.'[84] The missionary museum transported visitors back in time through the history of the evangelised countries, to show what progress had been made in their crusade. Because the objects were now in Britain, they signified that the system of beliefs which confused nature and the divine was no longer followed. The fact that Pacific islanders used to confuse these categories was expected to provoke reflection on the superiority of Christian civilisation.

Scientific ideas were implicated in this quest of demarcation, aided by their theological foundations. Missionaries used instruments such as telescopes and urged islanders to observe their gods with detachment. Scriptural passages presented visitors with explanations of the artefacts from inspired writ, while a concern with use allowed items to be related to each other. Ethnographic discussions of sacrifice and the nature of Pacific deities therefore operated alongside militaristic customs such as the ritualistic abandoning of gods to the fire. Superimposed on this narrative of transformation was the metaphor of light and darkness. This union between science, ethnography and theology is exemplified by the treatment of Pacific gods. 'Idols' were measured and displayed as specimens; but visitors to the museum were asked to see them as spoils from a spiritual war.

Just as islanders were urged to see their denunciation of objects as symbolic of their conversion, missionaries presented them with new objects that respected the value of industry and natural improvement. Clothing can serve as an example. The earlier forms of clothing adopted

---

[83] Ludmilla Jordanova, 'Objects of Knowledge: A Historical Perspective on Museums', in *The New Museology*, ed. Peter Vergo (London, 1989).

[84] James Clifford, *The Predicament of Culture: Twentieth-Century Ethnography, Literature and Art* (Cambridge, Mass., 1998), 244.

in the Pacific often incorporated birds' feathers and the bark of trees. Upon conversion, however, islanders were expected to master nature, by using processes of manufacture. Women were urged to make bonnets, for example, by using grass found on the islands. The islanders' appropriation of European clothes might be connected with the rules governing the attire of the religious in Britain. The possibility of making this comparison points to how missionaries sought to bring islanders out of isolation into the civilised world of commerce.

Stephen Greenblatt writes, 'Museums function, partly by design and partly in spite of themselves, as monuments to the fragility of cultures, to the fall of sustaining institutions and noble houses, the collapse of rituals, the evacuation of myths, the destructive effects of warfare, neglect, and corrosive doubt.'[85] The setting-up of the missionary museum and the appropriation of artefacts such as clothing in the Pacific marked the redefinition of what constituted the Pacific and Britain, in line with such categories as rational, superstitious, converted and unconverted. That reinscription marked the passing away of an older form of knowledge and an earlier set of identities, and this is why Greenblatt's point about fragility may be extended to any practice of exchange, collection and display in any historical period. Yet Greenblatt's statement also sum-marises the militarism of early nineteenth-century collecting practices. Throughout the missionary museum, and in the ceremonies that marked the acquisition of its objects, a pervasive rhetoric of militarism was com-bined with an attention to use and comparison. The transparency of this rhetoric should destabilise later nineteenth-century museums and modern-day collections, where objects continue to be taken from the people who made them, but where military language is seen to be distasteful. How militaristic is any museum in helping to bring about the demise of a parti-cular system of trade, belief or culture by the very display of those artefacts?

There was a system of organisation in the missionary museum and in the practices of collecting and display evidenced in the Pacific. All of these sites were used to instruct viewers to separate the material and the spiritual, and to consider the superiority of the Christian nation over the 'heathen'. The museum placed the peoples who produced artefacts on a continuum from savage to civilised. Thus, competing theologies of nature were at the centre of the encounter in the Pacific. Attitudes to nature could come to define progress, and could serve as the subject of public display. An individual's relation to an object could signify his or her religion. The way in which he or she exchanged objects denoted the practices that constituted that religion.

---

[85] Stephen Greenblatt, 'Resonance and Wonder', in *Exhibiting Cultures: The Poetics and Politics of Museum Display*, ed. Ivan Karp and Steven D. Lavine (Washington, 1991).

Conclusions

In urging South Pacific missionaries to focus their attention on civilisation, rather than indoctrination, the *Quarterly Review* for 1809 described a conversation between King Otoo of Tahiti and a resident missionary.[1] Otoo insisted on seeing the Saviour. If the missionaries could bring down the sun and moon by means of their quadrants, he asked, why could they not bring down their God? In reply, the missionaries insisted that their message involved the '*hidden man of the heart*, its nature, qualities, defilements' and 'exposure to God's wrath'. But because islanders did not trade in unseen deities, and because they believed that divine beings manifested themselves in nature, such a reply was classed as an 'idle tale'.

Nineteenth-century evangelicals held fast to the view that the heart changed at conversion, and that believers experienced spiritual sanctification through the course of their lives, leading to joy, peace and righteous obedience to the will of God. But these beliefs brought them to a dilemma. How could missionaries make Pacific islanders and subscribers to their cause *see* the results of unseen changes? Local people did not respond as the missionaries hoped if the divine message was not illustrated by seen phenomena. And if the success of unseen changes was not paraded in missionary pamphlets, statistical surveys, maps and illustrations of mission settlements, their livelihood was in danger.

Using nature to illustrate the means of personal salvation and the efficacy of societal transformation was the best solution. Pacific islanders already drew heavily on organic forms of thought, and evangelicals at home were steeped in a theology of nature. The manner in which nature was used to illustrate the unseen is exemplified by the comparison of Temoteitei's spiritual growth with a natural historical typology of change or the idealisation of a converted settlement in terms of its ordered plantations and beaming chapels. The need for tangible illustration is also evidenced in the conception of the resurrection as the

[1] *Quarterly Review*, 1809, 54.

seed passing to a twig, and in the representation of the spiritual growth of the educated mind as a natural historical process. But by relating the invisible to the natural, evangelicals entered dangerous epistemological territory.

Did this analogy imply that these two domains were equal? This reductionist anxiety came to the fore in the strict instructions given by Revd David Bogue for using illustrations, and in the prescription of rules for dressing in the Pacific. Such regulations suggest that evangelicals tried hard to keep the visible distinct from the unseen. Yet Tapeoe's imprisonment in a cage or the missionaries' belief that it was necessary to eradicate earlier forms of dress because of their similarity to 'heathen' religious customs indicate a more complicated story. In dealing with this complexity, it is useful to see the distinction between a figure of speech and what is described as unstable. Consequently, the assertion that evangelicals saw Temoteitei as nothing but a natural historical specimen, and conversion as nothing but the adoption of particular modes of dress, husbandry and settlement, is too simplistic. Natural history provided an ambiguous and scriptural language of illustration that made it possible to move between the seen and the unseen.

Missionaries also found natural history important because of the classificatory system that it provided. In 'The Children's Missionary Map of the World' (1844), published by James Nisbet, the various creatures of the world arranged in symmetry framed a map of the world coloured in shades ranging from black to white depending on the degree of evangelisation. In a similar map titled 'Pictorial Missionary Map of the World' (1861?) [Fig C.1], also published by Nisbet, cameo scenes from around the world demonstrated the manner in which societies changed from barbarity to civilisation in correspondence to their ascent to Christian truths [Fig C.2]. A pair of images depicted the 'North American Indians before the gospel' and the 'North American Indians under the influence of the gospel'. The first image shows a man on horseback planting an arrow into the back of his countryman; while the second depicts a scene of order as people help each other across the ice on their way to church. It is not only the colonised who are on display in this map. On the top left two images show scenes from England before and after the introduction of Christianity. The first is a sight of carnage as humans are sacrificed in a huge structure in the form of a giant man, which is about to be burnt. But after the introduction of the gospel, there is a scene of pious order as well-dressed English people make their way to church. The juxtaposition of these two images with the others that frame this map reveals how the progress of non-European societies from 'heathen' to converted was always related to events in England's own ancient past.

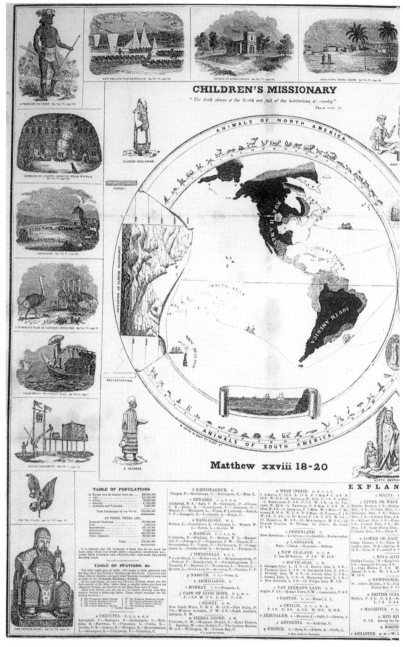

Figure C.1: James Nisbet, 'Children's Missionary Map' (1844).

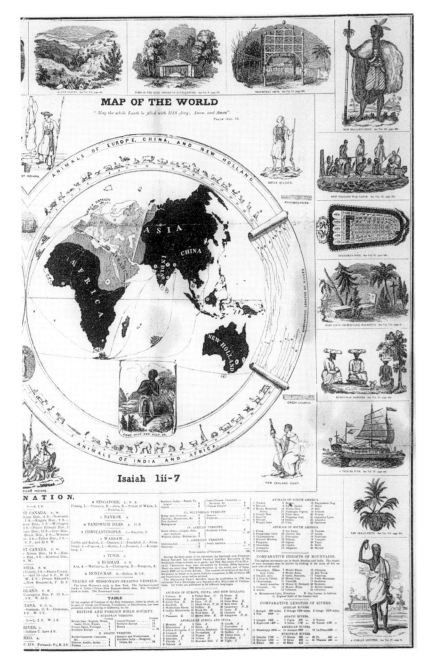

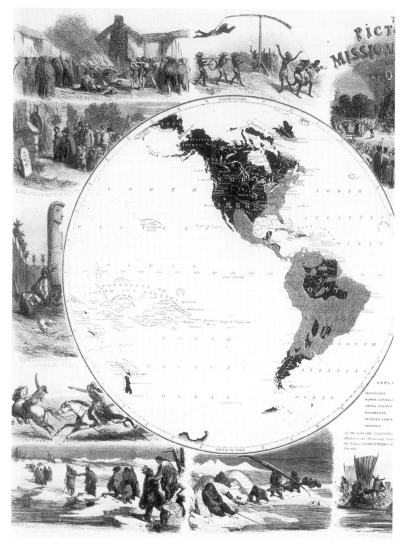

Figure C.2: James Nisbet, 'Pictorial Missionary Map' (1861?).

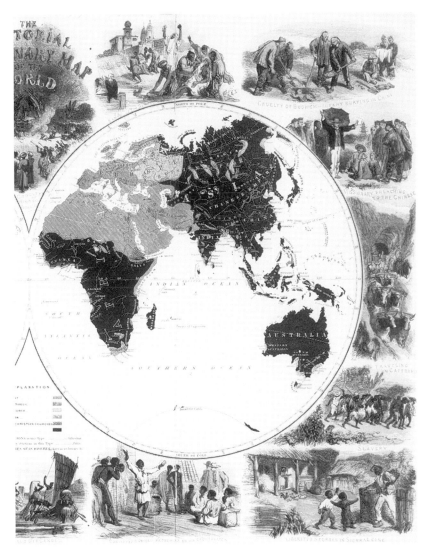

All peoples could be saved. All had once been sinners. And this was why it was necessary to send missionaries to every region of the world, including the poor slums of the metropolis. In the words of a sympathetic article in the *London Quarterly Review* of 1856:

City Missions, Ragged Schools, and many other branches of effort for classes of the population which lay beyond the ordinary and established ministrations of Christianity, are but an expression of the same feeling which has given birth to our Missions in New Zealand and Bengal. Missionary zeal is not anxiety for men who are removed by a certain distance, or distinguished by some savage or romantic peculiarities; but a concern for every man, whether far or near, who is a stranger to the fear and love of God.[2]

The narratives of conversion at home need to be related to those of the South Pacific. In the course of the book, I have related Joseph Lancaster's monitorial scheme for educating the poor in Britain to the education imparted to Pacific islanders. The web of correspondence between Revd Samuel Marsden, Sir Joseph Banks and Arthur Young was said to be vital in coming to terms with missionary agriculture. The displays of the London missionary museum were put into the context of missionary engagements with material culture in the Pacific.

The missionary maps also display an ambiguity between self and other. The act of comparison implies a difference, but since all the nations of the world are ranged on the same piece of paper, a shared humanity is also evidenced. Natural historical modes of classification also employ this concurrent rhetoric of similarity and distinction. By setting bounds to the categories of plant, animal and human, and by presenting typologies of change from seeds to trees, natural history reifies the whole system of nature, while identifying its stages and elements. Therefore, a classification system focuses attention on the compositions of individual members, while contextualising elements in the structure of the whole. In a similar vein, evangelicals could use nature to meditate on their own identity and calibrate their spiritual progress at the same time as they applied nature's categories outwards in order to distinguish converts from 'heathens', and display the benefits of belief to others. Nature could act as a private site at the same time as it publicised difference, and it could move between these various significations with ease. The primary focus of the first half of the book was on the private dimensions of evangelical organicism. I have discussed how believers conceived of conversion, death and the growth of the mind in relation to nature. The second half of the book then moved to the public domain, in order to suggest how the environment could

[2] *London Quarterly Review*, 1856, 216.

embody status in the natural sites of the plantation, the chapel, the museum and the clothed body.

The book has argued that these evangelical uses of natural history constitute a science that contested other forms of natural knowledge in the early nineteenth century. A view of scientific knowledge as material culture is central to this claim: missionaries' science was a scriptural form of seeing that related nature's processes to spiritual truths. By engaging with artefacts and commodities extracted from nature, and natural specimens, evangelicals in the Pacific came to an understanding of who they were, how they should relate to the Deity, and what made them distinct from 'heathens'. This was a genre of science that related to everyday experience and supported faith. The boundaries between diverse genres of science are difficult to trace, and their distinctions did not inhibit co-operation between different practitioners. This might be demonstrated by the carefully orchestrated correspondence between Sir Joseph Banks and Revd Thomas Haweis, and by Revd John Williams' hope that his *A Narrative of Missionary Enterprises* (1837) would attract the attention of many men of science.

Evangelicals aimed to colonise dangerously materialist philosophies of nature by constructing a system of natural history which fitted perfectly with their theologies of personal salvation and post-millenarianism. In an intriguing lecture presented by James Montgomery, an evangelical poet and ardent supporter of missions, who edited Tyerman and Bennet's travel journal to mission stations, this anxiety to contest secularised knowledge comes to the fore. Montgomery's lecture, published under the title *An Essay on the Phrenology of the Hindoos and Negroes* (1829), criticised phrenology so forcefully that it aroused an impassioned defence from Corden Thompson M.D., lecturer in physiology and the nature and treatment of disease at the Sheffield School of Anatomy and Medicine. Montgomery's primary critique of phrenology reveals an elaborate set of reasons for why evangelicals were concerned with constructing alternative forms of natural knowledge. 'If phrenology were like Hindooism, a system of *castes*, and every tribe of mankind, by a fatality of organization, were doomed to be, through all changes of society, savage, semi-barbarian, or civilized', Montgomery wrote, 'I for one, would abjure it without requiring any further evidence of its utter absurdity, point-blank contradiction to all the records of history, the testimony of living experience, and the whole result of man's knowledge of himself and his species.' But more important for Montgomery was phrenology's contradiction of scripture: 'A science of such anomalous consequences could not be of God, and would not stand.' The Bible held that all men had the capacity to be saved, and that all were made in the image of God, a doctrine that was allegedly ignored by phrenology's classification of people in terms of their cranial measurements. The doctrine of improvement, Montgomery urged, was visible even in the animal and vegetable kingdoms. 'If this be the case ... is it possible that the masterpiece of the Almighty should be the only incorrigibly defective work of his hand?'[3]

When evangelicals drew on natural history to classify the peoples of the world, the rhetoric of shared humanity and the desire to hold to the possibility of collective improvement is again visible. Pacific islanders were said to live in unity with nature, but if they respected the distinctions between the vegetable, animal and human and realised that nature pointed to God without embodying the divine, then they could progress in their understanding of Christianity and become like British Christians. In the words of the *Eclectic Review* of 1831: 'human nature, in those islands, may be considered as undergoing a most interesting process of experiment, every stage of which merits a watchful attention'.[4] The language of experimentation and the practices of observation, meditation, classification, cultivation, collection and display that constitute missionary natural history correspond to a competing form of knowledge. In the aftermath of the Enlightenment, evangelicalism was remoulded so as to give believers the confidence to theorise on nature using their own faculties; the increasing secularisation of knowledge made religious science an urgent necessity.

Ironically, though missionaries hoped that this evangelical view of nature would serve as a substitute for Pacific islanders' naturalism, there was a remarkable degree of consonance between the two. Exemplifying Pacific islanders' reliance on nature, in Tahiti the king's house was apparently called '*the Clouds of Heaven*, his double canoe the *Rainbow*, his torch *Lightning*, and the drum which is beat for his amusement *Thunder*'.[5] When Pacific missionaries urged local people to adopt European forms of dress, they hoped that islanders would renounce their naturalism and appropriate a referential view of nature. When Pacific islanders were taught to build chapels, missionaries hoped that they would become industrious in taming the land, and relinquish their connection with the dark and dreary *maraes*. In each of these cases evangelicals believed that one form of knowledge could be substituted for another. The situation was actually more complex. Missionaries encountered people who sought to make metal nails grow; who saw chapels as they had seen *maraes*; who used the alphabet as a prayer and chewed paper as food. It is unclear whether any of these reports are authentic. Nevertheless they reveal that the practices of evangelical

---

[3] James Montgomery, *An Essay on the Phrenology of the Hindoos and Negroes Together with Strictures Thereon by Corden Thompson, M.D.* (London, 1829), 30–1.
[4] Ibid., 93.   [5] *Quarterly Review*, 1809, 44.

natural history were not passively accepted in the islands; they were appropriated and reconstructed in accordance with existent views of nature. The manner in which Pacific islanders drew on crabs and rivers in their sermons to local congregations provides the strongest evidence for this claim.

According to Montgomery, 'Hindoos and Negroes' were not doomed to occupy a lowly status of civilisation because of their cranial characteristics; their idolatrous system of religion had degraded their mental capacity. Once their religions were brushed aside, they would allegedly move up the ladder of civilisation once again. It is just this message that is also presented by the missionary maps. The church of Gorruckpore and the appearance of Free Town, Sierra Leone, contrast in form with the 'Hindoo Amusement' and New Zealand war canoe in the 'Children's Missionary Map'. It was believed that the missionary churches could raise the 'heathen' to a civilised state only after the foundations of earlier systems were brushed aside and demolished. Yet, ironically, there was actually a marked similarity between Pacific islanders' reliance on natural terms and the missionaries' resort to natural history in order to picture the unseen. Though evangelicals subscribed to a doctrine of dramatic change, it seemed that they had discovered religions remarkably similar to their own. The *Quarterly Review* went to the extent of poking fun at how the South Pacific missionaries had found the Trinity in the mythical tales of the islanders, as chapter 4 demonstrates. While these similarities destabilised evangelical narratives of dramatic conversion they could, strangely, confer authenticity on the scriptural story of all humankind's descent from the same 'seed'. The *London Quarterly Review* of 1856 noted: 'Leaving it to the useful studies of the ethnologist to trace the physical indications of man's unity, we rejoice to receive evidence through missionary labour that the Negro is truly man, by tokens of *moral identity* far more conclusive than any physical or intellectual indications.'[6]

In addition to presenting natural history as a science, I have urged a view of missionaries as men of science. Williams' death in Eromanga characterises how an evangelical could read nature at his death. The memory of his death then became connected to the environment of Eromanga, as publicised in a popular print of the event. In the religious context of nineteenth-century Britain, the manner in which an individual died was central to the fulfilment of his or her vocation: Williams apparently mastered the environment in his death and therefore became a worthy man of science. In his *A Narrative of Missionary Enterprises* (1837),

---

[6] *London Quarterly Review*, 1856, 257.

Williams questioned the theories of the geologists Charles Lyell and William Buckland, writing that the 'rapidity of coral growth has been most egregiously overrated and overstated'. Instead he wrote that coral was not made by insects in the sea, but by 'the chemical precipitation of the minute calcerous particles'.[7] It was Williams' daily acquaintance with the landscape of the Pacific that made him a useful source of information for Charles Darwin before their meeting in London.[8] The map which folded out beside the frontispiece of Darwin's *The Structure and Distribution of Coral Reefs* (1842) used observations supplied by Williams, amongst others, to colour various reefs according to whether they were lagoon islands or barrier or fringing reefs. Williams' name, or the names of other informants, did not appear here or in the frontispiece. Instead, appeals were made to Darwin's credentials and the authority of the Lord Commissioners of Her Majesty's Treasury. A huge volume of information was by means of this map reduced to a sheet of paper, and the labours of exploration, observation and collection were obliterated. Williams was forgotten in the history of science as Darwin rose to prominence as a scientific genius.

If we are to come to a historical notion of science in the nineteenth century, it is important that we move beyond these processes of erasure, and avoid grand narratives that chronicle the passage of knowledge step by step in a chain of progress. Instead, this book has urged that missionary natural history could count as a credible form of science in the early nineteenth century and that missionaries could be men of science. It might seem unusual that this natural knowledge has been traced at sites such as the death scene, the museum, the periodical article and the missionary settlement, as opposed to the academic journal, the experiment or the scientific society. Yet if we are to reveal competing forms of knowledge, the manner in which we use our sources and the sources we select for study are crucial in framing our histories. Missionary natural knowledge was trustworthy precisely because it could give meaning to the whole of lived experience and this is why this set of sources is so revealing. In a conversion reported in the *Children's Missionary Magazine*, Edward asked his mother to explain the symbolism of the 'Children's Missionary Map'. 'I like these pictures that go around the map; this is a very curious one called, "Comparative heights of Mountains." What a long time it must have taken to measure them all. I thought some of them were so steep, that people could not get up to the very top.' Edward's mother quickly made him aware of his ignorance of the sciences of measurement. Edward's

<hr>

[7] Williams, *A Narrative of Missionary Enterprises*, 29.
[8] For Williams' meeting with Darwin, see South Sea Personal, Box 2, CWM, SOAS.

queries about the height of mountains fitted perfectly with his other observation: 'I have been looking at it, and have found out several things myself. I see these black parts mean, that the people who live in them are heathens.'[9] It was through such everyday exchanges that missionary natural history was constituted as a science.

Missionary natural history was a form of knowledge that cannot be strictly categorised as religion, science or colonialism; it co-existed in the early nineteenth century with other forms of more studied knowledge; and its practitioners saw themselves as more accurate and able observers than gentlemanly natural historians. By tracing the constitutive practices of missionary natural history, this book serves to show how it is possible to write a history of knowledge from below. While it is tempting to come to a retrospective view of science, where scientific practice is confined to an elite, it has been my aim to stimulate reflection on the diversity of activities that fell under the rubric of natural knowledge in the early nineteenth century.

[9] *Children's Missionary Magazine*, vol. 8, 6–7.

Bibliography

MANUSCRIPT SOURCES

Correspondence, Diaries and Ephemera of the London Missionary Society, The Council for World Mission Archives (CWM), School of Oriental and African Studies (SOAS), London.

Lecture Notes from the Missionary Seminary of the London Missionary Society. Dr Williams' Library (DWL), London.

Sir Joseph Banks Archive and Dawson Turner Correspondence (DTC), Natural History Museum, London.

Sir Joseph Banks Papers, Sutro Library, California.

Revd Thomas Haweis Papers, Australian National Library, Canberra.

PERIODICALS AND REPORTS

Annals of Agriculture
Annual Sermons and Report of the Missionary Society
Botanical Register
Congregational Magazine
Eclectic Review
Edinburgh Review
Educational Record
Evangelical Magazine
Illustrated London News
Lady's Newspaper
London Quarterly Review
Missionary Magazine and Chronicle
Morning Chronicle
Monthly Repository
Notes and Queries
The Patriot
Quarterly Review
Repository of Arts, Literature, Commerce, Manufactures, Fashions and Politics
The Times
Transactions of the Horticultural Soceity

Weekly Messenger
Westminster Review

PRIMARY SOURCES

Anon. *Observations Upon the Practicability and Importance of Applying Some of the Principles of Dr. Bell's System to the Education in Useful Science of the Sons of Those in the Middle and Higher Classes of Society.* London, 1823.
Catalogue of the Missionary Museum, Austin Friars. London, 1826.
Polynesia or Christianity in the Islands of the South Seas. Dublin, 1828.
The London Missionary Game, A Pack of Cards. London, 1837.
Polynesia, or Missionary Toils and Triumphs in the South Seas, a Poem. London, 1839.
The Lamented Death of the Rev. John Williams. London, 1841.
American Board of Commissioners for Foreign Missions on the Use of Missionary Maps at the Monthly Concert. Boston, 1842.
The Missionary Ship 'John Williams'. London, 1844.
Kumumua (in Hawaiian). Honolulu, 1846.
The Return to England of the Missionary Ship 'John Williams' Containing an Account of Her Voyages During Three Years as Related by Capt. Morgan, and Messrs. Barff, Buzacott and Mills. London, 1847.
John Williams, the Missionary. London, 1849.
Catalogue of the Missionary Museum Bloomsfield Street, Finsbury. London, 1900.
Our John Williams 1844–1944. London, 1944.
Practical Books: South Seas, a Handbook for Leaders. London, 1947.
Banks, Joseph. *A Short Account of the Cause of Disease in Corn Called by Farmers the Blight, the Mildew and the Rust.* London, 1815.
The Endeavour Journal of Joseph Banks 1768–1771, 2 vols. London, 1896.
Beechey, F. W. *Narrative of a Voyage to the Pacific and Beering's Strait to Co-Operate with the Polar Expeditions, Performed in His Majesty's Ship Blossom under the Command of Captain F. W. Beechey, R.N., F.R.S. &C. In the Years 1825–8.* London, 1832.
Bell, Andrew. *Extracts of a Sermon on the Education of the Poor, under an Appropriate System, Preached at St. Mary's Lambeth, 28 June 1807.* London, 1807.
Bennet, George, and Daniel Tyerman. *Journal of Voyages and Travels Deputed from the London Missionary Society to Visit the Various Stations in the South Sea Islands, China, India &C in the Years 1821 and 1829 Compiled from Original Documents by James Montgomery*, 2 vols. London, 1831.
Bennett, James. *The Memoirs of the Rev. David Bogue.* London, 1827.
Bingham, Hiram. *A Residence of Twenty-One Years in the Sandwich Islands or the Civil, Religious and Political History of the Islands.* London, republished 1969.
Bligh, William. *A Voyage to the South Sea, Undertaken by Command of His Majesty, for the Purpose of Conveying the Breadfruit Tree to the West Indies, in His Majesty's Ship the 'Bounty' ... Including an Account of the Mutiny on Board the Ship, Etc.* London, 1792.
Boddington, G. *St. Paul's First Epistle to the Corinthians Explained in Simple and Familiar Language.* London, 1839.

Bogue, David. *The Nature and Importance of a Good Education, a Sermon Preached before the Promoters of the Protestant Dissenters' Grammar School, Lately Opened at Mill Hill in the Parish of Hendon, Middlesex*. London, 1808.

Bonar, Andrew, ed. *Incidents of Missionary Enterprise Illustrative of the Progress of Christianity in Heathen Countries and of the Researches, Sufferings and Adventures of Missionaries*. Edinburgh, 1844.

Brown, John. *The Resurrection of Life: An Exposition of First Corinthians Xv*. London, 1852.

Buffon, Louis Leclerc. *Histoire Naturelle*. London, 1792.

Burder, George. *Missionary Anecdotes in Two Parts Exhibiting (I) the Idolatory of Superstition and Cruelty of the Heathen in All Ages and (Ii) the Efficacy of the Gospel in Their Conversion in the Successive Ages of the Christian Era*. London, 1821.

Butler, Joseph. *Analogy of Religion: Natural and Revealed to the Constitution and Course of Nature*, ed. W. E. Gladstone. London, 1907; first printed 1736.

Byron, George. *Voyage of the H. M. S. Blonde to the Sandwich Islands 1824–1825*. London, 1826.

Campbell, John. *The Missionary Farewell; Valedictory Services of the Rev. John Williams with His Parting Address to Which Is Now Added an Account of His Voyage to the South Seas and of His Mournful Death at Erromanga*. London, 1840.

Maritime Discovery and Christian Missions Considered in their Mutual Relations. London, 1840.

The Martyr of Erromanga or the Philosophy of Missions Illustrated from the Labours, Death, and Character of the Late Rev. John Williams. London, 1842.

Carey, William. *An Enquiry into the Obligation of Christians to Use Means for the Conversion of the Heathens*. London, 1792.

Cecil, Richard. *Faith and Purity. Two Charges Addressed to Missionaries Proceeding to the South Seas. To Which Is Added, a Letter Relative to the Preservation of Health*. London, 1838.

Collens, Robert. and Beryl Collens. *John Williams, a Sunday School Celebration*. London, 1949.

Cook, James. *A Voyage toward the South Pole and Round the World Performed in His Majesty's Ships the 'Resolution' and 'Adventure'*, 2 vols. London, 1777.

Cousins, G. *The Story of the South Seas*. London, 1894.

Darwin, Charles. *On the Structure and Distribution of Coral Reefs: Being the First Part of the Geology of the Voyage of the Beagle, under the Command of Capt. Fitzroy, R.N. During the Years 1832 to 1836*. London, 1842.

Darwin, Charles, and Robert Fitzroy. *Narrative of the Surveying Voyages of His Majesty's Ships 'Adventure' and 'Beagle' between the Years 1826 and 1836*. London, 1839.

Davidson, Norman. *John Williams of the South Seas*. London, 1925.

Dibble, Sheldon. *History and General View of the Sandwich Islands' Mission*. New York, 1839.

Ellis, J. J. *John Williams, the Martyr Missionary of Polynesia*, 3rd edn. London, 1890.

Ellis, William. *A Narrative of a Tour through Hawaii or Owhyhee*. London, 1826.

Polynesian Researches During a Residence of Nearly Six Years in the South Sea Islands, 4 vols. London, 1829.

A Vindication of the South-Sea Missions from the Misrepresentations of O. Von Kotzebue, Captain in the Russian Navy. London, 1831.

The History of the London Missionary Society. London, 1844.

Entwistle, Mary, ed. *Islands Everywhere: Stories for 7–9 Year Olds*. London, 1939.

Eveleth, Ephraim. *History of the Sandwich Islands, with an Account of the American Mission Established There in 1820*. Philadelphia, 1831.

Ferguson, R. *Affecting Intelligence from the South Sea Islands: A Letter Addressed to the Directors and Friends of Bible and Missionary Institutions in Great Britain and America*. London, 1839.

Fisher, James. *A Spring-Day: Or Contemplations on Several Occurrences Which Naturally Strike the Eye in That Delightful Season*. Edinburgh, 1808.

Flavell, John. *Navigation Spiritualized: Or, a New Compass for Seamen, Consisting of Xxxii. Points of Pleasant Observations, Profitable Applications, and Serious Reflections: ... Whereunto Is Now Added, 1. A Sober Consideration of the Sin of Drunkenness. 2. The Harlot's-Face in the Scripture-Glass, Etc.*, ed Revd C. Bradley. London, 1822; first printed 1682.

Husbandry Spiritualized: Or the Heavenly Use of Earthly Things, ed. Revd C. Bradley. London, 1822; first printed 1699.

Fox, Joseph. *A Comparative View of the Plans of Education as Detailed in the Publications of Dr. Bell and Mr. Lancaster*, 2nd edn. London, 1809.

An Appeal to the Members of the London Missionary Society against a Resolution of the Directors of That Society Dated 26 March 1810 with Remarks on Certain Proceedings Relative to the Otaheitan and Jewish Missions. London, 1810.

Gill, W. W. *Life in the Southern Isles or Scenes and Incidents in the South Pacific and New Guinea*. London, 1876.

Historical Sketches of Savage Life in Polynesia. London, 1880.

Jottings from the Pacific. London, 1885.

Hawkesworth, John. *An Account of the Voyages Undertaken by the Order of His Present Majesty for Making Discoveries in the Southern Hemisphere*, 2 vols. London, 1773.

Hayes, Ernest. *Wiliamu, Mariner Missionary*. London, 1922.

Horne, Melville. *Letters on Missions Addressed to the Protestant Ministers of the British Churches*. Bristol, 1794.

Hunter, D. D. *A Sermon and Charge Delivered at Zion Chapel, London on July 28, 1796, on Occasion of the Designation of the First Missionaries to the South Sea*. London, 1796.

Jack, Archibald. *Believing Consecration and Service, in Connexion with Missions to Heathen, a Sermon Occasioned by the Lamented Death of the Rev. John Williams, Missionary to the Islands of the South Seas, Delivered in St. Andrew's Chapel, Northshields, on the Lord's Day*. London, 1840.

Jarves, James Jackson. *History of the Hawaiian Sandwich Islands, Embracing their Antiquities, Mythology, Legends, Discovery by Europeans in the Sixteenth-Century, Rediscovery by Cook*. London, 1843.

Keynes, R. D., ed. *Charles Darwin's Beagle Diary*. Cambridge, 1988.

Kotzebue, O. von. *A New Voyage around the World in the Years 1823, 24, 25 and 26*. London, 1830.

Lancaster, Joseph. *Improvements in Education as it Respects the Industrious Classes of the Community.* London, 1803.

Langbridge, A. K. *Won by Blood: The Story of Erromanga, the Martyr Isle.* London, 1922.

Lee, Albert. *John Williams, the New Missionary Series.* London, 1921.

Love, John. *Address to the People of Otaheite with a Short Address to the Members of the London Missionary Society.* London, 1796.

Lovett, Richard. *The History of the London Missionary Society,* 2 vols. London, 1899.

Mathews, Basil. *Yarns of the South Sea Pioneers for Use of Workers among Boys and Girls.* London, 1914.

John Williams, the Ship-Builder. London, 1915.

The Ships of Peace. London, 1919.

If Only I Had a Ship: John Williams of the South Seas. London, 1937.

Matthewman, Phyllis. *John Williams.* London, 1954.

John Williams, a Biography for Children. London, 1954.

Melville, Herman. *Omoo, a Narrative of Adventures in the South Seas; Being a Sequel to the 'Residence in the Marquesas Islands'.* London, 1847.

Montefiore, Arthur. *Heroes Who Have Won Their Crown: David Livingstone and John Williams.* London, 1909.

Montgomery, James. *An Essay on the Phrenology of the Hindoos and Negroes Together with Strictures Thereon by Corden Thompson, M.D.* London, 1829.

Morrison, J. *The Fathers and Founders of the London Missionary Society.* London, 1839.

Moyle, Richard M., ed. *The Samoan Journals of John Williams, 1830–1832.* London, 1984.

Nisbet, James. 'The Children's Missionary Map of the World.' London, 1844.

'The Pictorial Missionary Map of the World.' London, 1861.

Northcott, Cecil. *Southward Ho!* London, 1935.

Glorious Company: One Hundred and Fifty Years Life and Work of the London Missionary Society. London, 1945.

John Williams Sails On. London, 1948.

South Sea Sailor, the Story of John Williams and his Ships. London, 1965.

Orme, William. *A Defence of the Missions in the South Sea and Sandwich Islands against the Misrepresentations Contained in a Late Number of the Quarterly Review in a Letter to the Editor of That Journal.* London, 1827.

Paley, William. *Natural Theology; or, the Evidences of the Existence and Attributes of the Deity ... Collected from the Appearances of Nature.* London, 1803.

Pearsall, Richard. *Contemplations on the Ocean, the Harvest, Sickness and the Last Judgement.* London, 1802.

Portlock, Nathaniel. *A Voyage Round the World, but More Particularly to the North-West Coast of America, Performed in 1785, 1786, 1787 and 1788.* London, 1789.

Pritchard, George. *The Missionary's Reward, or the Success of the Gospel in the Pacific.* London, 1844.

Prout, Ebenezer. *Memoirs of the Rev. John Williams.* London, 1843.

Reason, J., ed. *The Ship Book 1844–1944, Stories, Games, Models Etc.* London, 1944.

Robertson, H. A. *Erromanga: The Martyr Isle*. London, 1902.

Simeon, Charles. *Helps to Composition or Five Hundred Skeletons of Sermons, Several Being the Substance of Sermons Preached before the University*, 2 vols. Cambridge, 1802.

 The True Test of Religion in the Soul or Practical Christianity Delineated. Cambridge, 1817.

Sinclair, Sir John. *Proposals for Establishing by Subscription, a Joint Stock Farming Society for Ascertaining the Principles of Agricultural Improvement*. London, 1799.

Smith, William. *Journal of a Voyage in the Missionary Ship Duff to the Pacific*. New York, 1813.

Spurgeon, Charles. *Manasseh, a Sermon Delivered on Sabbath Morning, November 30, 1856 at the Music Hall, Royal Surrey Gardens*. London, 1856.

Steward, C. S. *Journal of a Residence in the Sandwich Islands During the Years 1823–1825, Including Remarks Upon the Manners and Customs of the Inhabitants; an Account of the Lord Byron's Visit in H. M. S. Blonde and a Description of the Ceremonies Observed at the Internment of the Late King and Queen of Oahu*. London, 1830.

Tolley, Joseph George. *A Paraphrase of Saint Paul's First Epistle to the Corinthians with Explanatory Notes*. London, 1825.

Warr, Winifred. *Practical Books No. 6. South Seas, a Handbook for Leaders*. London, 1947.

Wheeler, Daniel. *Extracts from the Letters and Journal of David Wheeler Now Engaged in a Religious Visit to the Inhabitants of Some of the Islands of the Pacific Ocean*. London, 1839.

Wilkes, Charles. *Narrative of the United States' Exploring Expedition, During the Years 1838–1842*, 5 vols. Washington, 1844.

 ed. *Narrative of the United States Exploring Expedition During the Years 1838–1842*, 5 vols. London, 1845.

Wilks, Marks. *Tahiti; Containing a Review of the Origin, Character and Progress of French Roman Catholic Efforts for the Destruction of English Protestant Missions in the South Seas; Translated from the French*. London, 1844.

Williams, John. *The Compassion of Christ for the Multitude, a Sermon*. London, 1821.

 The Sinner's Friend (in Tahitian). Maidstone, Kent, 1830.

 A Narrative of Missionary Enterprises. London, 1837.

 'The Missionary Pleading for the Perishing Heathen: A Sermon Preached at Surrey Chapel on Sunday Evening October 8th 1837', in *The Pastoral Echo: Nineteen Sermons by Eminent Dissenting Ministers and Others*. London, 1837.

Wilson, W. *A Missionary Voyage to the Southern Pacific Ocean Performed in the Years 1796, 1797, 1798 in the Ship Duff*. London, 1799.

Young, Arthur. *Political Essays Concerning the Present State of the British Empire*. London, 1772.

 An Enquiry into the State of the Public Mind Amongst the Lower Classes. London, 1798.

 Autobiography, ed. M. Betham Edwards. London, 1898.

Young, George. *The Life and Voyages of Captain Cook*. London, 1836.

SECONDARY SOURCES

Abrams, M. H. *The Mirror and the Lamp: Romantic Theory and the Critical Tradition*. Oxford, 1981.

Adas, Michael. *Machines as the Measure of Man: Science, Technology and Ideologies of Western Dominance*. Ithaca and London, 1989.

Agar, Jon, and Crosbie Smith, eds. *Making Space for Science: Territorial Themes in the Shaping of Knowledge*. Basingstoke, 1998.

Agrawal, Arun. 'Dismantling the Divide between Indigenous and Scientific Knowledge', *Development and Change* 25 (1995): 413–39.

Alam, A. 'Imperialism and Science', *Race and Class* 19 (1978): 239–51.

Allen, David. *The Naturalist in Britain: A Social History*. Harmondsworth, 1978.

Altholz, Josef L. *The Religious Press in Britain, 1760–1900*. New York, 1989.

Altick, Richard. *The English Common Reader: A Social History of the Mass Reading Public, 1800–1900*. Chicago, 1957.

Shows of London. Cambridge, Mass., 1978.

Ames, Kenneth. *Death in the Dining Room and Other Tales of Victorian Culture*. Philadelphia, 1992.

Anderson, Benedict. *Imagined Communities: Reflections on the Origin and Spread of Nationalism*. London, 1991.

Anderson, Patricia. *The Printed Image and the Transformation of Popular Culture*. Oxford, 1991.

Appleton, Jay. *The Experience of Landscape*. London, 1975.

Arens, William. *The Man-Eating Myth: Anthropology and Anthropophagy*. Oxford, 1979.

Arnold, David. *Colonizing the Body: State Medicine and Epidemic Disease in Nineteenth-Century India*. Berkeley, Calif., 1993.

The Problem of Nature: Environment, Culture and European Expansion. Oxford, 1996.

Arthur, Chris. 'Exhibiting the Sacred', in *Godly Objects: Museums, Objects and Religion*, edited by Crispin Paine, 1–27. Leicester, 2000.

Astore, William J. *Observing God: Thomas Dick, Evangelicalism and Popular Science in Victorian Britain and America*. Aldershot, 2001.

Baigrie, Brian S., ed. *Picturing Knowledge: Historical and Philosophical Problems Concerning the Use of Art in Science*. Toronto, 1996.

Baker, Lee D. *From Savage to Negro: Anthropology and the Construction of Race*. Berkeley and Los Angeles: University of California Press, 1998.

Ball, A., and M. Martin. *The Price Guide to Baxter Prints*. Woodbridge, Suffolk, 1974.

Banks, R. E. R., B. Eliot, J. Hawkes, D. King-Hele and G. L. Lucas, eds. *Sir Joseph Banks: A Global Perspective*. London, 1994.

Barker, Francis, Peter Hulme and Margaret Iversen, eds. *Cannibalism and the Colonial World*. Cambridge, 1998.

Barnes, Barry. 'Practice as Collective Action', in *The Practice Turn in Contemporary Theory*, edited by Karin Knorr Cetina, Eike von Savigny and Theodre R. Schatzi, 17–28. London, 2001.

Barreca, Regina. *Sex and Death in Victorian Literature.* Basingstoke, 1990.

Barrell, John. *The Dark Side of the Landscape: The Rural Poor in English Painting, 1730–1840.* Cambridge, 1983.

Barrett, Paul, ed. *The Collected Papers of Charles Darwin.* Chicago, 1977.

Basalla, George. 'The Spread of Western Science', *Science* 156 (1967): 611–22.

Baxandall, Michael. *Painting and Experience in Fifteenth Century Italy: A Primer in the Social History of Pictorial Style*, 2nd edn. Oxford, 1998.

Bayly, C. A. *Imperial Meridian: The British Empire and the World 1780–1830.* London, 1989.

  ed. *The Raj: India and the British, 1600–1947.* London, 1990.

  Empire and Information: Intelligence Gathering and Social Communication in India, 1780–1870. Cambridge, 1996.

Bebbington, David. *Patterns in History: A Christian Perspective on Historical Thought.* Leicester, 1979.

  Evangelicalism in Modern Britain: A History from the 1780s to the 1830s. London, 1989.

Becker, C. L. *The Heavenly City of Eighteenth-Century Philosophers.* New Haven, Conn., 1932.

Beer, Gillian. *Darwin's Plots: Evolutionary Narrative in Darwin, George Elliot and Nineteenth-Century Fiction.* Cambridge, 1983.

  'Travelling the Other Way', in *The Cultures of Natural History*, edited by Nicholas Jardine, James Secord and Emma Spary, 332–7. Cambridge, 1995.

Behrman, Cynthia. *Victorian Myths of the Sea.* Athens, Ohio, 1977.

Bermingham, Ann. *Landscape and Ideology: The English Rustic Tradition, 1740–1860.* London, 1986.

  'System, Order and Abstraction: The Politics of Landscape Drawing around 1795', in *Landscape and Power*, edited by W. J. T. Mitchell. Chicago, 1994.

Bertelli, Christopher. 'Theory and Practice: The Response of Farmers to Political Economy and "Scientific Agriculture" in Early Victorian England.' M.Phil. dissertation, University of Cambridge, 1987.

Bewell, Alan. *Wordsworth and the Enlightenment: Nature, Man and Society in the Experimental Poetry.* New Haven, Conn. and London, 1989.

Bickers, Robert A., and Rosemary Seton, eds. *Missionary Encounters: Sources and Issues.* Richmond, Surrey, 1996.

Bindman, David. *Ape to Apollo: Aesthetics and the Idea of Race in the 18th Century.* London, 2002.

Bittereli, U. *Cultures in Conflict.* Cambridge, 1989.

Bourdieu, Pierre. *Reproduction in Education, Society and Culture.* London, 1970.

  'Cultural Reproduction and Social Reproduction', in *Power and Ideology in Education*, edited by A. H. Halsey and Jerome Karabel, 87–8. New York, 1977.

  Outline of a Theory of Practice, translated by Richard Nice. Cambridge, 1977.

  Distinction: A Social Critique of the Judgement of Taste, translated by Richard Nice. London, 1986.

  Rules of Art: Genesis and Structure of the Literary Field. Cambridge, 1996.

Branagan, D. F. 'Samuel Stutchbury: A Natural History Voyage to the Pacific, 1825–27 and its Consequences', *Archives of Natural History* 20 (1993): 69–89.

Brantlinger, Patrick. "How Oliver Twist Learnt to Read and What He Read", in *Culture and Education in Victorian England*, edited by Pauline Fletcher and Patrick Scott, 59–81. London and Toronto, 1990.

Bravo, Michael. 'The Anti-Anthropology of Highlanders and Islanders', *Studies in History and Philosophy of Science* 29A (1998): 369–89.

'Precision and Curiosity in Scientific Travel: James Rennell and the Orientalist Geography of the New Imperial Age (1760–1830)', in *Voyages and Visions: Towards a Cultural History of Travel*, edited by Jas. Elsner and Joan-Pau Rubies, 162–83. London, 1998.

Bravo, Michael, and Sverker Sorlin, eds. *Narrating the Arctic: A Cultural History of Nordic Scientific Practice*. Canton, Mass., 2002.

Breckenbridge, Carol A. 'The Aesthetics and Politics of Colonial Collecting: India at World Fairs', *Comparative Studies in History and Society* 31 (1989): 195–216.

Briggs, Asa. *Victorian Things*. London, 1988.

Brooke, John Hedley. 'Natural Theology from Boyle to Paley', in *New Interactions between Theology and Science*, edited by John Hedley Brooke, R. Hookyaas and Clive Lawless, 8–54. Milton Keynes, 1974.

'The Natural Theology of the Geologists: Some Theological Strata', in *Images of the Earth: Essays in the History of the Environmental Sciences*, edited by L. J. Jordanova and R. Porter, 39–64. Chalfont St Giles, Bucks, 1979.

Science and Religion: Some Historical Perspectives. Cambridge, 1991.

'Religious Belief and the Content of the Sciences', *Osiris* 16 (2001): 3–28.

Brooke, John Hedley, and Geoffrey Cantor. *Reconstructing Nature: The Engagement of Science and Religion*. Edinburgh, 1998.

Brooke, John Hedley, Margaret J. Osler and Jitse M. van der Meer. 'Science in Theistic Contexts: Cognitive Dimensions', *Osiris* 16 (2001): 1–376.

Browne, Janet. *The Secular Ark: Studies in the History of Biogeography*. New Haven, Conn., 1983.

Buck, P. H. 'Arts and Crafts of the Cook Islands', *Bulletin of Bernice P. Bishop Museum* (1971).

Burnett, Graham D. *Masters of All They Surveyed: Exploration, Geography and a British El Dorado*. Chicago, 2000.

Butler, Marilyn. *Romantics, Rebels and Reactionaries: English Literature and its Background, 1760–1830*. Oxford, 1981.

Cain, Peter, and Anthony Hopkins. *British Imperialism*, 2 vols. London, 1993.

Calder, Alex. 'The Temptations of William Pascoe Crook: An Experience of Cultural Difference in the Marquesas, 1796–98', *Journal of Pacific History* 31 (1996): 144–61.

Campbell, I. C. *'Gone Native' in Polynesia: Captivity Narratives and Experiences from the South Pacific*. Westport, Conn., 1998.

Cannadine, David. *Ornamentalism: How the British Saw their Empire*. London, 2001.

Cannon, Susan Fye. *Science in Culture: The Early Victorian Period*. New York, 1978.

Cantor, Geoffrey. *Michael Faraday: Sandeminian and Scientist, a Study of Science and Religion in the Nineteenth Century*. London, 1991.

Cardinal, Roger, and John Elsner, eds. *The Cultures of Collecting*. London, 1994.

Carter, Harold. *His Majesty's Flock: Sir Joseph Banks and the Merinos of George III of England*. Sydney, 1964.

Sir Joseph Banks, 1743–1820. London, 1987.

Carter, Paul. 'Dark with Excess of Bright: Mapping the Coastlines of Knowledge', in *Mappings*, edited by Denis Cosgrove, 125–47. London, 1999.

Certeau, Michel de. *The Practice of Everyday Life*, translated by Steve Randall. Berkeley, 1984.

Chadwick, Owen. *The Victorian Church*, 2 vols. London, 1966.

Chambers, David Wade. 'Does Distance Tyrannize Science?' in *International Science and National Scientific Identity*, edited by R. W. Home and S. G. Kohlstedt, 19–38. Dodrecht and London, 1991.

Chartier, Roger. 'Texts, Printing, Readings', in *The New Cultural History*, edited by Lynn Hunt, 154–75. Berkeley, 1989.

Cultural History: Between Practices and Representations. Cambridge, 1993.

Christie, John, and Sally Shuttleworth, eds. *Nature Transfigured: Essays on Science and Literature, 1700–1900*. Manchester, 1989.

Cipolla, Carlo M. *European Culture and Overseas Expansion*. London, 1970.

Clarke, H. G. *Baxter Colour Prints Pictorially Presented*. London, 1920–1.

Clifford, James. *The Predicament of Culture: Twentieth-Century Ethnography, Literature and Art*. Cambridge, Mass., 1998.

Colley, Linda. *Britons: Forging the Nation, 1707–1820*. London, 1992.

Comaroff, Jean, and John Comaroff. *Of Revelation and Revolution: Christianity, Colonialism and Consciousness in South Africa*. Chicago, 1991.

Comaroff, John. 'Images of Empire, Contests of Conscience: Models of Colonial Domination in South Africa', in *Tensions of Empire: Colonial Cultures in a Bourgeois World*, edited by Laura Stoler. Berkeley, Calif., 1997.

Connerton, P. *How Societies Remember*. Cambridge, 1989.

Coombes, Annie. *Reinventing Africa: Museums, Material Culture and Popular Imagination in Late Victorian and Edwardian England*. New Haven, Conn., and London, 1994.

Cooter, Roger. *The Cultural Meaning of Popular Science: Phrenology and the Organization of Consent in Nineteenth-Century Britain*. Cambridge, 1984.

Cooter, Roger, and Stephen Pumfrey. 'Separate Spheres and Public Places: Reflections on the History of Science Popularization and Science in Popular Culture', *History of Science* 24 (1994): 242.

Cordingley, James. *Early Colour Printing and George Baxter*. London, 1950.

Cosgrove, Denis. *Social Formation and Symbolic Landscape*. London, 1984.

Cosgrove, Denis, and Stephen Daniels, eds. *The Iconography of Landscape: Essays on the Symbolic Representation, Design and Use of Past Environments*. Cambridge, 1988.

Courtney, C. T. *George Baxter, the Picture Painter*. London, 1924.

Crosby, Alfred. *Ecological Imperialism: The Biological Expansion of Europe 900–1900*. Cambridge, 1986.

Cunningham, Andrew, and Nicholas Jardine, eds. *Romanticism and the Sciences*. Cambridge, 1990.

Cunningham, Andrew, and Perry Williams. 'Decentring the 'Big Picture': The Origins of Modern Science and the Modern Origins of Science', *British Journal for the History of Science* 26 (1993): 407–32.

Daniels, Stephen. *Fields of Vision: Landscape Imagery and National Identity in England and the United States*. Princeton, 1993.

Darnton, Robert. *The Kiss of Lamourette: Reflections in Cultural History*. London, 1990.
    The Forbidden Best-Sellers of Pre-Revolutionary France. London, 1996.
Daws, Gawan. *A Dream of Islands: Voyages of Self-Discovery in the South Seas: John Williams, Herman Melville, Walter Murray Gibson, Robert Louis Stevenson, Paul Gauguin*. New York, 1980.
Dening, Greg. *Islands and Beaches: Discourse on a Silent Land, Marquesas, 1774–1880*. Honolulu, 1980.
    Mr Bligh's Bad Language, Passion, Power and Theatre on the Bounty. Cambridge, 1992.
    The Death of William Gooch: A History's Anthropology. Honolulu, 1995.
Desmond, Adrian. 'Artisan Resistance and Evolution in Britain, 1819–1848', *Osiris* 2nd series 3 (1987): 77–110.
    The Politics of Evolution: Morphology, Medicine, and Reform in Radical London. Chicago, 1989.
Dettlebach, M. 'Humboldtian Science', in *Cultures of Natural History*, edited by Nicholas Jardine, James Secord and Emma Spary, 287–304. Cambridge, 1996.
Dolan, Brian. 'Governing Matters: The Values of English Education in the Earth Sciences, 1790–1830.' Ph.D. dissertation, University of Cambridge, 1995.
Drayton, Richard. 'Science and the European Empires', *Journal of Imperial and Commonwealth History* 23 (1995): 503–10.
    Nature's Government: Science, Imperial Britain and the 'Improvement' of the World. New Haven, Conn., 2000.
Driver, Felix. *Geography Militant: Cultures of Exploration and Empire*. Oxford, 2001.
Dubow, Saul, ed. *Science and Society in Southern Africa*. Manchester, 2000.
Durrans, Brian. '(Not) Religion in Museums', in *Godly Things: Museums, Objects and Religion*, edited by Crispin Paine, 57–79. London, 2000.
Edmond, Rod. *Representing the South Pacific: Colonial Discourse from Cook to Gauguin*. Cambridge, 1997.
Edney, M. H. *Mapping an Empire: The Geographical Construction of British India, 1765–1843*. London, 1997.
Elliot, Brent. 'The Promotion of Horticulture', in *Sir Joseph Banks: A Global Perspective*, edited by R. E. R. Banks, B. Elliot, J. G. Hawkes, D. King-Hele and G. L. Lucas, 117–31. London, 1994.
Fagg, W. B. *The Tribal Image: Wooden Figure Sculpture of the World*. London, 1970.
Fan, Fa-ti. *British Naturalists in Qing China: Science, Empire and Cultural Encounter*. Cambridge, Mass., 2004.
Fara, Patricia. 'Isaac Newton Lived Here: Sites of Memory and Scientific Heritage', *British Journal for the History of Science* (2000): 407–26.
    'Images of a Man of Science', *History Today* (October 1998): 42–9.
Feaver, William. *The Art of John Martin*. Oxford, 1975.
Findlen, Paula. *Possessing Nature: Museums, Collecting and Scientific Culture in Early Modern Italy*. Berkeley, Calif., 1994.
Fleming, D. 'Science in Australia, Canada and the United States: Some Comparative Remarks', *Proceedings of the 10th International Congress of the History of Science* 18 (1962): 180–96.
Foster, Georg. *A Voyage Round the World*, 2 vols. London, 1777.

Foucault, Michel. *Discipline and Punish: The Birth of the Prison*, translated by Alan Sheridan. Harmondsworth, 1979.

Frasca-Spada, Marina, and Nicholas Jardine, eds. *Books and the Sciences in History*. Cambridge, 2000.

Frost, Alan, and Jane Samson, eds. *Pacific Empires: Essays in Honour of Glyndwr Williams*. Vancouver, 1999.

Frost, Alan, and Glyndwr Williams, eds. *Terra Australis to Australia*. Melbourne, 1998.

Fudge, Erica, Ruth Gilbert and Susan Wiseman, eds. *At the Borders of the Human: Beasts, Bodies and Natural Philosophy in the Early Modern Period*. Basingstoke, 1999.

Fyfe, Aileen. 'The Reception of William Paley's *Natural Theology* in the University of Cambridge', *British Journal for the History of Science* 30 (1997): 321–35.

    'Industrialised Conversion: The Religious Tract Society and Popular Science Publishing in Victorian Britain.' Ph.D. dissertation, University of Cambridge, 2000.

    'Reading Children's Books in Late Eighteenth-Century Dissenting Families', *Historical Journal* 43 (2000): 453–73.

    Science and Salvation: Evangelical Popular Science Publishing in Victorian Britain. Chicago, 2004.

Galison, Peter, and Caroline Jones, eds. *Picturing Science and Producing Art*. London, 1998.

Garrett, J. *To Live among the Stars: Christian Origins in Oceania*. Geneva, 1982.

Gascoigne, John. *Joseph Banks and the English Enlightenment: Useful Knowledge and Polite Culture*. Cambridge, 1994.

    Science in the Service of Empire: Joseph Banks, the British State and the Uses of Science in the Age of Revolution. Cambridge, 1998.

Gazley, John G. *The Life of Arthur Young*. Philadelphia, 1973.

Geertz, Clifford. *The Interpretation of Cultures: Selected Essays*. New York, 1973.

Gell, Alfred. *Art and Agency: An Anthropological Theory*. Oxford, 1998.

Gillespie, Richard, and David Wade Chambers. 'Locality in the History of Science: Colonial Science, Technoscience, and Indigenous Knowledge', *Osiris*, 2nd series 15 (2000): 221–40.

Gillispie, Charles. *Genesis and Geology: A Study in the Relations of Scientific Thought, Natural Theology and Social Opinion in Great Britain 1790–1850*. Cambridge, Mass., 1996.

Goodhall, Norman. *A History of the London Missionary Society, 1895–1945*. Oxford, 1954.

Greenblatt, Stephen. 'Resonance and Wonder', in *Exhibiting Cultures: The Poetics and Politics of Museum Display*, edited by Ivan Karp and Steven D. Lavine, 43–4. Washington, 1991.

    Marvellous Possessions: The Wonder of the New Age. Cambridge, 1991.

Greenhalgh, Paul. *Ephemeral Vistas: The Expositions Universelles, Great Exhibitions and World's Fairs, 1851–1939*. Manchester, 1998.

Grove, Richard. *Green Imperialism: Colonial Expansion, Tropical Island Edens, and the Origins of Environmentalism, 1600–1860*. Cambridge, 1995.

'Indigenous Knowledge and the Significance of South-West India for Portuguese and Dutch Constructions of Tropical Nature', in *Nature and the Orient: The Environmental History of South and South-East Asia*, edited by Richard Grove, Vinita Damodaran and S. Sangwan. Delhi, 1998.

Gunson, Niel. 'An Account of the Mamaia or Visionary Heresy of Tahiti, 1826–1841', *Journal of Polynesian Society* 71 (1962): 209–43.

'Co-operation without Paradox: A Reply to Dr Strauss', *Historical Studies Australia and New Zealand* 11 (1963–5): 513–34.

'Missionary Interest in British Expansion in the South Pacific in the Nineteenth Century', *Journal of Religious History* 3 (1964): 296–313.

'On the Incidence of Alcoholism and Intemperance in Early Pacific Missions', *Journal of Pacific History* 1 (1966): 43–62.

'The Out-going Correspondence of the Australasian Representatives of the London Missionary Society, 1866–1912', *Journal of Pacific History* 6 (1971): 161–3.

'John Williams and his Ship: The Bourgeois Aspirations of a Missionary Family', in *Questioning the Past: A Selection of Papers in History and Government*, edited by D. P. Crook, 73–95. St Lucia, Queensland, 1972.

Messengers of Grace: Evangelical Missionaries in the South Seas, 1797–1860. Melbourne, 1978.

'British Missionaries and their Contribution to Science in the Pacific Islands', in *Darwin's Laboratory*, edited by Roy Macleod and Philip Rehbock, 283–316. Honolulu, 1994.

Gutch, John. *Beyond the Reefs: The Life of John Williams, Missionary*. London, 1974.

Hall, Catherine. *Civilising Subjects: Metropole and Colony in the English Imagination, 1830–1867*. Oxford, 2002.

Harrison, J. F. C. *Learning and Living 1790–1960: A Study in the History of the English Adult Education Movement*. London, 1961.

The Second Coming: Popular Millenarianism, 1780–1850. New Brunswick, N. J., 1979.

Harrison, Mark. *Crowds and History*. Cambridge, 1988.

Hart, D. G., David Livingstone and Mark Noll, 'Introduction', in *Evangelicals and Science in Historical Perspective*, edited by D. G. Hart, David Livingstone and Mark Noll, 3–13. Oxford, 1999.

Headrick, Daniel. *The Tools of Empire: Technology and European Imperialism in the Nineteenth Century*. New York and Oxford, 1981.

Tentacles of Progress: Technology Transfer in the Age of Imperialism, 1850–1940. New York, 1988.

Healey, Chris. *From the Ruins of Colonialism: History as Social Memory*. Cambridge, 1997.

Hemingway, Andrew. *Landscape Imagery and Urban Culture in Early Nineteenth-Century Britain*. Cambridge, 1992.

Hepper, Nigel, ed. *Plant Hunting for Kew*. London, 1989.

Herbert, Chris. *Culture and Anomie: Ethnographic Imagination in the Nineteenth Century*. Chicago and London, 1991.

Hilton, Boyd. *Age of Atonement: The Influence of Evangelicalism on Social and Economic Thought, 1785–1865*. Oxford, 1988.

Hindmarsh, D. Bruce. 'Patterns of Conversion in Early Evangelical History and Overseas Mission Experience', in *Christian Missions and the Enlightenment*, edited by Brian Stanley, 71–98. Richmond, Surrey, 2001.

Hobsbawm, Eric, and Terence Ranger, eds. *The Invention of Tradition.* Cambridge, 1983.

Holderness, B. A., and Michael Turner, eds. *Land, Labour and Agriculture, 1700–1920: Essays for Gordon Mingay.* London, 1991.

Hooper-Greenhill, Eilean. *Museums and the Shaping of Knowledge.* London, 1992.

Hopkins, Anthony. 'Back to the Future: From National History to Imperial History', *Past and Present* 164 (1999): 198–243.

Horn, Pamela. *The Victorian and Edwardian Schoolchild.* Gloucester, 1989.

Hudson, Keith. *Patriotism with Profit: British Agricultural Societies in the Eighteenth and Nineteenth Centuries.* London, 1972.

Hunt, Lynn, ed. *New Cultural History.* Berkeley, Calif., 1989.

Hyam, Ronald. *Britain's Imperial Century, 1815–1914: A Study of Empire and Expansion*, 2nd edn. Basingstoke, 1993.

Inkster, Ian. 'Scientific Enterprise and the Colonial Model, Observations on Australian Experience in Historical Context', *Social Studies of Science* 15 (1985): 677–704.

Irschick, Eugene. *Dialogue and History: Constructing South India, 1795–1895.* Berkeley, Calif., 1994.

Jalland, Pat. *Death in the Victorian Family.* Oxford, 1996.

Jardine, Nicholas, James Secord and Emma Spary, eds. *The Cultures of Natural History.* Cambridge, 1995.

Jardine, Nicholas, and Emma Spary. 'The Natures of Cultural History', in *The Cultures of Natural History*, edited by Nicholas Jardine, Emma Spary and James Secord, 3–13. Cambridge, 1995.

Johns, Adrian. *The Nature of the Book: Print Knowledge in the Making.* Chicago, 1998.

'Science and the Book in Modern Cultural Historiography', *Studies in History and Philosophy of Science* 29A (1998): 167–94.

Jones, Max. *The Last Great Quest: Captain Scott's Antarctic Sacrifice.* Oxford, 2003.

Jordan, John, and Robert Patten, eds. *Literature in the Marketplace: Nineteenth-Century British Publishing and Reading Practices.* Cambridge, 1995.

Jordanova, Ludmilla. 'Objects of Knowledge: A Historical Perspective on Museums', in *The New Museology*, edited by Peter Vergo, 22–40. London, 1989.

Defining Features: Scientific and Medical Portraits 1660–2000. London, 2000.

Jupp, Peter C., and Clare Gittings, eds. *The Changing Face of Death: Historical Accounts of Death and Disposal.* Basingstoke, 1997.

Death in England: An Illustrated History. Manchester, 1999.

Knott, J. R. 'Characterising Protestant Martyrs', *Sixteenth Century Journal* 27 (1996): 721–34.

Kooiman, Dick. 'The Gospel of Coffee: Mission, Education and Employment in Travencore', in *Conversion, Competition and Conflict: Essays on the Role of Religion in Asia*, edited by Dick Kooiman, Otto van den Muijzenberg and Peter van der Veer, 185–214. Amsterdam, 1984.

Kuklick, H. *The Savage Within: The Social History of British Anthropology.* Cambridge, 1991.

Kuklick, Henrika, and Robert E. Kohler. 'Introduction to 'Science in the Field'', *Osiris* 2nd series, 11 (1996): 1–14.

Kumar, Deepak. 'Patterns of Colonial Science in India', *Indian Journal for History of Science* 15 (1980): 105–19.

ed. *Science and Empire: Essays in Indian Context 1700–1947.* Delhi, 1991.

Science and the Raj, 1857–1905. Delhi, 1997.

Kusamitsu, Toshio. 'Great Exhibitions before 1851', *History Workshop Journal* 9 (1980): 70–89.

Lamb, Jonathan. *Preserving the Self in the South Seas.* Chicago and London, 2001.

Latour, Bruno. *Science in Action: How to Follow Scientists and Engineers through Society.* Milton Keynes, 1987.

Latourette, K. S. *Christianity in a Revolutionary Age*, 5 vols. New York, 1958.

Lawrence, Christopher, and Steven Shapin, eds. *Science Incarnate: Historical Embodiments of Natural Knowledge.* Chicago, 1998.

Layton, David. *Science for the People.* London, 1973.

Lestringant, Frank. *Cannibals: The Discovery and Representation of the Cannibal from Columbus to Jules Verne*, translated by Rosemary Morris. London, 1997.

Lewis, C. T. Courtney. *George Baxter, his Life and Work.* London, 1972.

Lightman, Bernard. *The Origins of Agnosticism: Victorian Unbelief and the Limits of Knowledge.* Baltimore, 1987.

'"The Voices of Nature": Popularising Victorian Science', in *Victorian Science in Context*, edited by Bernard Lightman, 187–211. Chicago and London, 1990.

'The Visual Theology of Victorian Popularizers of Science: From Reverent Eye to Chemical Retina', *Isis* 91 (2000): 651–80.

'Victorian Sciences and Religions: Discordant Harmonies', *Osiris* 16 (2001): 343–66.

Lincoln, Margarette, ed. *Science and Exploration in the Pacific: European Voyages to the Southern Oceans in the Eighteenth Century.* Woodbridge, Suffolk, 1998.

Lindberg, David C., and Ronald L. Numbers, eds. *God and Nature: Historical Essays on the Encounter between Christianity and Science.* Berkeley, Calif., 1986.

Livingstone, David N. *Darwin's Forgotten Defenders: The Encounter between Evangelical Theology and Evolutionary Thought.* Grand Rapids, Mich., 1987.

The Geographical Tradition: Episodes in the History of a Contested Enterprise. Oxford, 1992.

'Situating Evangelical Responses to Evolution', in *Evangelicals and Science in Historical Perspective*, edited by D. G. Hart, David Livingstone and Mark Noll, 193–219. Oxford, 1999.

Llewellyn, Nigel. *The Art of Death: Visual Culture in the English Death Ritual, c.1500–c.1800.* London, 1991.

Lorimer, Douglas. *Colour, Class and the Victorians: English Attitudes to the Negro in the Mid-Nineteenth Century.* Leicester, 1978.

Lowenthal, David. *The Past is a Foreign Country.* Cambridge, 1985.

McCalman, Ian. *Radical Underworld: Prophets, Revolutionaries and Pornographers in London, 1795–1840.* Cambridge, 1988.

McCann, Philip. 'The Newfoundland School Society 1823–55: Missionary Enterprise or Cultural Imperialism?' in *Benefits Bestowed: Education and British Imperialism*, edited by J. A. Mangan, 94–112. Manchester, 1998.

McCormick, E. H. *Omai, Pacific Envoy*. Auckland, 1977.

Mackay, David. *In the Wake of Cook: Exploration, Science and Empire*. London, 1985.

MacKenzie, John, ed. *Propaganda and Empire: The Manipulation of British Public Opinion 1880–1960*. Manchester, 1984

   Imperialism and Popular Culture. Manchester, 1986.

   Imperialism and the Natural World. Manchester, 1990.

   The Empire of Nature: Hunting, Conservation, and British Imperialism. Manchester, 1998.

McLeish, John. *Evangelical Religion and Popular Education: A Modern Interpretation*. London, 1969.

Macleod, Roy. 'On Visiting the "Moving Metropolis": Reflections on the Architecture of Imperial Science', in *Scientific Colonialism: A Cross Cultural Comparison*, 1–15. Washington, D.C., 1987.

   'Passages in Imperial Science: From Empire to Commonwealth', *Journal of World History* 4 (1993): 117–50.

   'Nature and Empire: Science and the Colonial Enterprise', *Osiris* 2nd series, 15 (2000): 1–317.

Macleod, Roy, and Fritz Rehbock, eds. *Nature in its Greatest Extent: Western Science in the Pacific*. Honolulu, 1988.

   eds. *Darwin's Laboratory: Evolutionary Theory and Natural Selection*. Honolulu, 1994.

McManners, John. *Death and the Enlightenment: Changing Attitudes to Death among Christians and Unbelievers in Eighteenth-Century France*. Oxford, 1981.

Mangan, J. A. 'Introduction', in *Benefits Bestowed: Education and British Imperialism*, edited by J. A. Mangan, 1–22. Manchester, 1998.

Marshall, P. J., ed. *The Oxford History of the British Empire*, vol. 2: *The Eighteenth Century*, edited by Wm. Roger Louis. Oxford, 1998.

Martin, Roger. *Evangelicals United: Ecumenical Stirrings in Pre-Victorian Britain, 1795–1830*. London, 1983.

Maxwell, Anne. *Colonial Photography and Exhibitions: Representations of the 'Native' and the Making of European Identities*. Leicester, 1999.

Maxwell, Ian Douglas. 'Civilization or Christianity? The Scottish Debate on Mission Methods, 1750–1835', in *Christian Missions and the Enlightenment*, edited by Brian Stanley, 123–40. Richmond, Surrey, 2001.

Miller, Charles, ed. *Missions and Missionaries in the Pacific*. New York, 1985.

Miller, D. P., and P. H. Reill, eds. *Visions of Empire: Voyages, Botany and Representations of Nature*. Cambridge, 1996.

Mingay, G. E. *A Social History of the English Countryside*. London, 1990.

   Land and Society in England 1750–1980. London, 1994.

   Rural Life in Victorian England. London, 1998.

Mitchell, W. J. T. 'Imperial Landscape', in *Landscape and Power*, edited by W. J. T. Mitchell, 5–34. Chicago, 1994.

   Picture Theory: Essays on Verbal and Visual Representation. Chicago, 1997.

Mitchison, R. *Agricultural Sir John: The Life of Sir John Sinclair of Ulster 1754–1835*. London, 1962.

Moore, James. *The Post-Darwinian Controversies: A Study of the Protestant Struggle to Come to Terms with Darwin in Great Britain and America, 1870–1900*. Cambridge, 1979.

    History, Humanity and Evolution: Essays for John C. Greene. Cambridge, 1989.

    'Religion and Science', in *Modern Biological and Earth Sciences*, edited by David Livingstone and Ronald Numbers, forthcoming.

Moorehead, Alan. *The Fatal Impact: The Invasion of the South Pacific, 1767–1840*. London, 1968.

Morley, John. *Death, Heaven and the Victorians*. London, 1971.

Morrell, W. P. *Britain in the Pacific Islands*. Oxford, 1960.

Morus, Iwan. 'Currents from the Underworld: Electricity and the Technology of Display in Early Victorian England', *Isis* 84 (1993): 50–69.

Murray, David. *Museums, their History and their Use*. Glasgow, 1904.

Nandy, Ashis. *The Intimate Enemy: Loss and Recovery of Self under Colonialism*. Oxford, 1983.

Neill, Stephen. *A History of Christian Missions*. Harmondsworth, 1964.

Newton, Michael. 'Bodies without Souls: The Case of Peter the Wild Boy', in *At the Borders of the Human: Beasts, Bodies and Natural Philosophy in the Early Modern Period*, edited by Erica Fudge, Ruth Gilbert and Susan Wiseman, 196–214. Basingstoke, 1999.

Nicholson, M. 'Alexander Von Humboldt, Humboldtian Science, and the Origins of the Study of Vegetation', *History of Science* 25 (1987): 167–94.

Nicholson, M. H. *Mountain Gloom and Mt Glory*. New York, 1959.

Noll, Mark. *The Rise of Evangelicalism: The Age of Edwards, Whitefield and the Wesleys*. Leicester, 2004.

Numbers, Ronald, and John Stenhouse, eds. *Disseminating Darwinism: The Role of Place, Race, Religion and Gender*. Cambridge, 1999.

Obeyesekere, Gananath. *The Apotheosis of Captain Cook*. Princeton, N.J., 1992.

    '"British Cannibals": Contemplation of an Event in the Death and Resurrection of James Cook, Explorer', *Critical Inquiry* 18 (1992): 630–54.

Orchard, Stephen. 'English Evangelical Eschatology, 1790–1850', Ph.D. dissertation, University of Cambridge, 1969.

    'The Origins of the Missionary Society', *Journal of the United Reformed Church History Society* 24 (1996): 440–8.

Ospovat, Don. *The Development of Darwin's Theory: Natural History, Natural Theology, and Natural Selection, 1838–1859*. Cambridge, 1981.

Outram, Dorinda. 'The Languages of Natural Power: The "Eloges" of Georges Cuvier and the Public Language of Nineteenth Century Science', *History of Science* 16 (1978): 153–78.

    Georges Cuvier: Vocation, Science and Authority in Post-Revolutionary France. Manchester, 1984.

Pagden, A. *European Encounters with the New World*. New Haven, Conn., and London, 1993.

Palladino, P., and M. Worboys. 'Science and Imperialism', *Isis* 84 (1993): 91–102.

Pang, Alex Soojung Kim. 'Visual Representation and Post-Constructivist History of Science', *Historical Studies in the Physical Sciences* 28 (1997): 139–71.

    Empire and the Sun: Victorian Solar Eclipse Expeditions. Stanford, Calif., 2002.

Pearce, Susan. *On Collecting: An Investigation into Collecting in the European Tradition*. London, 1994.

Pearson, B. *Rifled Sanctuaries: Some Views of the Pacific Islands in Western Literature to 1900, the Macmillan Brown Lectures, 1982*. Auckland, 1984.

Pendered, M. *John Martin, Painter, his Life and Times*. London, 1923.

Petitjean, P., C. Jami, and A. M. Moulin, eds. *Science and Empires: Historical Case Studies about Scientific Development and European Expansion*. Dordrecht, 1992.

Piggin, Stuart. *Making Evangelical Missionaries 1789–1858: The Social Background, Motives and Training of British Protestant Missionaries to India*. Abingdon, 1984.

Porter, Andrew. 'Commerce and Christianity: The Rise and Fall of a Nineteenth-Century Missionary Slogan', *Historical Journal* 28 (1985): 597–621.

   ed. *Atlas of British Overseas Expansion*. London, 1991.

   'Religion and Empire: British Expansion in the Long Nineteenth Century, 1780–1914', *Journal of Imperial and Commonwealth History* 20 (1992): 370–90.

   '"Cultural Imperialism" and Protestant Missionary Enterprise, 1780–1914', *Journal of Imperial and Commonwealth History* 25 (1997): 367–91.

   The Council for World Mission and its Archival Legacy: A Special Lecture Given on 18 March 1999. London, 1999.

   ed. *The Nineteenth Century*. vol. III of *The Oxford History of the British Empire*, edited by Wm. Roger Louis. Oxford, 1999.

   'Religion, Missionary Enthusiasm, and Empire', in *The Oxford History of the British Empire*, vol. III: *The Nineteenth Century*, edited by Andrew Porter, 222–45. Oxford, 1999

   Religion Versus Empire? British Protestant Missionaries and Overseas Expansion, 1700–1914. Manchester, 2004.

Prakash, Gyan. *Another Reason: Science and the Imagination of Modern India*. Princeton, N.J., 1999.

Pratt, Mary Louise. *Imperial Eyes: Travel Writing and Transculturation*. London, 1992.

Pyenson, Lewis. 'Pure Learning and Political Economy: Science and European Expansion in the Age of Imperialism', in *New Trends in the History of Science*, edited by H. J. M. Bos, L. C. Palm, H. A. M. Snelders and R. P. W. Visser, 209–78. Amsterdam, 1989.

   'Cultural Imperialism and Exact Sciences Revisited', *Isis* 84 (1993): 10–108.

Qureshi, Sadia. 'Displaying Sara Baartman, the Hottentot Venus.' M.Phil. dissertation, University of Cambridge, 2001.

Reingold, N., and M. Rothenberg. *Scientific Colonialism: A Cross Cultural Comparison*. Washington, D.C., 1987.

Richardson, Alan. *Literature, Education and Romanticism: Reading as Social Practice 1780–1832*. Cambridge, 1994.

Richardson, Ruth. *Death, Dissection and the Destitute*. London, 1998.

Rosenthal, A. 'She's Got the Look! Eighteenth Century Female Portrait Painters and the Psychology of a Potentially Dangerous Employment', in *Portraiture: Facing the Subject*, edited by Joanna Woodall, 147–66. Manchester, 1997.

Rosman, Doreen. *Evangelicals and Culture*. Aldershot, 1992.

Rousseau, G. S., ed. *Organic Form: The Life of an Idea*. London and Boston, 1972.

Rowell, G. *Hell and the Victorians: A Study of Nineteenth Century Theological Controversies Concerning Eternal Punishment and the Future Life*. Oxford, 1974.

Royle, E. 'Mechanics' Institutes and the Working Classes, 1840–1860', *Historical Journal* 14 (1971): 305–21.

Rudwick, Martin. 'The Emergence of a Visual Language for Geological Science, 1760–1840', *History of Science* 14 (1976): 149–95.

    'Senses of the Natural World and Senses of God: Another Look at the Historical Relation of Science and Religion', in *The Sciences and Theology in the Twentieth Century*, edited by A. R. Peacocke, 241–61. Stocksfield, Northumberland, 1981.

Rugg, Julie. 'From Reason to Regulation, 1760–1850', in *Death in England: An Illustrated History*, edited by Peter Jupp and Clare Gittings, 202–27. Manchester, 1999.

Russell, Colin. *Science and the Social Change 1700–1900*. London, 1983.

Ryan, James. *Picturing Empire: Photography and the Visualisation of the British Empire*. London, 1997.

Sahlins, Marshall. *Islands of History*. London, 1987.

    How 'Natives' Think About Captain Cook for Example. Chicago, 1995.

Said, Edward. *Orientalism*. Harmondsworth, 1991.

    Culture and Imperialism. London, 1993.

Salmond, Anne. *Between Worlds: Early Exchanges between Maori and Europeans 1773–1815*. Honolulu, 1997.

Samson, Jane. *Imperial Benevolence: Making British Authority in the Pacific Islands*. Honolulu, 1998.

    'Ethnology and Theology: Nineteenth-Century Mission Dilemmas in the South Pacific', in *Christian Missions and the Enlightenment*, edited by Brian Stanley, 99–122. Richmond, Surrey, 2001.

Samuel, R. *Theatres of Memory: Past and Present in Contemporary Culture*. London, 1994.

Sanborn, Geoffrey. *The Sign of the Cannibal: Melville and the Making of a Post-Colonial Reader*. Durham, 1998.

Sangawan, S. 'Indian Response to European Science and Technology 1757–1857', *British Journal for the History of Science* 21 (1988): 211–32.

    'The Strength of a Scientific Culture and 19th Century India: Interpreting Disorder in Colonial Science', *Indian Economic and Social History Review* 34 (1997): 217–50.

Sangster, Paul. *Pity My Simplicity: The Evangelical Revival and the Religious Education of Children 1738–1800*. London, 1963.

Scarr, Deryck. *The History of the Pacfic Islands: Kingdoms of the Reefs*. Melbourne, 1990.

Scarry, Elaine. *The Body in Pain: The Making and Unmaking of the World*. Oxford, 1987.

Schaffer, Simon. 'Scientific Discoveries and the End of Natural Philosophy', *Social Studies in Science* 16 (1986): 387–90.

    'The Earth's Fertility as a Social Fact in Early Modern Britain', in *Nature and Society in Historical Context*, edited by Bo Gustafsson, Roy Porter and Mikulas Teich, 124–47. Cambridge, 1997.

Schmitt, Robert C. 'The Missionary "Censuses" Tahiti', *Journal of Polynesian Society* 76 (1967): 27–34.

Scott, Colin. 'Science for the West, Myth for the Rest?: The Case of James Bay Cree Knowledge Construction', in *Naked Science: Anthropological Inquiry into the Boundaries, Power and Knowledge*, edited by Laura Nader. New York, 1996.

Secord, Anne. 'Corresponding Interests: Artisans and Gentlemen in Nineteenth-Century Natural History', *British Journal for the History of Science* 27 (1994): 383–408.

'Science in the Pub: Artisan Botanists in Early Nineteenth-Century Lancashire', *History of Science* 24 (1994): 270–315.

'Pleasure and Power of Pictures in Early Nineteenth-Century Popular Science', *Isis* 93 (2002): 28–57.

'Artisan Naturalists: Science as Popular Culture in Nineteenth-Century England.' Ph.D. dissertation, University of London, 2002.

Secord, James. 'King of Siluria: Roderick Murchison and the Imperial Theme in Nineteenth-Century British Geology', *Victorian Studies* 25 (1982): 413–42.

'Newton in the Nursery: Tom Telescope and the Philosophy of Tops and Balls, 1761–1838', *History of Science* 23 (1985): 127–51.

'The Big Picture', *British Journal for the History of Science* 26, special edited volume (1993): 387–483.

Victorian Sensation: The Extraordinary Publication, Reception, and Secret Authorship of Vestiges of the Natural History of Creation. Chicago, 2000.

Sekora, John. *Luxury: The Concept in Western Thought from Eden to Smollett.* London, 1977.

Shapin, Steven, and Barry Barnes. 'Science, Nature and Control: Interpreting Mechanics' Institutes', *Social Studies of Science* 7 (1997): 31–74.

Sharpe, Jim. 'History from Below', in *New Perspectives on Historical Writing*, edited by Peter Burke, 24–41. Cambridge, 1991.

Shattock, Joanne, and Michael Wolff, eds. *The Victorian Periodical Press: Samplings and Soundings.* Leicester, 1982.

Shaw, B. D. 'Body/Power/Identity and Christian Perceptions of the Passions of the Martyrs', *Journal of Early Christian Studies* 14 (1996): 269–312.

Sheets-Pyenson, Susan. 'Popular Science Periodicals in Paris and London and the Emergence of a Low Scientific Culture, 1820–1875', *Annals of Science* 42 (1985): 549–72.

'Cathedrals of Science: The Development of Colonial Natural History Museums During the Late Nineteenth Century', *History of Science* 25 (1987): 279–300.

Shineberg, D. L. *They Came for Sandalwood: A Study of the Sandalwood Trade in the South West Pacific, 1830–1865.* Melbourne, 1967.

Shortland, Michael, and Richard Yeo, eds. *Telling Lives: Essays on Scientific Biography.* Cambridge, 1996.

Silver, Harold. *Education as History: Interpreting Nineteenth and Twentieth Century Education.* London, 1983.

Simon, Brian. 'The History of Education: Its Importance for Understanding', in *The State and Educational Change: Essays in the History of Education and Pedagogy*, edited by Brian Simon, 3–19. London, 1994.

Sivasundaram, Sujit. 'Making Science: Man, Nature and British Missionaries in the South Pacific, 1820–1880', M.Phil. dissertation, University of Cambridge, 1998.

'Natural History Spiritualized: Civilizing Islanders, Cultivating Breadfruit and Collecting Souls', *History of Science* 32 (2001): 417–43.

'Nature Speaks Theology: Colonialism, Cultivation and Conversion in the Pacific, 1795–1850', Ph.D. dissertation, University of Cambridge, 2001.

'John Williams', in *Dictionary of Evangelical Biography*, edited by David Bebbington, Timothy Larsen and Mark Noll, 737–9. Leicester, 2003.

'The Periodical as Barometer: Spiritual Measurement and the *Evangelical Magazine*', in *Culture and Science in the Nineteenth-Century Media*, edited by Geoffrey Cantor, Louise Henson, Sally Shuttleworth and Jonathan Topham, 43–55. Woodbridge, Suffolk, 2004.

'Redeeming Memory: The Martyrdoms of Captain James Cook and Reverend John Williams', in *Captain James Cook: Explorations and Reassessments*, edited by Glyndwr Williams, 201–29. London, 2004.

Smith, Bernard. *European Vision and the South Pacific*. New Haven, Conn., 1985.

Imagining the Pacific: In the Wake of the Cook Voyage. New Haven, Conn., 1992.

Smith, Bernard, and Alwyne Wheeler, eds. *The Art of the First Fleet and Other Early Australian Drawings*. New Haven, Conn., and London, 1988.

Smith, Vanessa. *Literary Culture and the Pacific: Nineteenth-Century Textual Encounters*. Cambridge, 1998.

Snobelen, Stephen. 'Of Stones, Men and Angels: The Competing Myth of Isabella Duncan's *Pre-Adamite Man* (1860)', *Studies in History and Philosophy of Biology and Biomedical Sciences* 32 (2001): 59–104.

Sorrenson, Richard. 'The Ship as Scientific Instrument in the Eighteenth Century', *Osiris* 2nd series, 11 (1996): 221–36.

Spadafora, David. *The Idea of Progress in Eighteenth-Century Britain*. New Haven, Conn., and London, 1990.

Spary, E. C. *Utopia's Garden: French Natural History from Old Regime to Revolution*. London, 2000.

Stafford, Robert. *Scientist of Empire: Sir Roderick Murchison, Scientific Exploration and Victorian Imperialism*. Cambridge, 1989.

Stanley, Brian. 'Commerce and Christianity: Providence Theory, the Missionary Movement and the Imperialism of Free Trade, 1842–1860', *Historical Journal* 26 (1983): 71–94.

The Bible and the Flag: Protestant Missions and British Imperialism in the Nineteenth and Twentieth Centuries. Leicester, 1990.

'Christian Missions and the Enlightenment: A Reevaluation', in *Christian Missions and the Enlightenment*, edited by Brian Stanley, 1–21. Richmond, Surrey, 2001.

'Christianity and Civilization in English Evangelical Mission Thought, 1792–1857', in *Christian Missions and the Enlightenment*, edited by Brian Stanley. Richmond, Surrey, 2001.

Star, Susan Leigh, and James R. Griesemar. 'Institutional Ecology, "Translations" and Boundary Objects: Amateurs and Professionals in Berkeley's Museum of Vertebrate Zoology', *Social Studies of Science* 19 (1989): 385–420.

Stepan, Nancy Leys. *Picturing Tropical Nature*. London, 2002.

Stephens, W. B. *Education in Britain 1750–1914*. Basingstoke, 1998.

Steven, Margaret. *Trade, Tactics and Territory: Britain in the Pacific, 1783–1823*. Melbourne, 1983.

Stewart, Garrett. *Death Sentences: Styles of Dying in British Fiction*. Cambridge, Mass., 1984.

Stewart, Larry, and Paul Wiendling. 'Philosophical Threads: Natural Philosophy and Public Experiment among the Weavers of Spitafields', *British Journal for the History of Science* 28 (1995): 37–62.

Stewart, Susan. *On Longing: Narratives of the Miniature, the Gigantic, the Souvenir and the Collection*. Baltimore, 1984.

Stocking, George. *Observers Observed: Essays on Ethnographic Fieldwork*. London, 1983.

Victorian Anthropology. New York, 1987.

Strauss, W. P. 'Paradoxical Co-operation: Sir Joseph Banks and the London Missionary Society', *Historical Studies Australia and New Zealand* 11 (1963–5): 246–52.

Taylor, Joyce. *Joseph Lancaster: The Poor Child's Friend: Educating the Poor in the Early Nineteenth Century*. West Wickham, Kent, 1996.

Thirsk, Joan, ed. *Agricultural Change: Policy and Practice 1500–1750*. Cambridge, 1990.

Chapters from the Agrarian History of England and Wales 1500–1750. Cambridge, 1990.

Alternative Agriculture: A History from the Black Death to the Present Day. Oxford, 2000.

Thomas, Keith. *Man and the Natural World*. Harmondsworth, 1984.

Thomas, Nicholas. *Entangled Objects: Material Culture and Colonialism in the Pacific*. Cambridge, 1991.

Colonialism's Culture: Anthropology, Travel and Government. Oxford, 1994.

'Licensed Curiosity: Cook's Pacific Voyages', in *Cultures of Collecting*, edited by Roger Cardinal and John Elsner, 116–36. London, 1994.

Out of Time: History and Evolution in Anthropological Discourse, 2nd edn. Ann Arbor, Mich., 1996.

Thompson, E. P. *The Making of the English Working Class*. London, 1988.

Thorne, Susan. '"The Conversion of Englishmen and the Conversion of the World Inseparable": Missionary Imperialism and the Language of Class in Early Industrial Britain', in *Tensions of Empire: Colonial Cultures in a Bourgeois World*, edited by Laura Stoler. Berkeley, Calif., 1997.

Congregational Missions and the Making of an Imperial Culture in Nineteenth-Century England. Stanford, Calif., 1999.

Todd, J. 'Science at the Periphery: An Interpretation of Australian Scientific and Technological Dependency and Development Prior to 1914', *Annals of Science* 50 (1993): 33–58.

Tomlison, B. R. 'Empire of the Dandelion: Ecological Imperialism and Economic Expansion, 1860–1914', *Journal of Imperial and Commonwealth History* 26 (1988): 84–99.

Topham, Jonathan. 'Science and Popular Education in the 1830s: The Role of the Bridgewater Treaties', *British Journal for the History of Science* 25 (1992): 397–430.

'"An Infinite Variety of Arguments": The Bridgewater Treatises and British Natural Theology in the 1830s, Ph.D. dissertation, University of Lancaster, 1993.

'Beyond the "Common Context": The Production and Reading of the Bridgewater Treatises', *Isis* 89 (1998): 232–62.

'Science, Natural Theology, and Evangelicalism in Early Nineteenth-Century Scotland: Thomas Chalmers and the Evidence Controversy', in *Evangelicals and Science in Historical Perspective*, edited by D. G. Hart, David Livingstone and Mark Noll, 141–74. Oxford, 1999.

'Scientific Publishing and the Reading of Science in Nineteenth-Century Britain: A Historiographical Survey and Guide to Sources', *Studies in History and Philosophy of Science* 31A (2000): 559–612.

Twells, Alison. 'A Christian and Civilised Land: The British Middle Class and the Civilising Mission, 1820–42', in *Gender, Civic Culture and Consumerism: Middle-Class Identity in Britain 1800–1940*, edited by Alan Kidd and David Nicholls, 47–64. Manchester, 1999.

Vaughan, Michalina, and Margaret Scotford Archer. *Social Conflict and Educational Change in England and France 1789–1848*. Cambridge, 1971.

Vera, Eugenia Roldan. 'Useful Knowledge for Export', in *Books and the Sciences in History*, edited by Marina Frasca-Spada and Nicholas Jardine, 338–53. Cambridge, 2000.

'Book Export and the Transmission of Knowledge from Britain to Early-Independent Spanish America.' Ph.D. dissertation, University of Cambridge, 2001.

Vergo, Peter, ed. *The New Museology*. London, 1989.

Viswanathan, Shiv. *A Carnival for Science: Essays on Science, Technology and Development*. New Delhi, 1997.

Wallis, Helen. 'Publication of Cook's Journals: Some New Sources and Assessments', *Pacific Studies* 1, no. 2 (1978): 163–94.

Walls, Andrew F. 'The Eighteenth-Century Protestant Missionary Awakening in its European Context', in *Christian Missions and the Enlightenment*, edited by Brian Stanley, 22–44. Richmond, Surrey, 2001.

Watson, J. R. *The Victorian Hymn*. Durham, 1981.

Wess, J. Dustin. *Darkness Invisible: The Prints of John Martin*. Williamstown, Mass., 1986.

Wheeler, Michael. *Death and the Future Life in Victorian Literature and Theology*. Cambridge, 1990.

Heaven, Hell and the Victorians. Cambridge, 1994.

Williams, Raymond. *The Country and the City*. London, 1973.

Williams, Samuel Tamatoa. *Missionary Stories from the South Sea Islands*. London, 1849.

Willis, Justin. 'The Nature of a Mission Community: The Universities' Mission to Central Africa in Bonde', *Past and Present* 140 (1993): 127–54.

Winks, Robert W., ed. *Historiography*, vol. V of *The Oxford History of the British Empire*, edited by Wm. Roger Louis. Oxford, 1999.

Winter, Alison. *Mesmerized: Powers of the Mind in Victorian Britain*. Chicago, 1998.

Wood, Gillen D'Arcy. *The Shock of the Real: Romanticism and Visual Culture, 1760–1860*. New York, 2001.

Woodall Joanna. 'Introduction', in *Portraiture: Facing the Subject*, edited by Joanna Woodall, 1–25. Manchester, 1997.

Yarrington, Alison. *The Commemoration of the Hero 1800–1864: Monuments to the British Victors of the Napoleonic Wars*. New York and London, 1998.

Yarwood, A. T. *Samuel Marsden: The Great Survivor*. Melbourne, 1977.

Yeo, Richard. *Defining Science: William Whewell, Natural Knowledge, and Public Debate in Early Victorian Britain*. Cambridge, 1993.

Index

A'a, 189–92, 190, 191
agriculture, 150–4, 166–9
  agricultural missionaries, 166–9, 202
  and conversion, 95, 150, 159, 164–6, 173–4
  exchange of specimens, 154–9, 160
  indigenous response, 161, 162–3
  meditations on, 152
  teaching of, 63
Aitutaki, 164, 181, 185
alcohol, 50, 53, 79, 87, 112, 124, 162, 168
alphabet, 62, 63–4; *See also* education
Altick, Richard, 180
Anglicanism, 20, 22, 23, 24, 25
  and education, 66
  Elland Society, 150
  in London Missionary Society, 2, 18, 28
Ann, 150
Annals of Agriculture, 152
anthropomorphism, 92, 136–8, 140, 141, 208,
  beaver and sloth, 80, 81, 82–3
Arminianism, 19, 23, 28
Armitage, Elijah, 166–9
arrowroot, 197–8
artefacts, *see* material culture
Astore, William, 4
astronomy, v, 63, 112
  indigenous response, 184, 202
  teaching of, 68, 76–7, 87, 88
atonement, 20, 22, 25, 163
Austral Islands, *see* Rurutu

Banks, Sir Joseph, 3, 5, 96–102, 150, 150–1,
  208, 209
baptism, 27, 114
Baptist Magazine, 46
Baptist Missionary Society, 19, 27
Baptists, 24, 28, 46
Barff, Revd Charles, 67
barometer, 77–9
barter, 196
Baxter, George, 137, 138–44

Bayly, Christopher, 7
beavers, 79–83, 81
Bebbington, David, 19, 20, 24
Bell, Andrew, 66–71
Bennet, George, 153, 154–61, 184, 187, 188
Bingham, Revd Hiram, 123–4
birds, 92, 93, 134, 136, 163–4, 186
Bligh, Captain, 97, 100, 158
Blonde, 123, 126
Blossom, Thomas, 166–9
Board of Agriculture, 150
body, 133–8
Bogue, Revd David, 71–7
  connection with London Missionary
    Society, 18, 27
  Missionary Seminary, 36, 71–7, 103–4
  on civilisation, 164
  on ideal missionary, 116, 119
  on preaching, 89–90, 203
Bounty, 97–8
Bourdieu, Pierre, 59
Boyle, Robert, 37
breadfruit, 97, 157, 158, 196, 197
British Museum, 188, 189
Brooke, John Hedley, 5
Buchanan, Ebenezer, 86–8
Buckland William, 211
Burder, Revd George, 28, 45, 123
burial, 135–6
Butler, Bishop Joseph, 136–8, 151
Buzacott, Revd Aaron, 63–4, 84

Calvinism, 2, 19, 34
  Calvinist–Arminian controversy, 23,
    25, 28
Camden, 53
Campbell, Revd John, 145
cannibalism, 126, 132
  representation of, 6, 35, 43, 45, 109
  social change from, 112
  theology of, 97

238